PROTESTANT CHURCHMANSHIP

for RURAL AMERICA

PROTESTANT CHURCHMANSHIP *for* RURAL AMERICA

by C. R. McBRIDE

THE JUDSON PRESS

Chicago   Valley Forge   Los Angeles

Printed in the U.S.A.

4

PREFACE

As THE HANDS OF TIME HURRIED past the middle of the twentieth century, America, rural as well as urban, found itself in
the throes of three revolutionary movements. These movements
were not small rumblings but ground swells that bade fair to
alter the lives of men and women of every nation on the earth.
These were not the revolutions of armed violence, though violence might and did erupt at different times and places; but
they were the revolutions of scientific progress in meeting the
basic needs of the human race.

I

The first revolution was and is in the realm of technology
in food production. For millenniums men had scratched the
surface of the earth with crude plows, planted open pollinated
seeds, and hoped for a return sufficient to feed themselves and
provide a little over to share with those engaged in other pursuits. Early in the twentieth century the bright light of science
was focused on agriculture. At first significant changes came
slowly; and then, like a torrent, they engulfed the American
farmer. The magic of electricity and the internal combustion
engine brought machinery of every description to replace
horses and mules and to relieve farmers of backbreaking labor.
The effectiveness of a single farmer was so multiplied that he
sought larger areas to cultivate.

Plant breeders were busy developing new varieties that bore
more fruit and were resistant to disease and insects. In 1955,
96 per cent of the crop varieties used on American farms and
gardens had been developed in the 20 years previous. Great

strides were made in the control of insects and in fertilizers. As acres in cultivation were reduced at great expense to the government, the farmers added more fertilizer and produced larger yields. The increased yield was not totally a matter of more fertilizer but was due in part to the control of disease and insects that previously had decimated the crops. To a considerable degree agriculture was set free of complete dominance by the weather, as irrigation came to the rescue and fertile but barren acres were made to produce abundantly. Progress in agriculture was not confined to plant life, but invaded the barn and hennery. Scientific breeding and the use of biotics resulted in the production of more milk, more beef, more pork, and more eggs *on less feed and in less time* than ever before.

For the first time in human history the earth, as far as America was concerned, was producing more food and fibers than man could use. The cry had changed from "How can we feed our people?" to "How can we be rid of the surplus food supplies now spoiling in the storage bins?" Indeed, this was a very pleasant revolution; pleasant, that is, until one sees the millions of underfed peoples in other parts of the world!

II

The second revolution of the twentieth century was economic. In the rural America of the nineteenth and early twentieth centuries economics was comparatively simple. The government had what seemed to be an unlimited amount of land. A citizen of the country might have 160 acres by asking for it and agreeing to remain on it for a short period of time, meanwhile improving the land. With this free land, a span of mules, a plow, and a few other tools, a young man and his wife were in business. While he tilled the acres "by the sweat of his brow" she bore the children, processed food, made the clothes for the family, took care of the garden plot and the chickens, and made butter to be exchanged at the village grocery store for food staples.

Such economic simplicity vanished from the American scene about 1950. The 23 million horses and mules of 1910 were reduced to four and a half million by 1958, while the one thousand tractors of 1910 increased to nearly five million in the same period. Although the horses produced colts by a natural process, the tractors did not produce baby tractors. New tractors had to be purchased at a high price which was determined by urban standards.

Except in the depression days land values had constantly increased. There being no more land for the asking, those desiring to farm were compelled to pay high prices for it. Many young men who wanted to farm could find no desirable land for sale.

Agriculture became a 90 billion dollars-a-year business before 1960: sixteen to service and supply the farmer, fourteen to the farmer for his produce, and sixty for transporting, storing, processing, and merchandising! And while industry had only $7,866 invested per worker, agriculture had $21,115 invested for each worker. A farm in the corn belt, equipped, might be valued easily at $50,000 to $100,000, or even more.

Many farmers with small acreages were unable to earn enough on their farms to provide the standard of living they desired. The securing of a "good paying job" in the nearby town or city looked attractive. For them farming was reduced to a part-time job as they commuted to a 40-hour-a-week job in town.

Change in the economic nature of agriculture brought the federal government into the picture. There was a great demand on the part of the farmer for price support of agricultural products in order that his buying power might be on a parity with that of the industrial worker. In an effort toward equalization billions of dollars were poured into the economic stream of rural life. That it profited the farmer, in the long run, is debatable.

Meanwhile industry was finding that towns and small cities offered certain advantages which could not be secured in the larger cities. More and more, factories were being located in villages and towns, so that while the farm population continued to decrease, the overall rural population was increasing.

The villages and towns that secured industry often profited at the expense of the hamlets, villages, towns, and the nearby farms that failed to attract industry. The places without industry were high producers of children, and, at considerable expense brought them to maturity only to lose them to the industrialized places. It has been correctly observed that when a town stands still or loses population it loses part of its income earners, while the older people, dependents, stay on. Conversely, when a town or city is growing it tends to keep a healthy ratio between income earners and dependents. Thus a part of rural America was enriched at the expense of other parts.

III

The third revolution was sociological. The early pattern of settlement in America was the family homestead with its social, educational, and religious life centered in the small, compact, neighborhood. Through the Midwest, schools were located at about four-mile intervals; thus no child needed to *walk* more than two miles to school. Churches were similarly located. Life was unhurried and self-contained in these neighborhoods until the close of World War I. Then young men who had gone from these neighborhoods to fight in Europe for their country were reluctant to return to the former pastoral way of life. During the period of their restlessness came the automobile, hard-surfaced roads, the airplane, radio, and television. Rapidly the old patterns began to disintegrate. The technological improvement in agriculture called for fewer farmers, so that by 1958 only 10 per cent of the farm-born males had a chance to enter farming. Hamlets and smaller villages offered few opportunities for employment. The population movement to the larger village, town, and city was accelerated, as annually places for 15,000 new jobs in nonfarm rural areas were developed.

Because travel became easy and fast, and under the impetus of alluring advertisements, rural people were no longer content to confine their shopping to the local general store. They sought out the larger towns and cities where selections were larger and where they imagined the prices were lower. Interestingly, the city people became unhappy with their downtown shopping areas and enterprising merchants accordingly built shopping centers which were not altogether unlike the old village general store, and attracting both rural and urban people.

A steady consolidation of schools developed and children were transported in modern buses several miles each day to attend school. Often this necessitated that children leave home before daylight and return after dark during the winter months. As the farm population declined, many open-country and neighborhood churches were faced with the alternative of closing or merging their interests with other neighborhood churches. Too many of them preferred slow death to merging with a church of another, or even their own, denomination.

City people were restless too. The inner city did not offer them hoped-for advantages. In great numbers they moved to the rural areas circling the cities. Many hamlets and villages near cities found their populations doubled, tripled, or quadrupled in a few years' time. Thus suburbia and exurbia came into being as the city-sprawl reached farther and farther into the rural domain.

One of the most significant changes came in the rural home, especially the farm home. Farming had once been a family enterprise. The technological revolution provided less work for members of the family. Mother soon found it convenient to secure out-of-the-home employment. The children did likewise as soon as they could find part-time jobs. With the demands of the consolidated schools, employment, and out-of-the-home recreation, thousands of homes deteriorated to little more than a service station for the family. With the breakdown of a closely-integrated family life social evils developed with which neither the schools nor the homes found themselves able to cope.

IV

Hurriedly we have tried to sketch the three revolutions that characterize American rural life near the beginning of the second half of the twentieth century. The changes have come rapidly, some for better and some for worse. They are far-reaching. But the story is not ended. A fourth revolution is needed immediately, lest the gains of the other three be lost. The fourth revolution must come in the realm of the Spirit. There is need for a spiritual awakening by which men become God's trustees of the good things of rural life and use them for the advance of his kingdom throughout the whole world. The church of rural America has not yet begun to understand the nature of its responsibility amid the new rural conditions. Like the nation that prepares to fight new wars by using the methods of the wars of the past so the church stumbles along on the brink of defeat. The church is in need of dynamic leaders who will courageously lead it into a spiritual revolution that will establish the known good and develop new areas of righteousness. To that end *Protestant Churchmanship for Rural America* has been prepared. On its pages we have tried to gather together those things a young minister and his church should know as they go about their business.

This book has been prepared in three parts. The first part is an introduction to the rural church movement which started in 1908 and 1909 when President Theodore Roosevelt's Commission on Country Life made its report. This report triggered action on several fronts. In this introduction we are concerned not only with history and current programs, but with the nature of certain areas to be served by rural churches, and the church's philosophy of responsibility.

The second part of the book is a fresh look at church administration. Its foremost question is "How can a church organize itself so as to best use its resources in bringing its neighborhood, community, and the world under the leadership of Jesus, the Christ?"

In the final part, we look at the minister and attempt to indicate his behavior as a leader in the church and as the architect of the emerging town-country community. The minister is the key person in the creation of a spiritual climate that will properly evaluate and direct the technological, sociological, and economic revolutions into the development of a truly great Christian civilization.

C. R. McBride
Central Baptist Theological Seminary,
Kansas City, Kan.

May 1, 1961

ACKNOWLEDGMENTS

IT IS IMPOSSIBLE adequately to acknowledge all the persons and institutions who have contributed to the writing of this book. All the authors of the many books and articles read have had a large part in forming the philosophy expressed in these chapters. The number of these contributors is legion and, while we are extremely grateful for their help, it is impossible to call them all by name.

Much credit must be given to the members of two rural churches: The First Baptist Church of Sandborn, Indiana, and The Community Baptist Church of Honey Creek, Wisconsin. Patiently and with consecration the former endured the ministries of a young pastor for eleven years. Without this the author would probably have given up the rural ministry before he was well started. The latter church had a great sense of vision that made experiments in community work possible over a nine-year period.

Neither should the American Baptist Home Mission Society be overlooked, for it has contributed richly to this writing. It was the privilege of the author to serve for nine years on the Society's Board of Managers, and for three years on its staff. These experiences made it possible for him to extend his horizons and to become acquainted with churches and pastors from coast to coast in many different situations.

The author is deeply indebted to two colleagues, Dr. Eric G. Haden and Dr. Robert Torbet for their helpful counseling, and to Mrs. Irene Barr for the many hours spent at her typewriter.

These people and institutions we gratefully acknowledge, and offer a hearty "Many, many thanks."

C. R. M.

CONTENTS

PART ONE

AN INTRODUCTION TO THE RURAL CHURCH MOVEMENT

PART TWO

TOWN-COUNTRY CHURCH ADMINISTRATION

PART THREE
PASTORAL ADMINISTRATION

PROTESTANT CHURCHMANSHIP

for RURAL AMERICA

PART ONE
AN INTRODUCTION
to the
RURAL CHURCH MOVEMENT

I

BEGINNINGS
OF THE RURAL CHURCH MOVEMENT

THE RURAL AREAS OF AMERICA have troubled and challenged Protestant churchmen for more than half a century. The standings and privileges enjoyed by ministers in the cities are rooted deep in a rural heritage. On a Sunday morning they read rural parables spoken by a Man who lived with rural people. As a city pastor lifts his eyes from the reading and looks into the faces of his parishioners he knows that sixty, seventy, or perhaps eighty per cent of them were born in rural America, and there they received their education and religious faith. At dinner he may note that the food on his table is the product of America's prolific acres. And, in the evening time he may experience a nostalgic urge for the warm, deep, informal fellowship of the rural people he knew when serving his first church as a young and inexperienced pastor. In a poetic vein he may long to experience again the quiet countryside and with the Psalmist say;

"The heavens are telling the glory of God;
 and the firmament proclaims his handiwork."

If the churchman is the pastor of a rural church, after reading from the Book and looking into the faces of his people, he may be aware of their problems and opportunities and how desperately they cry out for constructive, consecrated, Christian leadership. However, he may have in his pocket an invitation to candidate in a small-city church. To accept the call will be, in the words of the world, a promotion. And in doing so he may think it will mean a more significant service, greater

17

prestige, better schooling and opportunities for his children, and a larger salary. He knows that if the call comes he will rationalize until, accepting it, he moves to the city. But he will not easily free himself from the challenge of doing his share in the religious nurture of the seventy million people of rural America.

If the churchman is no longer a pastor, but fills one of the many denominational offices in which matters and concerns for the church in America are expressed, he may feel that the time has come to be of greater service to rural people. He speaks in various ways of their importance and of their need for a consecrated ministry. He often tells of the days when he was pastor of a rural church, and he refers to them as "the happiest days of my ministry." If his position permits, and funds are available, he may allocate money for the help of rural churches. In doing these things he is not hypocritical, but is only giving utterance to the fact that the problems of the rural church are troubling him and he is challenged by both their needs and the opportunity they present for the work of the kingdom of God.

No matter where the Protestant churchman lives the rural areas challenge his religious philosophy and behavior. That he receives such a challenge is no accident, for concerned men have been busy propagandizing the needs and opportunities of rural people. Today, there is a well defined rural church movement. It has permeated the colleges and seminaries of the major denominations; it is spoken of in conventions and church meetings; books are written and literature is distributed where religious minded people meet; and once each year a national convocation on church in town and country is held somewhere in the nation.

This outpouring of rural propaganda has come as concerned Protestant churchmen have tried to meet the needs of rural people and to capitalize for kingdom purposes on their unique opportunities.

EARLY THINKING

For a better understanding of the challenge, let us go back to the year of 1908 when President Theodore Roosevelt appointed a commission of five distinguished authorities to study American country life and report to him on the conditions they found, for this act is considered the beginning of the modern rural church movement. In his letter to Dr. Liberty Hyde Bailey, chairman of the commission, the President indicated his belief that permanent greatness for any nation must be based on the well-being of its farmers. He pointed out that the lot of American farmers was superior to that of other generations and although it was improving it was not keeping pace with the rest of the country. Living conditions, especially in the South, were not worthy of the American ideal. He said that, while better methods of farming were needed, the real problem was a better life for country people, farmers and villagers alike.

The members of the commission applied themselves to their task, mailing out more than a half million questionnaires. They carefully studied and analyzed the more than one hundred thousand returns from this mailing. They held thirty regional meetings in which they discussed with rural people their problems and hopes. As they traveled over country roads all across the nation they talked with rural people, and looked at their farms and villages. In the end they disclosed six underlying problems of rural life. There was a lack of knowledge on the part of farmers of the exact agricultural conditions and possibilities of their regions. Specific training in the schools for country life was lacking. They found that the farmer was at a disadvantage or handicap against established systems and interests, and this prevented him from securing adequate returns for his products. The lack of good highways was evident to them. There was a widespread continuing depletion of soils, resulting in an injurious effect on rural life. They found a general need of new and active leadership in rural areas.

From their analysis they determined that a four-pronged program should be launched: (1) the farmer should receive exact knowledge of his business and of the particular conditions under which he works; (2) a scheme of public education should be organized which would be adapted to the needs of farming people; (3) there should be a vast enlargement of voluntary organized effort among farmers; and (4) a revitalizing of the institutions of religion was needed.

The report of the commission was a stimulus to individuals and organizations interested in a better rural America. Churchmen who had been pleading for departments and programs to minister to rural people found sympathetic listeners and a place in the budgets of their organizations. Shortly, through the pioneer studies of Charles Josiah Galpin, rural sociology was born, nurtured, and brought to maturity. Not immediately, but soon thereafter, short courses for the aid of rural pastors were set up on the campuses of the land-grant colleges. At the same time organizations of many hues sprang up across the country, through which laity and clergy might and did contribute to the betterment of rural life. The rural movement was under way.

THE RURAL PROBLEM

There were a number of factors which created, or helped to create, a rural problem in the world's most prosperous nation. A knowledge of these factors is important to a fair consideration of the development of the rural movement in America. The European influence, for instance, must be understood if a full picture of the problem is to be seen. There was an overwhelming desire among Europeans of the seventeenth and eighteenth centuries to migrate to America, the land of new opportunity. Many came in search of religious freedom. Later great numbers came seeking freedom from the Prussian military machine. From Ireland came hordes to escape the famine when potato crops failed. All these people had two things in common: a passionate desire for freedom, and confidence that they could work out their own salvation in a new land.

Because primogeniture was the custom or law in some European countries, those who were not first-born sons sought uninherited land. America, a great unexplored continent, seemed to offer these people hope for becoming landowners. They came, and took the land. Weather conditions were different in the new land, and the settlers were unprepared for the torrential downpours of rain, the droughts, and the strong winds they encountered. If they treated the land as they had done in Europe, it blew and washed away. They had to learn by experience, and experience takes time. True to human nature, they tried to reproduce the customs and practices of their homeland. They sought to create cultural units which would remind them of their European homes. Thus a German Settlement, an English Settlement, and a Swiss New Glarus, all appeared in Wisconsin.

Europe, with its good and bad, was set down on a new continent. From this new human venture as well as from other backgrounds came problems and solutions which we shall now try to delineate.

Let us choose 1908 and the report of Roosevelt's Commission on Country Life as a dividing line and go behind it for a quick look at the formation of the nation.

In 1790, in spite of considerable opposition, the first United States census was made, recording a total of 3,929,214 people. Of this number only 201,655 or 5.1 per cent were urban. The remaining number (3,727,559, or 94.9 per cent) were rural. Perhaps never again were the rural people of America to be so numerous *in comparison* with the urban segment of the population. While the actual number of rural people has steadily risen, the number of urban people has increased more rapidly in proportion to the total population. This has been caused largely by immigration into the cities.

In 1908, the dividing year, the population was close to a balance with 45.7 per cent urban and 54.3 per cent rural, but the rural majority was soon to disappear. By 1950 the rural people, totaling 54 million, were only 36 per cent of the population. Rural dominance at the polls had been lost. Attitudes and values were being shaped more by urban interests.

Between 1790 and 1908 the country was expanding westward to the Pacific and southward to Mexico. Much of the new territory was rich expanses of land that had never before been occupied by white men. The plains, forests, swamps, and streams challenged men to subdue them.

The vastness of the enlarged nation endangered, or made exceedingly difficult, essential communications. Roads were but dusty trails. It was in 1903 that the first automobile crossed the United States under its own power. It took H. Nelson Jackson sixty-three days to make the trip, averaging 125 miles a day, and it cost him $8,000.

In the winter many roads were passable only on foot or by horseback. Families in southern Indiana made their last fall trip to town, just five miles away, late in October or early in November. Except in direst emergency the family would not return to town until April. Against such a background of isolation it is understandable why farm families sought eagerly the fellowship of the neighborhood church.

The Homestead Act of 1862 helped people to settle on the land. The requirements for receiving the land included improving and living on it. This system made for isolation quite contrary to man's natural desire to live with others of his own kind. While homesteading settled the country, at the same time it led to much unhappiness, especially on the part of the women.

Such great expansion, geographical and numerical, called for schools wherever there were children. Where possible in the East and Midwest, the citizens built a school every four miles so that no child would need to travel more than two miles. Naturally, such schools were small. Because families were large, and there were more families in a given area than now, the school attendance was much larger than it is in the same localities today. School hours were arranged according to the farm needs for labor. Many schools operated during only three or four months a year; even when they were open for six or eight months, some of the pupils could attend for only part of the time, so great was the need for their labor on the family farm.

Usually there was a shortage of teachers, books, and materials for the pupils in the more isolated areas. There was little lacking, however, in religious instruction. In many places school teachers and parents felt that it was not wrong to open a school day with Bible reading and prayer. Frequent use was made of Bible stories and stories with "a moral." Out of Ohio came the famous McGuffey Readers and Spellers to mold the character of a generation of children. Many children, in some but not all areas of the nation, grew up with a wholesome respect for religion as they were instructed in the public school by Christian teachers using Christian literature.

To complicate further the development of a nation, the states engaged in a fratricidal war from 1861 to 1865. While the war abolished slavery and determined that the United States was a nation rather than a loose federation of states, it left in its wake much suffering and desolation. The economy of the South was blighted as unscrupulous men took advantage of its weakened condition and imposed high freight tariffs and questionable business schemes. In this period of travail, religious denominations, torn in their sympathies before the war, remained divided, some even to the present day.

There grew up the policy of racial segregation with facilities for the races to be "separate but equal." Even had it been possible to make all facilities equal, the burden of two sets of schools, churches, and recreational projects was too heavy to bear. In 1954 the Supreme Court ruled that segregation was illegal and ordered public schools integrated. The process of integration is going on, but not without controversy. The aftermath of the War Between the States has produced in some southern rural areas a well-nigh unbearable condition.

That which has been said of the schools can be repeated with few changes for the churches. In many areas the churches were of necessity close together, for they had to be within reach of the people. A day's travel was considered to be the distance a man could drive a team of horses and return in the same day. There was bitter competition by the denominations for the better sites. The church leadership, by and large, was untrained, and some denominations were afraid of schools for their ministers. Nevertheless, many denominational colleges were established in these early days.

Ministers were recruited from each local church's area. Since the greater number were unschooled, and those that did go to school attended in the proximity of their homes, they had neither the vision nor the skill to alter the thinking of the rank and file of church members. Each thought and lived as the parishioners. As far as any knew, the practices and the poverty of his area were universal. The mores of the community were the practices of the church. If challenged, as on the subject of slavery, they "proved conclusively" from the Scriptures the rightness of their conduct. The church was thrown into the impossible plight of trying to cause the community to lift itself by tugging at its own bootstraps.

However, the rural church was at the center of the interests of the people. It was their primary institution, socially as well as religiously. It was the one place where they could gather and share in fellowship. It was not at all unusual for a congregation to have a "protracted meeting" lasting six weeks. Many people were genuinely converted to Christ in these meetings. There were also, as might be expected in the isolation of the frontier, many queer things happening under the guise of the Christian religion. It was in this period that camp meetings became popular in some areas. The whole family and the dog would leave home for a week or two to attend a camp where religious services were held day and night. Some unnatural and immoral things happened at these camps as emotional fervor rose and took unintended directions under the preaching of "called-of-God men."

In a competitive society it is natural and comparatively easy for people to take unfair advantage of one another's weaknesses. As the years progressed and their numbers grew, the urban people began to feel their strength. They passed laws favoring themselves. They bought from the farmer at the lowest possible price. They sold back to the farmer at as high a price as possible.

Geographically united, the urban people could, and frequently did, have better schools and churches than the rural people. They enjoyed more social life and better financial opportunities. Industries promised high wages to those who would come to the cities to work, although nothing was said about the higher costs of living and other inconveniences the workers would have to endure once there.

Farm girls, knowing the isolation and drudgery their mothers had endured, were not anxious to remain on land that promised little more than a premature death. They visualized better schools and a finer social environment for their children. In increasing numbers they migrated to the larger towns and cities. Naturally the young men followed, and took over such work and businesses as they could handle. Their rustic vigor, independence, and initiative soon placed many in favorable positions. Not a few were happy with their new status in life, and the cities grew.

Land conservation was an afterthought with people who had an abundance of undeveloped natural resources. Valuable timber was burned to clear the ground for field crops. Wasteful farm practices often resulted in serious soil erosion. Some farmers even boasted of the number of farms they had worn out, a practice which they called "conquering the wilderness."

The poorer rocky farms of the northeastern states were abandoned for the more fertile and tillable soil of the Midwest or the far West. For years the South depended on cotton as its principal crop. Immense amounts of it were shipped abroad. The crop was frequently referred to as "King Cotton." Like most tyrants, King Cotton exacted a heavy price from his subjects, this time in the form of soil erosion. When the prices dropped the people were left with depleted farm lands, no place to sell their cotton, and no knowledge of what they could do with their idle, impoverished, acres.

Thus, as the country expanded westward, there grew up the American "rural problem"— isolation, drudgery, poor communications, limited school and church facilities, and exploitation of the natural resources, along with the tantalizing promise of better living conditions in the cities. Here was a deterioration of life and land that threatened the security of the country's future and called for action.

By 1908, rural unrest had reached such a peak that the President appointed the Commision on Country Life. The report of the Commission was carefully read, not only in government circles, but by educators, economists, sociologists, and churchmen. The Commission's analysis of conditions and recommendations for reform were carefully noted; then, slowly at first, but rapidly gathering speed, remedial measures were introduced. School curriculums were revised, schools for ministers on campuses of land grant colleges were established, the extension agencies of the United States Department of Agriculture and land grant colleges were strengthened, rural sociology was lifted up, conservation societies were formed, and church mission boards appointed committees and organizations to minister to the rural areas of the nation. The modern rural church movement was under way.

II

DYNAMIC PERSONALITIES

It may be helpful to the student of the rural church movement to pause long enough to consider briefly the contribution of several dynamic personalities who have given the present movement its form and direction. To do this, we shall need to look again to Europe, then to the Orient, and back again to our homeland. Although this survey of personalities must be selective, it will illustrate the rich background of the town-country movement.

John Frederick Oberlin (1740-1826)

If rural Protestants believed in patron saints, surely they would nominate John Frederick Oberlin for that honor.

Born in a family of culture and religious faith, he attended the University of Strassburg where he studied under eminent professors. At twenty-three he received the Doctor of Philosophy degree and became a Lutheran minister. He did not accept a pastorate because he felt unqualified. His restless, inquisitive spirit was searching for a task that seemed to need his full attention. In his seeking, he was visited by Pastor Stuber of the Walbach parish in the Vosges Mountains, a man who was looking for someone to succeed him because of his wife's declining health. His description of the parish made an indelible impression on Oberlin. It is said that years later he reported the conversation somewhat as follows:

"I do not wish to exaggerate anything, my dear Oberlin. Six months of winter: at times the cold of the shores of the Baltic; a wind like ice sometimes comes down from the mountain tops above us; the sick and dying are to be visited in remote, wild, solitary places among the forests. My wife often is almost dead with terror, supposing me lost in the snow storms. It is like the passages of the Alps."

"And your parishioners, are they well disposed?" asked Oberlin.

"Not too much, not too much, I must say without calumniating them! There are some good souls there who are much attached to me; but they are all frightfully ignorant and untractable and proud of their ignorance. It is an iron-headed people, a population of cyclops. When I went there, the schoolmaster was a swineherd in the summer: in the winter he taught the children in a miserable shack the little he knew.

My parishioners have nothing. I myself have very little. My wife's small fortune is already exhausted in relieving a little the general misery. Four districts even poorer than the mother parish are also to be served; not a single practicable road from the village; deep mud holes among the cabins and huts; the fruit, wild cherries, apples, and pears fit only for swine; and the inhabitants, abandoned to the completest indifference, have not the least concern to ameliorate their condition." [1]

John F. Oberlin had once said, "I do not want to labor in some easy pastoral charge where I can be at ease. I want a work no one else wishes to do; and which will not be done unless I do it." Walbach seemed to be such a place, and after prayer and meditation he accepted the challenge.

Understanding the gospel as being something for all of life, Oberlin worked in the fields, the schools, at road building, and vocational training, while giving "moral lectures" in the church, administering the ordinances, and preaching. God's love and grace went to work through this consecrated man. Slowly the parish began to change. For almost sixty years he labored and saw the complete transformation of the village and its people. His consecrated endeavors have become a pattern for the modern rural church.

N. F. S. GRUNDTVIG (1783-1872)

The second European to engage our attention was a Dane. The military defeat of 1864, with the loss to Germany of Slesvig, seemed to doom Denmark to oblivion. But in those dark hours there began to grow up in the rural districts a vigorous movement which was destined to create a new and greater Denmark. "Outward loss, inward gain" became the new watchword.

[1] Beard, August Field, *The Story of John Friederich Oberlin*. New York: Christian Rural Fellowship, 1946.

A deeply religious man, Nikolai Frederik Severin Grundtvig, was wrestling with the problems of his rural people. It became a strong conviction with him that in addition to their religious faith his people needed enlightened, inquiring minds. They needed the opportunity to study in a voluntary, adult manner and not in the rote or catechetical methods used in teaching children. He saw the people being lectured by men who had the right to lecture because they had seen and handled, had discovered and experimented with, their subjects; in short, because they knew of that which they spoke. His people needed to learn by equally experimental methods.

With this thought, he started the Danish Folk Schools to prepare rural people for a wholesome existence where they were. This plan of adult education so enlisted the energies of the people that a new and better Denmark came into being. At the outbreak of World War II, the Danes had the highest standard of living in all Europe. In many respects it surpassed the vaunted American standard.

Not directly, perhaps, but indirectly, Americans owe to Bishop Grundtvig the inspiration that has resulted in our far-flung Extension Service and other adult educational projects. Those who first established the Extension Service, (and those who now develop it), were not unaware of the great change that came to Denmark when men's minds were opened and stimulated by new facts.

FREDERICK WILLIAM RAIFFEISEN (1818-1888)

The third European of note is Frederick William Raiffeisen. He is neither known as the previously mentioned, nor is his contribution as extensively accepted in rural areas. But as time has led an increasing number of people to understand the fullness of the gospel for the whole man, Raiffeisen's contribution becomes more fully appreciated and more widely used.

Frederick William Raiffeisen, a Lutheran layman, organized the first co-operative credit association in Flannersfeld, Germany, in 1849. He first used the term "brotherhood credit" when referring to the services of the organizations in which he was interested. Thus he is the father of the modern credit union.

These three Europeans, so far removed in time and distance from the rural churches of America, pioneered in serving rural people. They did not falter in the strenuous tasks laid before them. Years later, when men of kindred spirits sought to remedy the ills of a new generation of ruralites on a new continent, they had before them the inspiration and experiences of these men. In varying degrees they have used them, but always for the betterment of mankind.

SAM HIGGINBOTTOM (1874-1958)

The rural movement is not confined to twentieth century United States. It is world-wide and spans the ages. We may now look briefly at two missionaries sent from America, who have profoundly affected Christianity's approach to rural people.

Sam Higginbottom was born in England where he learned the merits of hard and sustained work. In early youth he became a Christian. Migrating to America, he put his former experiences to good use as he worked his way through school, expecting to be a clergyman.

He was recruited by the Presbyterians and sent to India where he was to teach school. He was not in the new country long before he saw that one of India's greatest needs was food, and another was a new approach to, and philosophy of, manual work. His students were horrified when he suggested they should work with their hands. They eventually capitulated when he led the way in making a garden for the school. He experimented with organic gardening and found that he could raise superior vegetables by this method. From this humble beginning he enlarged the scope of his agricultural interests and organized an Agricultural Institute at Allahabad.

The princes (maharajahs) would gladly have paid him large sums of money to work for them in reforming the agriculture of their areas. He preferred to remain a Christian missionary, using agriculture as the approach to "the more abundant life" of Jesus. Unfortunately, during his first years in India his colleagues shared neither his vision nor his consecration and sent back to America reports denouncing him for not "preaching the gospel." For a while his work was suspended, only to be reopened. The Agricultural Institute continues to this day and his example is spreading to other mission fields.

BRAYTON C. CASE (1887-1944)

Another Christian missionary leader in the agricultural field was Brayton C. Case, one of the truly great men of the twentieth century. Until his untimely death in 1944 he served as an agricultural missionary in Burma for the American Baptists, where he had founded the Christian Agricultural School at Pyinmana, Burma.

Brayton C. Case was born of missionary parents in Burma, August 18, 1887. Until he was twelve, he lived among Burmese children, attending mission school with them. He learned to speak the Burmese language better than the Burmese. He was sent to America for college and seminary training. He attended the University of California, where he majored in agriculture. He took his master's work at Columbia University and Union Theological Seminary.

On his return to Burma in 1913 he saw with new eyes the poverty, hunger, and misery of the Burmese people. He understood that while man cannot live by bread alone, *man must have bread to live*. He began to think in terms of a four-point program: preaching, teaching, healing, and feeding the people. But feeding the people could be accomplished only as they mastered better agricultural techniques. He set himself to teaching the people better methods of raising food and fibre.

In 1915 he wrote to the Board of the American Baptist Foreign Mission Society that three-fourths of the Burmese people earn their living by means of agriculture. He pointed out that the people were very poor, not even owning the cattle with which they cultivated their fields. They had little to eat beyond their staple grain crop. Under such conditions it would be impossible to establish a strong, self-supporting, self-propagating church. The Board was sympathetic and it carefully considered his plea. Soon he was authorized to find a place for a school, and after some time he selected Pyinmana (Lazy-man-rest-not) as the best-located of all the stations he had visited. The work began slowly, but each year saw an advance. The Burmese government became interested in the project and began to underwrite about half its cost. Enlargement was then possible.

It was Brayton Case's dream that the school might reach farmers' sons who were able to get only a common school education. His aim was to educate boys who would return to their villages and raise the level of living there. He wanted to keep the education simple enough to be applied to village conditions. Even the tools the boys learned to handle would need to be cheap enough to be within the means of the village people. It was his aim to help as large a number of the plain people as possible.

With this brief background of European and missionary activities, we may now turn to the men who labored directly on the American rural scenes and whose contributions gave shape and substance to the developing rural movement.

MALCOLM DANA (1869-1940)

Malcolm Dana was one of the bright lights of the rural church movement. As a pastor in the East and Midwest, he won honor and respect as a constructive community leader. He believed that a church could not live apart from the community where it was located. Therefore he took an active interest in everything that concerned the welfare of the community. He pleaded for laymen to express their religion in daily living thus making the church the most fundamental conditioning factor in community life. These concerns and theories made him a leader in interdenominational co-operation. His excellent pastoral work was cut short by World War I. Through the war he served with the Y.M.C.A. and organized a fellowship among soldiers which was a forerunner of the American Legion.

On his return to the states (1919), he was asked to become director of the new Town and Country Department of the Congregational Church's Extension Board. He held this position for twenty years, one year short of his demise. His aim was to strengthen religious forces in town and country and to improve the quality of rural life. He developed the larger parish plan, demonstration parishes, projects for training rural ministers, and visual aids for religious education. Ideas such as these are described in later chapters of this book.

As a pastor of pastors with the whole country as his parish, and a teacher-at-large of rural churches everywhere he stimulated others to undertake new ventures in community services. He was one of the first to apply a knowledge of sociology to the church. He felt that the rural church should reach all people in the community, and that social and personal services should be rendered wherever need arose. To him the rural church was more than a preaching station. It was a focal point for all community life, and its influence and services should radiate to cover the entire community.

He believed seminaries should more definitely prepare men for the rural pastorate. He secured the support of John D. Rockefeller, Jr., in experiments along this line. Through their efforts, five New England seminaries were organized in 1929 into the Inter-seminary Commission for Training the Rural Ministry. The co-operating seminaries were Hartford, Yale, Andover Newton, Bangor, and Boston University School of Theology. A sixth, Union Theological Seminary of New York City, joined some years later.

Thus Malcolm Dana left upon the new rural church movement the imprint and lasting marks of his ideas, ideals, and personality.

CHARLES JOSIAH GALPIN (1864-1947)

Although he was not an ordained clergyman, Charles Josiah Galpin, son of one rural Baptist minister and brother of another, made a distinct contribution to the American rural church movement by his careful study of the nature of rural communities. To the best of our knowledge he was the first American university pastor. In 1905 he was persuaded to work with the students of the University of Wisconsin by his brother, who was then a pastor in Madison, Wis. From his scores and hundreds of contacts with students from the country areas he came to know the country church as a rural social problem.

One hearing of the Commission on Country Life was held at Madison. The term "social forces" sang itself over and over in Galpin's ears. He wanted to know more about these forces. He secured the service of the librarian in Belleville, N. Y., population 600, and collected data over a three months period. He chose Belleville because it had been his home and he knew the area. He wanted to see what kinds of homes contained large, few, or no memberships in the various organizations in the community. When the data arrived he put the results on maps: Tenant homes, owners' homes on back roads, and so forth. This was the first modern attempt at studying the rural community sociologically.

In 1911, as a professor at the University of Wisconsin, he made another study, working out of Delavan, a trading town for farmers. Here he began to see the social significance of goods, services, and trade. He decided to make trade and service central in his study. In a week he went to every farm house in the area and filled in 3000 questionnaires. Back at the University, he mulled over the data, and later wrote, "I saw enough to convince me that rural society is a reality; that it was a virgin vein for research; and that both in and for itself and for urban society, a body of knowledge about rural life was worth while."

KENYON L. BUTTERFIELD (1868-1935)

Kenyon Leech Butterfield was already well known in rural circles when President Roosevelt appointed him a member of the Commission on Country Life. From his vantage ground as former president of Rhode Island College of Agriculture (1903-06), and president and head of the Division of Rural Social Sciences of Massachusetts Agricultural College (1906-24), he was making an earnest and effective plea for the rebuilding of American rural life.

In his first book, *Chapters in Rural Progress*, published in 1908, he defined "rural" as being synonymous with "farm," a definition which he later modified to include village life. He pleaded for an educational system that would give rural children a keener appreciation of nature and prepare them spiritually to live on the farms and in the villages. He urged the federation of all rural social agencies for the welfare of the whole body of rural people. He was not unmindful of soil erosion and clearly indicated its deleterious effect on national life.

His second book, *The Country Church and the Rural Problem* (1911), enlarged upon his former observations. He clarified his thinking in a summary statement on the rural problem, saying, "The total rural problem is nothing more or less than to develop a new rural civilization." Of the church he wrote, "It is hopeless to expect that the church can fulfill its mission among the people who live upon the land unless it can conceive its function in terms of the fundamental needs of these people."

Dr. Butterfield called the first Country Life Conference, January 6 and 7, 1919, at Baltimore, Md., and was elected president of the American Country Life Association, which office he held for ten years. He was a delegate to the International Missionary Conference at Jerusalem in 1928, and gave one of the principal addresses. He traveled extensively in the Near East, Africa, and the Orient as counselor on rural work for the Conference.

As a pioneer and prophet in the field of rural education, he was influential in promoting legislation resulting in enlarged federal support of extension services and home economics.

For his outstanding work on behalf of rural people everywhere, he was decorated by the King of Belgium.

Warren H. Wilson (1867-1937)

Warren Hugh Wilson made his chief contribution to improved rural living through the medium of the secretaryship of the Department of Church and Country Life, Board of Home Missions of the Presbyterian Church, U.S.A. a position he occupied for almost thirty years (1909-1937).

Although regarded as a philosopher, Wilson's writings and works indicate that he was also a man of action. Indeed he seemed to be more interested in parish organizations, church methods and relationships, and the problems of the rural community, than he was in rethinking Christian theology.

Wilson entered rural work a decade before World War I, before rural America became conscious of the world, while half the population of the nation was in rural areas, and a high percentage of this on the farms. Even in those halcyon days, his keen mind and sensitive heart were struck by the terrific forces of decay in rural society. He pleaded eloquently that churches become federated to meet the challenge. He wanted churches to be concerned for the communities in which they lived. He called for the church to take the lead in wholesome recreation, for he observed that many of the ills in community life were due to farmers not having learned to play together. With Dr. Wilson, the idea of federation went beyond church organization; it was for the economic survival of farm people, too. He counseled rural people to solve economic problems together.

He saw the Pennsylvania Germans' church as their Labor Union, and wrote, "It is impossible for people who are divided in their economic life to be united in their religious life . . . ."[1] "Therefore the sum of the whole matter is this, the Christian man or woman in America, especially in the open country, must learn to devote himself to the community, and to this end must magnify the church as the community center."[2]

In his second book he continued his emphasis on federation, as he did until the end of his life, but threw responsibility for existing conditions upon the prevailing school curriculum. He felt that the weakness of the common schools showed itself in their failure to educate the upper and lower marginal people of the community, in their failure to train average men and women for life in that community, in their robbing the community of leadership by training many to go out from the community never to return, and in their general disloyalty to the local community with its needs and its problems. To help correct this unwholesome condition he proposed for examination the Danish folk schools started by N. F. S. Grundtvig.

Of the pastoral work, he wrote in 1927,

> If one were to look to the future, it would be that some day rural America will be mapped anew for church work, and in every "trade-basin," where commerce and industry center around a bank and a store, there will be placed a pastor who will serve without discrimination all who live in an area. His presence will not exclude other ministry, but he will patiently establish his relations with all who live on that land. He will give no preference to his own members, but will put upon them the burden he shares himself. He will constrain no one and will condition his service in no degree by membership, but he will include all in the care of the gospel.[3]

[1] From *The Church of the Open Country*, Missionary Education Movement, New York, 1911. Page 110. Used by permission.
[2] *Ibid.* Page 198.
[3] From *Rural Religion and the Country Church*, Fleming H. Revell, New York, 1927. Used by permission.

Wilson died on March 2, 1937, honored and revered by all who knew him.

LIBERTY HYDE BAILEY (1858-1954)

Dr. Bailey served with distinction on President Roosevelt's Committee on Country Life. He understood fully the place of land in the program of the church and produced a significant little book, *The Holy Earth*. This book has served as a source of inspiration, information, and instruction to hundreds of rural workers. From his place in the classroom of Cornell University hundreds of men were sent out with a new appreciation of the earth as God's gift to men.

RALPH A. FELTON (1882-   )

The one man usually considered, unofficially, to be the dean of rural ministers is Dr. Ralph A. Felton, former professor of Rural Church at Drew Theological Seminary, Madison, N. J. Dr. Felton held this chair for many years and from it made a remarkable contribution to the rural cause. Prior to holding this position he was director of the Rural Extension Department of the Methodist Board of Extension and Missions.

Early in his teaching career, Ralph Felton traveled to China, Japan, and Korea, where he made a study of rural churches and people. His study was made for the Tambaram meetings of the International Missionary Council and published under the title, *The Rural Church In the Far East* (1938).

From his wide and long experience in the rural church movement, he compiled and published a series of pamphlets that are invaluable to students of the rural church. His studies are factual and as enlightening as anything available at present.

The work of Dr. Felton accounts for much of the progress of the Methodists in the rural field.

MARK A. DAWBER (1881-   )

Another Methodist who should be mentioned in any roll call of dynamic rural leaders is Mark A. Dawber. He was born in England and came to this country as a young man. He entered the ministry and took a circuit of four small churches in Pennsylvania. His work was so conspicuous that in 1918 he was called to Boston University as Professor of Rural Church. It was here that he developed the idea of the church-centered community. He was soon appointed to head the Department of Rural Work of the Methodist Board of Missions and Church Extension.

In 1938 the Home Missions Council of North America selected him as its executive secretary. From this position he fathered the National Convocation on Church in Town and Country. This convocation has become the most significant gathering of rural Protestant Christians of our day.

MARK RICH (1899-   )

Dr. Mark Rich came to the position of Secretary of Town and Country Work Department of the American Baptist Home Mission Society in 1938, after serving the larger parish of Groton, N. Y. He had received his Ph.D. from Cornell University in 1937.

One feature of his work was the issuing of over forty rural church bulletins. These are brief bulletins, each dealing with one phase of the rural church's interest. They form a small but significant addition to a rural pastor's library.

A second Rich contribution is the schools for Town and Country ministers held each winter at Green Lake, Wis., on the American Baptist Assembly grounds. The schools started as one-month schools in fall, winter, and spring. Each school now lasts sixteen days. Since the schools are of short duration, it is possible to have outstanding rural leaders of the nation participate as lecturers and discussion leaders. This scheme makes the schools extremely valuable, and over the years an impressive number of pastors have attended.

From the eighteenth century to the present, the ideas of rural-minded men of the highest calibre from Europe, Asia, and America have met in the rural areas of America to give the world a new concept of Christian civilization.

III

A SURVEY OF RURAL CHURCH
PROGRAMS

THERE ARE, APPROXIMATELY, 200,000 Protestant churches in
rural America. They have a combined membership of twenty-
seven million people. This would average one church of 145
members for every 387 residents. However, the distribution
of churches is most uneven, for in areas of declining population there may be one or more churches for every 100 or 150
people. At the other extreme, in rapidly growing areas there
may be less than one church for a thousand people. And there
are also many hamlets, perhaps as many as 10,000, that have
no regular Christian ministry, though some of them still have
churches.

The denominations used in this study have different defini-
tions for "rural." Some hold to the United States Bureau of
the Census definition, while others increase their count by
including the towns (2,500 to 10,000 population) in their cal-
culations. The table (page 39), in so far as possible, indicates
the way the denominations divide their areas of responsibility
and the number of rural churches each reports.

In the Southern Baptist Convention, the most rural of the
major denominations except the Cumberland Presbyterians, 83
per cent of the churches and four million members (50%) are
reported in rural areas. Fourteen denominations report 96,652
rural (town and country) churches, which is 70 per cent of all
the churches of these denominations. About sixteen million
people belong to these churches, which is 45 per cent of the
total membership of the fourteen reporting denominations.

Denomination	T. & C.* Churches	% of all Churches	Membership in T. & C. Churches	% of all Members	Definition of T. & C. Area
Baptist					
American Baptist	3,514	61	535,597	34.5	10,000
Southern Baptist	23,146	83	3,921,052	50	2,500
Church of the Brethren	680	69	145,065	77	2,500
Church of God	893	42	30,089	26	2,500
Disciples	4,624	65	587,895	30	2,500
Evangelical United Brethren	3,294	73	326,443	45	2,500
National Lutheran Council (10 Synods)	9,143	59	2,153,860	37	10,000
Methodist	32,400	81	6,000,000	66	10,000
Presbyterian					
Cumberland	895	89	47,150	57	2,500
United Presbyterian Church in the United States	5,502	59	603,620	20	10,000
United States	2,700	73	300,000	37	5,000
Protestant Episcopal	4,145	56	413,606	25	10,000
Reformed Church in America	355	45	75,000	38	5,000
United Church of Christ in America	5,361	65	622,347	33	2,500
	96,652	70	15,872,224	45	

* Town and Country.

This indicates, among other things, that rural churches are usually small. Therefore they have fewer total resources at their disposal. Many of them have fewer than fifty members, which is not enough to support a full-time resident pastor and a church program. Such churches cannot effectively minister to their communities. Nevertheless, it must never be inferred that these churches are useless. Even the smallest unit can contribute something to the welfare of the community in which it is located.

Neither should one reach the conclusion that all rural churches are small, for there are some with memberships of a thousand. But generally speaking, the number of members in a rural church is more likely to be under one hundred than over two hundred.

Small as some rural churches are, they supply the nation with a high percentage of its religious leaders. In a large urban church one has to ask only a few questions concerning the birthplace of its leaders to be assured that a city church is an extension of a large number of rural churches. In one home mission office it was found that seven of the ten executives were rural-born. A preponderance of men in the ministry have been rural-born. One little open-country church in Kansas produced ten ministers and missionaries or their wives in less than a generation, while its sister church in a small city could claim not a single one in its seventy-five-year history.

As a study of the denominations' programs indicates, there is a more favorable atmosphere for the development of rural churches now than at any time in the past fifty years. However there is growing opposition to rural work from another direction. The improvement in communications, the declining percentage of people engaged in agriculture, and the increase of the rural non-farm segment of the rural population, cause some leaders to argue that there are no significant differences between rural and urban churches except in size. They infer that only the difference in the size of churches calls for different programs. This criticism will be dealt with later.

We may then note from a study of fourteen denominations that 70 per cent of the churches of Protestantism are found in town and country areas. These churches hold in their membership approximately 45 per cent of the total church membership of these denominations. In past years these churches, because of their small membership rolls, inadequate leadership, and a false concept of ministerial success, were neglected; but a new day is dawning. In spite of ecclesiastical neglect, the churches in rural areas have shown such remarkable vitality that much expansion of the denominations may be credited to them, and even more may be anticipated in the future. Let us, then, review the programs which the denominations have developed for their rural churches.

The majority of Baptists belong to one of four Baptist Conventions: The American (formerly Northern) Baptist Convention, The Southern Baptist Convention, and the two Negro Conventions, The National Baptist Convention, U. S. A., Inc., and The National Baptist Convention of America. The first two of these groups recognize rural church work with specially assigned workers and programs.

AMERICAN BAPTIST CONVENTION

As early as 1911, the attention of the American Baptist Convention was being directed to the plight of the rural churches by such men as Charles Josiah Galpin, Walter Rauschenbusch, and Samuel Zane Batten.

The Department of Social Service and Rural Community Work of the American Baptist Home Mission Society was established on January 1, 1919. In 1929 Rev. Edwin E. Sundt became the secretary of the Society's Department of Town and Country Work and definite advances, formerly advocated, began to be realized. The first annual award given to an outstanding rural pastor was made in 1932 with the presentation of "The Rosa O. Hall Honor Award for Distinguished Service to Town and Country Churches." This award has been presented every year since. The larger parish plan of church grouping was publicized and advanced in some areas of the Convention.

In 1938 when Dr. Mark Rich became secretary, the work was expanded with the appointment of Town and Country Work Directors in twenty states. Sensing that one of the greater needs of town and country churches was for trained pastoral leadership, Mr. Rich embarked on an in-service educational program. A portion of the American Baptist Assembly at Green Lake, Wis., was set aside as the Rural Church Center, and buildings for classrooms, chapel, dining and office space were provided. From the Home Mission Society and the Board of Education, funds were secured to subsidize the travel, lodging and board of pastors and their families from over the Convention area. Three schools, each of a month's duration were set up, one in late fall, one in the winter and one in early spring. However, because a month proved too long for pastors to be away from their churches, the schools were later shortened to 16 days each.

Schools are limited to an enrollment of 30 students. To date more than 1000 pastors have studied for two or more weeks at the Rural Church Center.

The schools cover the gamut of town and country church interest, dealing with such subjects as the pastoral ministry, group dynamics and church leadership, community-type and cooperative Baptist churches, and the church in the rural-urban fringe.

Professors from state colleges, as well as denominational colleges and seminaries, are co-opted for the teaching. Only one professor appears at one time in a school. For five days he offers three hours of class work each morning, two hours each afternoon and one hour each evening. He then leaves, and another professor with another subject appears. This system makes for intensive, concentrated study.

Sometimes very practical and far-reaching results come from these sessions. For example, one of the earlier schools, while studying finances, developed the idea of a minimum salary plan for American Baptist churches. Some other schools followed suit, with the result that the plan has now been adopted by several state Baptist conventions.

A Baptist Town and Country Fellowship was organized in 1944, composed of both clergymen and lay people.

In 1948 a significant National Planning Conference for Northern (American) Baptist Churches in Town and Country was held at Green Lake. One hundred twenty rural pastors, laymen and laywomen, and denominational leaders in town and country work developed a *Platform of Rural Advance*, which led to the creation of the Commission on Rural Advance by the Associated Home Mission Agencies.

In 1949 the Board of Education and Publication, in making a grant to the Central Baptist Theological Seminary at Kansas City Kan., suggested that the school might experiment with the launching of a Deparment of Rural Leadership Training. The work of the Department of Rural Leadership Training as now developed divides itself into four parts:

Teaching, in which two professors are used, offering a total of forty semester hours of rural work. *Literature,* in which the Department is engaged in the production of literature for the rural-minded student and for the use of town and country churches. *Extension service* is provided, in part, by one-day and week-end institutes. An annual Rural Church Emphasis Week is held during the third week before Easter for the school's student body and the Baptist laity and clergy of the Midwest. During this week, a rural pastor is honored by being invited to give the chapel addresses, and one outstanding rural church is declared to be Central's Rural Church of the Year, and is awarded a plaque. *Missionary service* is rendered, in co-operation with state conventions, in sending and then supervising theological students' services to churches.

The seminary has been generous in its allotment of funds for the purchase of books pertaining to town and country life, thus creating a large, well housed, and properly catalogued collection in the seminary library.

In the reorganization of the American Baptist Home Mission Societies in 1958 the Department of Town and Country Work, of which Dr. Clayton A. Pepper had become director, was absorbed into the Division of Church Missions. This change was not intended to lessen the interest in rural people; in fact it has strengthened it by incorporating rural interests more adequately within the work of the whole denomination. For instance, under the leadership of Rev. Lawrence H. Janssen, whose services were formerly available to city churches, church-and-community studies have more recently been conducted in rural areas. In conjunction with Central Seminary such a study of the Kansas City (Kan.) Rural-Urban Fringe was completed and mimeographed. Other services which became available to town-country churches with this administrative change included in-service training for pastors, under the leadership of Rev. Robert T. Frerichs, and Church Strategy, under Selwyn Smith.

Dr. Paul O. Madsen, Associate Executive Secretary of the Division of Church Missions, outlined a four-point program for the denomination in his address at the 12th annual Rural Church Emphasis Week, March 14, 1961. In brief this calls for the following:

1. Fields that are large enough to demand the best of a man who is called to serve.

2. Resident, full-time ministers, well trained.

3. Adequate support for ministers.

4. An adequate program of community service and Christian education, with a building and program for all ages.

The Home Mission Boards took a major policy action in January of 1960, with the decision that anyone appointed to a Town and Country field will be classified as a fully commissioned missionary, with the same rights and privileges and standards as that of any other missionary who goes out to serve. This action adds dignity, self-respect and even more—a sense of value and permanence in being backed by the Home Mission Societies.

SOUTHERN BAPTIST CONVENTION

The Southern Baptist Convention began its specifically rural work in 1943.

Considerable progress has been made in advancing the rural church program through the colleges and seminaries of the Convention. Southeastern Baptist Theological Seminary, Wake Forest, N. C., has a department dedicated to preparing students for a rural ministry, and Southwestern Baptist Theological Seminary, Fort Worth, Tex., co-operates with the Texas Baptist Convention in the employment of a man for seminary classes and field work.

A four-point program is being used by the denomination in developing the churches and their leaders: better pastoral leadership, better buildings and grounds, better trained lay leaders, and a good kingdom program.

In order to gather more detailed information on the needs and opportunities of the rural churches the Home Mission Board appointed The Long Range Planning Committee, representing pastors, associational missionaries, teachers, state convention workers, and representatives from boards and agencies of the Southern Baptist Convention. Through the use of surveys selected churches were encouraged to study their communities and their church programs. From the information gathered it is hoped that a permanent program for church development may be stated in definite terms and offered to all Southern Baptist Churches in rural areas.

The Long Range Planning Committee set up the following goals, on the basis of a twenty-five-year program:

1. All Southern Baptist pastors adequately trained and supported, living in the community, and giving full time to it.

2. Each rural church of the Southern Baptist Convention properly located, having adequate grounds and facilities to meet the needs of the community.

3. Every Southern Baptist rural church seeking to make the greatest possible contribution in lifting the level of the total life of the community.

4. Every Southern Baptist rural church teaching the Bible plan of stewardship; giving a percentage of its total budget to missions through the Co-operative Program, and increasing that percentage each year.

5. The expansion of Southern Baptist rural work to make a church accessible to the people of every community in the Convention area.

6. The Long Range Committee co-operating with minority groups, such as Indians, Spanish-speaking, and Negroes, in the development of their rural churches and mission stations.

7. All Southern Baptist colleges and seminaries including in their curricula specialized courses in community life and development and practical training of rural leadership.

CHURCH OF THE BRETHREN

Two Brethren colleges are giving special emphasis to rural life developments: Manchester College, North Manchester, Ind., and McPherson College, McPherson, Kan.

A few years ago, a sum of $50,000 was set aside as a special loan fund to young Brethren farmers needing financial aid in setting up their farm operations. This practice has immensely benefited the rural churches.

In some churches the Brethren have farm locating committees that help young people settle on farms, provide them with financial backing and other help, and attempt to keep farms within the church membership. Two such churches are the Panther Creek Church of Adel, Iowa, and the South Waterloo Church of Waterloo, Iowa.

In pastoral leadership, the Brethren provide supplemental funds for pastors' salaries to ensure better pastoral care in rural churches.

Nine characteristic objectives are discussed under the following headings in *Rural Life Objectives,* by I. W. Moomaw: Building the Christian Community, Foresight in Settlement of Estates, Preserving the Family Type Farm, Improved Methods of Renting, Father and Son Partnerships, Wise Use of Coöperative Organizations, Direct Mutual Aid, Education for Rural Life, The Church and the "Farm Problem."

CHURCH OF GOD

The most recent of the denominations to establish a department of rural work is the Church of God, with headquarters in Anderson, Ind. As early as 1941 the denomination had a Committee on Town and Country Church. Then in 1956, the denomination employed Rev. Louis F. Meyer to set up a program of work for town and country churches and to teach rural work in their seminary.

The secretary of the Town and Country Church Department issues a quarterly bulletin, "Rural Fellowship Dispatch," which contains news, instruction, and inspiration. It is planned to make this a monthly publication.

Eight goals and objectives are: (1) To present a serious appeal for proper recognition of the small town and country church as the vital source of leadership for the church; (2) To challenge town and country people to cultivate their heritage and possibilities for Christ and his Church; (3) To help conserve and strengthen existing town and country churches spiritually, financially, and organizationally. To make them a growing, serving part of the kingdom by helping each church serve all the needs of all members of the family; (4) To give direction and guidance in the development of new churches in the town and country areas of America through a planned program of evangelism; (5) To devise ways to conserve the migrating town and country Christian for the Church of God as he moves to the city; (6) To encourage pastors to look upon the town and country church as a lifework; (7) Realizing that all of life is sacred, help to improve all levels of life in the town and country areas of America — moral, spiritual, educational, social, and economic; (8) Since the community is the "soil" out of which the church grows, seek to help each town and country church find ways of greater witness to its total community.

DISCIPLES OF CHRIST

In 1912 there came into being the Commission on Social Service and the Rural Church, which was organically related to the American Christian Missionary Society. The Commission strongly urged (1) grouping of churches for ministerial support; (2) full-time rural ministers trained and fitted to meet the needs of rural congregations and communities.

Under the leadership of Professor E. C. Cameron of Butler University (Indianapolis) there was issued in 1929 a "Suggested Standard for Town and Country Churches of the Disciples of Christ." But the rural movement gained only marginal attention and support, and was curtailed by the untimely death of Professor Cameron.

In 1939 the rural movement gained status when the Home and State Missions Planning Council was organized with a standing Committee on Town and Country Church. Since that date all the State Missionary Societies and the United Christian Missionary Society have been committed to make rural work a major interest in their planning and administration. In 1944 there was added to the staff a National Director of Town and Country Church.

The Committee on Town and Country Church is composed of fifteen members, rural pastors, professors of rural sociology and rural church, state secretaries, and the national director. The Committee has two-day meetings each year for review and planning, making recommendations to the state missionary societies and to the United Christian Missionary Society for their consideration and action.

From recent recommendations of the Committee the following directives may be gleaned:

Rural churches must become community institutions and not denominational enterprises or sectarian clubs. In the end the rural church will become a community institution, uniting the people for worship and service, or it will die.

The great need is for pastors, lay and ordained. To help in the training of pastors the committee has prepared a three-year reading course for those with limited training. Each man taking the training is required to read six books a year and to consult with an appointed counselor.

The Church Enlargement Crusade in Town and Country Churches is planned to be an evangelistic endeavor with certain features added so that the churches will be left with plans for an enriched and expanded program. The program is wrapped as a twelve-day package. Three nights are given to consideration of the church's needs and opportunities in evangelism, Christian education, and stewardship. Two or three days are spent in visitation evangelism; and there are six nights of evangelistic preaching.

A uniting of churches for more adequate pastoral leadership has been furthered under the Pastoral Unity plan. In this plan two or more churches commit themselves to work under common ministerial leadership. There are 300 churches in 100 pastoral units.

Four seminaries are recognizing the need for training men for rural work.

The Rural Fellowship of the Disciples of Christ was organized in 1941 for the purpose of providing fellowship among rural pastors and promoting their interests.

In summary, the Disciples of Christ advocate that the rural church must accomplish two things:

1. Build Christian community where it lives.
2. Prepare Christian leadership for city churches.

The Evangelical United Brethren Church

The denomination has had a Commission on Town and Country Church since 1957, with the following directive: "It is the commission's duty to keep uppermost, at all times, the spiritual meaning of life, in relation to rural living, the land, the home, the community, the church, Christ and God; striving by an inclusive, long term strategy, based on thorough study and sound planning, to bring into existence the abundant life in Christ Jesus for all who are a part of rural communities, through strengthening the ministry and influence of the rural parishes throughout the Evangelical United Brethren Church." To implement the work of the Commission the denomination has a full time director of town and country work.

It is the aim of this church to have a resident pastor in each local church, who will build and lead in a program that meets the needs of both the church and the community. The program is to be of such a nature that successive pastors will continue with it rather than try to launch the church on another path. In general, the local church program should strengthen the spiritual values of the rural family by encouraging and aiding the young people to establish homes in rural areas and become constructive Christian forces in their respective communities.

The Commission on Town and Country Church, through the Department of Home Missions and Extension of the Board of Missions, publishes a monthly six-page paper, *Our Church in Town and Country*. This is the bulletin of the Rural Fellowship, and the town and country director is the editor.

The Lutheran Church

The National Lutheran Council's Division of American Missions has undertaken to establish and strengthen the Lutheran witness in rural areas by starting, in 1945, a rural church program with a full-time secretary. Part of the work has been a comprehensive study of Lutheranism in America. The goal is to develop a Lutheran program that ministers to a cross section of the nation. The following quotations are drawn from *A Profile of the Lutheran Church in the United States.*

The Church is the body of Christ. It can not be labeled rural and urban. However, the Lutheran Church ministers to people living in the open country and in the city and it must recognize the special needs of the different types of community.

The Lutheran Church has no desire to be a class church but in the true sense to be an American church whose membership profile coincides with the profile of the nation.[1]

Three general objectives are, as stated by Dr. E. W. Mueller in *Lutheran World,*

1. *To alert* the church to carry on an energetic mission program in rural America, to push out from the areas of strength, and to claim the unchurched areas for God by sharing with the people in these areas that which we have in Christ.

2. *To arouse* our constituency to the task of building a generation of God-fearing country folk who, together with their offspring will serve as leaven in their own communities and in the urban communities to which many of their children will migrate.

3. *To mobilize* as many of our 6,000 rural congregations and pastors as possible in a sustained effort to secure our rural heritage. The mobilized rural church needs to make use of every legitimate resource to aid it in the building of Christian communities as it continually weaves the red thread of divine redemption into the fabric of community living.

The Lutherans in building a rural church program are not unaware of the ecology of rural life. Emphasis is placed upon stewardship of the land, the sanctity of the home, and the importance of community life, with the church energizing, spiritualizing, and directing human conduct.

Among other things, special attention has been given to the 4-H club. An annual "God-Home-Country Award" is made to Lutheran young people who have outstanding records as 4-H'ers.

THE METHODIST CHURCH

Before the Roosevelt Commission on Country Life made its report (1909), Methodists were interested in rural life. Early the plight of rural people and their churches was championed by the bishops. As a result the Town and Country movement has been an integral part of the church's planning.

The Town and Country Department has as its basic purpose:

[1] Mueller, E. W., *A Profile of the Lutheran Church in the United States* (Chicago: Division of American Missions, National Lutheran Council, 1954).

To help strengthen the small churches now in existence in town and country areas; To co-operate in establishing new churches in unchurched areas; To serve mission areas within continental United States, such as coal fields, mountain areas, sparsely settled and isolated areas, low-income farm groups, and migrant labor.

The Town and Country Department has a clearly defined program outlined as a guide for the work of the Methodist Church in town and country areas.

1. Co-operate with the various boards and agencies of the church in an effort to create in the ministry a deep sense of mission and evangelism.

2. Co-operate with the Methodist seminaries and Methodist colleges in the establishing of professors of town and country work in these schools. The professor of town and country work to have an open channel to the Annual Conference boards and agencies, and to the local churches through the Commission on Town and Country work in the Annual Conference.

3. The Department joined with the Annual Conference boards of missions and commissions on town and country work for the adoption of a minimum salary plan and a general improvement of the financial program in the local church.

4. Relating every interest of the Methodist Church to meet the rural church problem through representation on the Town-Country Commission of representatives from all boards and agencies of the denomination; each Annual Conference having a Commission on Town and Country Work.

5. Co-operate with the section of Church Extension on improving rural church buildings, providing adequate parsonages, and helping small churches to make provision in their programs, and for fellowship and religious education, as well as worship.

6. Develop the Group Ministry Plan of work as one of the major ways of reaching the small church with an adequate leadership and a sustaining program. The Group Ministry is an adaptation of the Larger Parish Plan to fit the Methodist plan of work and polity.

7. Establish Methodist families in town and country communities and champion the family farm as a sacred institution. Promote father-son partnerships as a means for young men to stay in their rural communities.

8. Provide a ministry for areas of special mission need such as coal fields, low-income farm groups, and sparsely settled and other neglected areas.

9. Relate town and country church programs to the life of the community more than ever before. Believing that the church pros-

pers when it works on the theory that a good community must possess all the elements necessary for the good life, develop a vigorous program of assistance in establishing a wholesome working relationship between the local churches and all the worthy national, state, and local community agencies.

10. Materials. A *Newsletter* published from time to time serves to keep town and country leaders informed, describes new literature available, and shares information on various programs and methods being employed throughout the church.

THE PROTESTANT EPISCOPAL CHURCH

In 1935 Bishop Fenner of the Protestant Episcopal Church wrote: "More than any other religious body, the Episcopal Church is thought of as a 'city church,' and while she cannot be proud of the title, she must admit that she has earned it." Since then this Church has formed some definite rural policies, though it is still predominantly urban. In a sense it has attempted to go back to its origins, for from ancient times the Church of England has been a great rural church.

The National Advisory Committee on Town and Country Work of the Protestant Episcopal Church proposes seven major emphases to be made in national and local work:

1. Provide a pastoral ministry, including preaching and the sacraments for Episcopalians in small towns and open country areas.

2. Provide continuous Christian education to Episcopalians of all ages.

3. Strengthen the existing organized work of the Church.

4. Establish the organized work of the Church in areas of need and opportunity.

5. Aggressively evangelize and win to Christian conviction and Episcopal Church membership the unchurched who live in rural areas.

6. Bring Christian influence to bear on all phases of rural community life: government, economics, education, recreation, health, social, and religious life.

7. Co-operate with other church bodies and all other agencies which strive to improve the rural general welfare.

These are being implemented with considerable rapidity.

On a 410-acre farm near Kansas City the Protestant Episcopal Church has developed the Roanridge Rural Training Institute. It was first organized in 1943 to provide a summer program for seminary students residing at Park College in Parkville, Mo.

Then, four years later, the Roanridge Rural Training Foundation was organized.

The property now includes modern farm buildings and machinery, greatly improved land under complete soil and water management, a central administration building, and two staff residences. Roanridge demonstrates two types of agriculture; it includes a large, well-run modern farm raising registered Shorthorn cattle, and a small, one-acre project developed with hand tools and a minimum of expense, to show the possibilities available to any rural clergyman in his own back yard.

Although Roanridge is the national center for rural church training, several regional institutes, patterned after Roanridge, are equally important. Each has its own director and its own staff, but the entire program is co-ordinated by the director of Roanridge.

The Rural Church Training Program has existed in its present form since 1945, a co-operative program involving the seminaries, training institutes, the provinces, dioceses, parishes, and missions. Through these institutes, seminarians are given a practical introduction to rural life. They are guided and supervised in learning how the church can best minister to people living in rural areas.

In collaboration with the National Council Unit of Research and Field Study, the Division of Town and Country maintains a continuous service to make surveys and field studies in local areas in response to requests from bishops in those areas. After the studies have been made, the Division continues a co-operative plan of action with the diocese to develop the type of church program which will best serve that area.

The Division both initiates action and co-operates with other Divisions of the National Council and other agencies in the production of literature for Christian educational use, for pastoral and devotional uses, correspondence ministry to the isolated, and for Rogation and Harvest Festival services.

The following visual aid sets have been made, and more are contemplated: *The Cross and Plow Series,* showing some steps the church is now taking to develop a more effective ministry in town and country; *Sharpening Rural Church Tools,* portraying the Church's program for assisting clergy and church workers in improving their methods of work; and *Learning Which Fork to Use,* showing the work of the Rural Church Training Institute. Special emphasis is placed also on the production of motion pictures.

Close co-operation and a program of mutual helpfulness are maintained between the Division of Town and Country and the Episcopal Rural Workers' Fellowship, a voluntary membership society of clergy and laity interested in advancing the best interests of rural church work and providing a bond of fellowship for workers in the town and country areas. The Fellowship issues a quarterly journal, *Cross Roads.*

UNITED CHURCH OF CHRIST

The union of Congregational and Christian Churches, completed in 1931, brought into one denominational framework 5,425 churches with 1,298,000 members. This union then merged with the Evangelical and Reformed Church in 1957 to form The United Church of Christ in the United States and thereby added 2,735 congregations and 761,842 members.

Rural work was established by the Congregationalists as early as 1919, when Dr. Malcolm L. Dana was appointed secretary of the Town and Country Church Department. It continued in unbroken succession through Dr. Thomas A. Tripp (1937-1954) and Dr. Wesley A. Hotchkiss (1954-1958) until the forming of The United Church of Christ. The rural work of the two denominations is now combined in the Department of Town and Country Work.

The activities of the Department include continuous consultations with state committees concerning their direct contacts with the rural churches in their respective areas. Guidance is offered to rural pastors and churches regarding the best known ways of parish work. Research, particularly field research which is the study of specific parishes, communities, and larger areas, is treated as a matter of importance. Published materials, both pamphlets and magazine articles, are provided in a steady stream for pastors and laymen who seek improvement of their understanding of rural society and parish methods. Training of the rural ministry is done through numerous institutes, summer short courses, and experimental projects.

The Congregational and Christian churches pioneered in several projects, among which was a Life Ministry to Town and Country Churches. Invented by the New Hampshire Congregational Christian Conference for service to rural churches in difficult areas, the plan solicits the life rural minister to make an agreement with the state conference to devote his entire professional life to going where the conference assigns him, and in turn the conference assures his support. The first life rural ministry was established in 1944. In 1951 there were three ordained men serving as life ministers in New Hampshire. The encouraging factor in the life rural ministry is that rural churches and areas have responded with fine good will and co-operation to a vigorous and progressive leadership.

A second project is the securing and training of lay preachers for rural churches. The New Hampshire Conference has a lay preachers' fellowship. Sixteen laymen are or have been members. This fellowship is attracting considerable interest. Its program includes a week-end meeting every other month and a ten-day lay preachers' school each summer.

The Conference holds that the Christian layman should be able to preach the gospel. He has a religious faith and at least can give a testimony. To be sure, an ordained ministry is essential to the church. There is no consideration of lessening the emphasis on fully-trained professional ministers. It is pointed out, however, that there are not, and probably will not be, enough ordained men to serve all the churches. The emphasis is on lay preachers, not lay ministers. The administration of the sacraments and other rites, such as marriage ceremonies, in a parish whose pulpit is filled by a lay preacher can be done by a neighboring ordained minister.

It is understood that the lay preacher is not a person who looks toward ordination and takes the course of lay-preacher training as a back-door entrance into ordination. Nor does the lay preacher expect to compete with ordained men. The lay preacher anticipates making his own distinctive, separate, and different place in the ministry of the church.

The ten-day summer school of the New Hampshire Conference and the Board of Home Missions is planned by the lay preachers' fellowship. The course of study is designed to prepare them to be lay preachers, better laymen in their own churches, better informed, and better equipped for church work. It prepares them to serve in their respective regions as leaders in the development of churchmanship among the other laymen. It fits them to assist in church extension programs which reach out to neglected neighborhoods with a ministry of worship, preaching, teaching, and fellowship. It prepares them to serve as pulpit supplies and as preachers in local churches.

Bible study and discussion are basic to the curriculum. The lay preacher is led to understand the times in which he lives, the community, the social forces which are at work in his world, and the nature of the struggle which is taking place before his eyes. He anticipates coming to know intimately what religion has to offer, what religion does when it is at work, what its powers are, and what its achievements have been. He learns something about the use of his voice in Scripture reading and in preaching. He shares in the planned evening programs of the school, including intimate discussions with teachers on problems vital to them.

One of the problems of the church is that of serving rural areas which have clustered and scattered populations. The population distribution pattern of the Great Plains is a principal example of this problem, where settlement is clustered in the towns which are far apart, and it is sparse among the farming sections which lie between.

Rural pastors, churches, and the denomination are experimenting with the various modern means of mass communication for serving scattered populations. In the early 1940's South Dakota Conference, in co-operation with the Board of Home Missions, originated a program of rural religious extension service among churches in sparsely settled counties. This program experimented in the use of radio and religious literature to serve scattered families. The radio broadcasts in this program made contacts with isolated families by the pastors of the town churches possible. Throughout western South Dakota, particularly, the scattered ranch families ordered information booklets which were delivered by nearby pastors who organized schoolhouse churches and home study groups.

The Evangelical and Reformed branch of the new denomination has always maintained high standards of scholarship for its ministry. A survey has shown that only 14 per cent of the rural pastors were without college training, and only 2 per cent without seminary training.

College and seminary training does not necessarily mean that a pastor is fully trained to lead rural people. The Church works closely with the Michigan State College of Agriculture, encouraging rural pastors to enroll for three summers of study. Generous scholarships to cover expenses are offered. In addition to this training on an agricultural campus the seminary has a professor of rural church.

The Secretary of Town and Country Work is assisted by a synodical committee that counsels with him on the work. In the new denomination the strengths of both Churches are merged.

THE UNITED PRESBYTERIAN CHURCH IN THE UNITED STATES

One, if not the first, of the major denominations to consider seriously the rural church as an important segment of its corporate life, demanding special attention and program, was the Presbyterian Church. The pioneer leader, Warren H. Wilson, gave not to that Church alone but to all protestantism a thrust in the right direction during his thirty years as Director of the Department of Town and Country Work.

The areas of responsibility and major objectives of the Department were outlined by Henry S. Randolph in a paper read before the Committee on Management of the Town and Country Department of the National Council of Churches of Christ, October 15, 1956, at Merom, Ind.

In all communities where the Church has a responsibility the Department seeks to make available a comprehensive gospel, integrating community agencies and activities, and providing necessary activities not provided by other agencies. While continually trying to eliminate discrimination at home they seek to give rural Presbyterians a world vision so that they will try to meet human needs from their stores of food, clothing, and technical knowledge. It has expressed a deep concern for farm life and seeks to build a sense of security through land settlement programs, and a spiritualization of farm life through which farmers recognize themselves as God's stewards of the land and tillers of the soil. The concern for people reaches beyond the farmer to the non-farm element of rural life as the Department strives to help people to become successful in such trades as will develop their personalities, provide for their families, and help them become well integrated in community life. Because a sizable proportion of rural people will migrate to urban areas it seeks to help orient them in the urban way of life and develop good working relations between rural and urban churches. At the same time it seeks out the marginal people of the rural area and brings to them the services of the church. Toward the building of strong churches, the area each church serves is broadened to correspond with the sociological community. This in turn calls for a strong rural church program in each synod.

In order to accomplish these high aims the Department provides the churches and synods with such services as literature, conferences, schools, workshops, surveys, counseling, and the recruiting and training of a rural-minded ministry.

The rural program of United Presbyterians who merged with the Presbyterian Church, U.S.A. was highly important to the 400 rural churches of that denomination. Under the leadership of Dr. George Kerr many parsonages and church buildings were improved. The method of procedure was to make a direct grant of $2,000 to any church that would undertake a major improvement on its equipment. Under this incentive contracts totaling several millions of dollars were let.

IV

THE LAND AND ITS PEOPLE

IT IS VERY DIFFICULT, if not utterly impossible, to describe the American ruralite. Once he was thought by some to be a one-gallused, straw-chewing, ignoramus which they deigned to call a "clodhopper" or a "hayseed." Only in a few cases was this even remotely true. Farm people have been and are quite intelligent. They are in the midst of a highly successful revolution in food production in which more constructive changes have taken place in 30 years than in the past 300 years.

An adequate description of rural people is further complicated because two-thirds of them are not farm people. They live in villages and towns, operating businesses, manning the professions and services, and working in industries. Yet, by definition they are rural people.

Agriculture has a way of coloring the life of people who, in making a living, are removed several steps from it. Even cities are colored by the type of prevailing agriculture in their regions. The several major crop types of agriculture have their own peculiar contributions to make to the customs, habits, and prosperity of those who live within their respective areas. The vitality and structure of rural churches have, through the years, been determined by the agriculture of their areas. Therefore it is well for the minister to know the location and characteristics of these areas.

The United States Census divides the country into three regions, namely, north, south, and west. In turn, these regions include nine further subdivisions. Dr. Carl C. Taylor, of the United States Department of Agriculture, has divided the country into seven regions according to the major types of farming. For the purposes of the rural church this is a more satisfactory way to divide the country. By dealing with a major type of farming in any region, the work habits, income, health, and social practices of the people of any one area will be reasonably uniform. Thus, workable solutions may be established for each region.

THE CORN BELT

> The corn belt is the heart of what is known in broad terms as the great Middle West. Consisting of 469 counties lying within the eleven states of Ohio, Indiana, Illinois, Iowa, Michigan, Wisconsin, Minnesota, South Dakota, Nebraska, Kansas and Missouri, its core is in the first four states while only in Iowa are all counties classified as belonging to the belt.[1]

For the most part its 818,000 farms are family-sized, family-operated, commercial farms. The population in 1950 was over fourteen million people. However, only 24 per cent, about four million people, live on farms. About three million are rural non-farm, and some seven million are urbanites. In this belt are such larger cities as Chicago, Indianapolis, and Omaha, with smaller cities where small industries and businesses flourish. The people speak of this land in superlatives. According to them it has the richest soil, ideal weather for corn-livestock production, and the most up-to-date farms in the nation. Its wealth is more equitably distributed than elsewhere, and the independence of its people is zealously guarded. Statistics seem to justify the conclusions of the natives.

The area has seen a heavy turnover in population. A generation ago Americans of pioneer stock sent their sons and daughters to high school and college. Many of these entered business and the professions instead of returning to the farms. Newly arrived or second-generation immigrants who took over the farms gave their children a common school education but kept them on the farms. Consolidated schools are, for the most part, accepted in the corn belt and are growing in numbers with the steady improvement of roads. Farm organizations flourish throughout the belt.

[1] Taylor, Carl C., and Others, *Rural Life in the United States* (New York: A. A. Knopf, 1949), p. 360.

The wealth of the people, the feeling of self-sufficiency, and the changing cultural background make this one of the most difficult areas for churches. Churches which once served the original settlers have closed and new churches to serve the later farmers have been established. However, there are some strong churches in the area, notably among the Lutheran and the Evangelical and Reformed groups. These, it should be noted, are the "land-loving" groups.

THE COTTON BELT

The cotton belt lies in a great crescent stretching from eastern North Carolina across the lower Mississippi basin to Oklahoma and western Texas. This belt covers 690 counties and has a population of seven million. It is more exclusively a farming area than any other. It has a higher birth rate than any other region, a circumstance which would provide a rapid increase of population were it not offset by the migration of the people to other parts of the nation.

The people of the south are comparatively young. About thirty per cent of the population is made up of children and youths between the ages of five and nineteen. This age group makes up only 25 per cent of the population of the rest of the nation. In the cotton belt the nation has the highest proportion of its total population living on farms, the highest tenancy rate, and the lowest farm level of living index. [2] Here also is the highest percentage of non-whites.

The cotton belt is rich in natural resources, but years ago cotton became "king," and other resources were disregarded. Soil depletion has been great, and many farms have been abandoned. The raising of cotton demands so much time that a family garden is often neglected, and malnutrition results. Nowhere else in the nation are tractors so few and horse plows so numerous.

As might be expected, many of the institutions in the cotton belt are below the national standard. Rural schools are too frequently housed in dilapidated buildings and manned by

[2] Many factors account for the variations in the levels of living found in rural areas. Drs. Schuler and McKain in *Rural Life in the United States* (p. 306) list them under three headings: (1) income differentials; (2) variations in needs and desires; (3) locality differences.

untrained teachers. Libraries and other equipment for schools are conspicuous by their absence. In many communities the policy of segregation demands two sets of schools, thus doubling the expense. More than anywhere else in the nation, the people of this region are most conscious of the county unit.

Except in Louisiana the people are largely Protestants. The Baptists lead in the number of church members, with the Methodists a close second. Many churches have preaching services only once a month, though they may claim a membership of two hundred or more. Pastors are untrained, many of them being farmers who feel "called to preach," and who do so now and then. But for all of its inadequacies, the church is highly respected and is the chief integrating force in many communities.

In recent years there has been forced upon many cotton belt people a sense of their responsibility for the proper use and care of natural resources. Abandoned farms are being reclaimed, and reforesting is going on apace. Mechanization of farm work is on the increase. Industry is moving into the area. Those who know the cotton belt are quick to say a new day is dawning for it.

THE DAIRY LAND

A dot on a map of the United States for each million gallons of milk produced on farms indicates the well-nigh universal production of milk. Where the population of the nation is the heaviest, there the dots become a solid mass. This is the dairy land of the nation, another major farm type area.

There are 269 counties in Minnesota, Wisconsin, Michigan, Ohio, Pennsylvania, New York, Maryland, Vermont, New Hampshire, Connecticut, Maine, Massachusetts, and Rhode Island that form the dairy land. While the farm people of this area are of varied origins, the nature of their work molds them into a fairly uniform culture.

Of the total population of this area, only 8 per cent live on farms. Another 20 per cent are classified as rural nonfarm. This is the great urban area of the nation where such activities as manufacturing, business, and stocks and bonds take the time of 70 per cent of the people. The rural people of the dairy land are closely related to city life. Here, more than anywhere else in the nation, there is a mingling of the new urban ways of life with the rural mores. The result is not unpleasant.

Dairy herds demand constant care, but they assure a stable income throughout the year. In the average herd there are from ten to forty milch cows, plus the young stock. At an early age children begin to help with the milking, and care for the stock. Dairying is a family enterprise, and the children profit from their close association with their parents in work and the early acceptance of responsibilities.

It is in the dairy land, more than in other types of farming, that rural life is characterized by stability. For the most part the farms are owned by their operators. In 1945 only 12 per cent of all the farmers in the area were tenants, and many of these were renting from relatives with the intention of buying later. In not a few cases, the contracts were for cash rent, which is the most desirable and nearest to ownership of any tenant agreement.

The level of living is relatively high. These people not only produce milk, butter, and cheese, but they have their own fruit trees and berry bushes, and the vegetable garden is well-nigh universal with them. They usually have poultry flocks and raise their own meat. Their houses, for the most part, are well-built and well-furnished. Electricity is a necessity in their barns as well as in their homes, and with it come the many modern appliances we associate with pleasant living.

Milk must be taken to the processing plant regularly. Roads therefore must be passable the year round. Snow removal equipment of the latest design is maintained, and with the first snow the highway crews go to work.

It is in the dairy land that the farmers put a high value on co-operation. Early they learned that this was the only way by which they could get a fair price for their milk. They formed co-operatives for the sale of milk and its products. The volume of business done through these co-ops is enormous, and the market is kept at a high and stable level. From these producers' co-ops, others have come into being, so that the dairy land is truly the co-op land.

The sense of security and stability which characterize the dairy land is reflected in the religious beliefs of the people, for here religious expressions are more rational, more liberal, more socially emphatic than in most other type-farming areas. In this area "gospel" sects are at a minimum.

THE GENERAL AND SELF-SUFFICING AREA

In the east-central part of the United States, embracing 552 counties, there is a strip of land that does not specialize in any one farm crop. In this area, where one-fifth of the farm families live, the people produce many things primarily to feed themselves. The area includes most of Kentucky, Tennessee, West Virginia, Virginia, and Pennsylvania, about one-half of Missouri and Ohio, parts of Vermont and New Hampshire, plus portions of eleven other states from Oklahoma to Maine.

The farms in this area are usually small, and most of the farm tools are simple. Mechanization of farms is at a minimum. Farm incomes are lower than in any other type of farming area. But since the people produce what they consume, they live much better than their cash income would seem to indicate. There is a great deal of off-farm work here. The people are inclined to get along with what they have. They are proud of their independence and resourcefulness. They have a deep attachment to their homes and their way of life, and about three-fourths of the farms are owned by their operators. When they move to cities, they have difficulty in making satisfactory adjustments. Such a mode of living has a tendency to increase the number of small farms as larger units are subdivided to accommodate children who want to farm.

As the name of the area indicates, there is no single dominant crop or livestock in the area. The farmers raise corn for meal, feed, and fodder; also potatoes, vegetables, fruits and honey. They have on each family unit a cow or two, chickens, and hogs. They do their own butchering and curing of meats. There are sawmills in the area, and a steady harvest of timber.

Living standards are low, houses usually small, and many are unpainted. Educational attainments are low. In some areas many of the adults above forty years of age can neither read nor write. The level of farm living is 74, as measured by the

United States Department of Agriculture, below the national index level of 100 by 26 points. It is, however, above the cotton belt level of 53 points. The mountains, hills, forests, and streams make communications most difficult. Poor roads make for little travel, compact neighborhoods, and predominant family units. Here life is still unhurried, less crowded, and more independent than anywhere else in the United States.

Churches are highly respected in the area, with the Baptist and Methodist denominations in great numbers. However, it should be carefully noted that there is a steady increase of new and highly emotional sects through the whole area. These are, in some places, supplanting the older churches. Most of the ministers of the area have little formal training, and spend much of their time farming or working at other jobs.

THE RANGE-LIVESTOCK AREA

The range-livestock area has been described as that which is left after the other farm areas have been taken out. It is a belt from 500 to 1,000 miles wide extending from Mexico to Canada and taking in about 30 per cent of all lands in the United States. It includes western Texas, New Mexico, most of Utah, most of Colorado, a fourth of Nebraska, half of South Dakota, Wyoming, Montana, Idaho, and about one-half of Oregon, plus a small area in Kansas and in North Dakota. For all of its wide expanse, less than 14 per cent of the cattle and only 45 per cent of the sheep of the country are raised in this area.

This is the area of many cultures. Here are descendants of Coronado's caravan that entered the country in 1541. Here are Indians whose ancestors antedated the earliest white man's entrance by hundreds of years. Here on fifteen million acres of poor land is the Navajo reservation, with the Hopi reservation near its center. The Navajo Indians for the most part follow a semi-nomadic life, tending their flocks of sheep, while the Hopi people reside in villages on the mesas. Other Indians live in their pueblos, with a bit of livestock and thin patches of corn, squash, and melons as their only visible means of sustenance. Mexicans are found usually in their own settlements. They may work on ranches owned by Caucasians, but they usually live apart and seldom own ranches. Finally there is the Caucasian, or white culture, which is considerably different from that of the romantic days of the cattle kings of 1840 to 1885.

For the reasons found in the other areas, the people are moving from the farms into the small towns where they can have schooling for their children. Of the 4,400,000 people in the area in 1950 only 836,000 were living on farms.

The level of living index, except for non-whites, is high in this area. For the entire area it is 105. For many local areas it is much higher. But for the Spanish American it is 62, and for the Navajos it is 19.

Though the cities are not large, they exercise considerable influence. The small towns are community centers, and people will drive 200 miles to a trading center. It is not unusual for people to go 100 miles to a dance or picture show and return the same evening.

Open-country churches are nonexistent. Even in towns, churches are few in number, because of the sparsely settled condition, but the people are not irreligious. Colporters and missionaries minister to many people. Churches with adequate staffs are needed to reach, not only the people in town, but those on the farms and the non-white groups. Large churches can seldom, if ever, be built here, but a type of dispersed, mobile ministry could render invaluable service in kingdom work. The radio, with mail follow-up, is occasionally used in ministering to these people.

THE WESTERN SPECIALTY-CROP AREA

In what was once the most desolate part of the United States, there are today gardens producing both necessities and luxuries for the nation. In 88 counties of Arizona, California, Utah, Idaho, Oregon, and Washington eight million acres have been claimed from the desert by irrigation. This new land produces the nation's almonds, apricots, alfalfa, asparagus, carrots, cantaloupes, cherries, lettuce, prunes, walnuts, lemons, and grapes. These products are called "specialty-crops." In no other farm area are there so many different farm enterprises. Because of the nature of their farming, farm families buy most of their food. They consume in their homes less of the food they grow than those in any other major agricultural region.

Farming here is big business, with three interrelated characteristics, namely: (1) dependence upon irrigation, (2) intensive use of the land, (3) speculation. In intensive farming, large acreages are seldom desirable. Over half of the farms in California consist of less than thirty acres. Many fruit, dairy, and poultry farms on the West Coast have only ten to forty acres.

The process of urbanization is carried farther here than elsewhere, except in the dairy land. Twelve per cent of the people are listed as rural farm, 23 per cent rural non-farm, and 65 per cent urban.

There is a wide variation in the levels of living. Incomes are high, but the distribution is extremely uneven. Wealth and poverty exist side by side. There is a social barrier between the farm operators and the hired laborers, the latter being Indians from the mountains, or white migrants. This is interesting, for there are few social differences between the farm owner-operator and the farm tenants. The lot of the migrant laborer is hard. His stay in one place is short so that his housing is always of a temporary nature, and modern conveniences are seldom available. His children miss months of school and drop out at an early age.

Most of the early settlers (about 1850) came from the northeastern states. A few years later, the major source of origin was the Midwest. These two sections established the early pattern of rural life: general or self-sufficient farming, free public schools, Protestantism, the virtue of hard work, and the unity of the farm family. Then came a wave of immigrants from the cotton belt, with their habits of leisure and a deep consciousness of class lines. In the 1930's there came the dust-bowl refugees from the parched plains of Oklahoma, Arkansas, and Texas. In addition to these are many settlers from England, Germany, Portugal, Holland, Switzerland, Russia, Italy, China, Japan, Armenia, India, and Mexico. Each brought his own religious beliefs. Church work can be exceedingly difficult in this region.

THE WHEAT AREA

Although wheat is grown in all farm areas of the nation, it is the dominant crop in only 250 counties with approximately

260,000 farms. The wheat belt is in three separate areas. Winter wheat raising is centered in western Kansas and spring wheat in North Dakota. In addition to these, there is a wheat area in the Columbia Basin. There is enough similarity in these three to call them one type of farming area.

This is the land of large farms, the average being 531 acres. In the Grand Coulee valley they average 3,000 acres with some reaching 8,000. Wheat farming is highly mechanized and the farmers are proud of their big machines. Once they depended upon an army of migrant laborers to harvest the wheat crop, but today they depend upon their own labor and custom combines.

There is a barrenness about the wheat area that usually depresses a person from the corn belt. Farm houses are not surrounded by groves, orchards, barns, and cribs as in other farm-type areas. An occasional small windmill breaks the monotony of the landscape. Here the density of population is only 6 persons to the square mile, and in some areas it is less than one to the square mile. (The average for the nation is computed at about 54.) There are no large cities in the wheat area. The migration, in and out, has been very heavy. When the weather is right the country is rich, but when the droughts come and the winds blow many must leave. But people of the wheat area love the apparent barrenness, and their homes are well-equipped and livable.

There are almost no open-country schools and churches. Those which do exist were established by the early settlers, but as farms have grown larger and farm families smaller, some have, of necessity, been closed. The farm families may divide for the school year, the father and older boys staying on the farm while the mother keeps house for the children in town during the school months. This system has proven so unsatisfactory that many are moving from farm to town, whence they commute to the farm to work.

A few churches are slowly adapting themselves to give a satisfactory ministry to these people. There is a tendency for the churches in town to confine their ministry to the town folks. They may, but usually do not, maintain neighborhood churches or units in the open country. It has been suggested that here the rural churches need a strong program on a county-wide basis. This seems to be one place where larger parishes might profitably be developed.

DISPOSSESSED PEOPLES

There are two classes within American agriculture that, because of their depressed condition, have a special claim on the rural church. In the final analysis it is only the church in their midst that can minister adequately to them. These classes are the North American Indians and the migrant agricultural laborers.

Christians, through their missionary organizations, have been aware of the needs of the Indians. In an effort to help them they have established schools and churches. But these efforts plus those of the Federal Government have not eliminated the Indian problem. To be sure, through the eastern part of the nation Indians have been to a large degree assimilated into the prevailing culture. But in the Southwest and part of the Far West the story is different. On their reservation in Utah, Arizona, and New Mexico dwell some 65,000 Navajos. Near the center of their territory is the Hopi reservation of small villages with about 2,500 Indians. Scattered through the rest of the Southwest are other small tribes.

It is difficult to describe the conditions under which the Southwestern Indian lives. Dr. Clarence Salisbury, as a young Presbyterian medical missionary, returned to America on his first furlough. He had occasion to visit the Navajo reservation. On seeing the poverty and physical condition of the natives he said in effect: "Why go back to a foreign field when the need here is as great as there?" Thereupon he gave himself to the Navajos as a medical missionary. He was stationed at Ganado, Ariz., where he developed a Christian settlement. He invested his professional life ministering to the Indians, and he established an excellent hospital.

The Indians of the Southwest need from Christians the kind of help that will make it possible for them to attain a decent level of living, educate their children, and know Jesus Christ as Lord and Savior. They need to enter the full stream of American Christian life. For the Gospel to be truly effective, the people must be aided in their economic and educational life. Brayton C. Case's formula for mission work in Burma: preach, teach, heal, and feed, might well be used with America's Indians.

In the United States, one million or more families, totaling five million people, are classed as migrant agricultural laborers. By their labors American tables are set with fresh string beans, lettuce, onions, radishes, and other delicacies, as well as with such staples as fruits, potatoes, and sugar. Yet the life of the migrant laborer, and the hope of his children are barren.

There are four major streams of migrating workers in the United States. The first stream rises in South Florida and flows north along the Atlantic seaboard to New Jersey, New York, and the New England states. For the most part it is composed of Negroes. Two streams originate in Texas, one flowing northward into the fruit and vegetable harvests of Michigan, Wisconsin, Indiana, and Illinois. The other stream moves up the western plains area for work in sugar beets, potatoes, and fruits of Colorado, Montana, and North Dakota. These two streams consist largely of Spanish-American people. The fourth and oldest stream moves up and down the western coast. Generally speaking, it too is made up of Spanish Americans, although there are Indians, Negroes, and "poor whites" in the caravans. There is hardly a state in the nation that does not, at some time, employ migrant agricultural labor.

It is almost impossible for one man to support a family on the pay received by migrant laborers. The pay may seem to some to be sufficient, but this sufficiency is offset by the days not worked because of drought, flood, or frost, plus the time spent in travel from one section of the country to another. The low income means that a laborer's wife and children must work the fields beside him. Preschool children are denied the loving care of a mother, as they play along the edges of the fields, or stay in the car nearby. The school-age children often receive no more than two or three months schooling in a year, and the majority drop out of school before finishing the sixth grade. In too many communities the migrants are wanted for labor, but are not wanted in schools, churches, or other places of public gathering. Because of their migrating, they are usually without the help of Social Security, and when unemployed have no source of sustenance. Their housing is often makeshift and without satisfactory sanitation.

The President of the United States appointed a Commission on Migratory Labor (1951) to make a study of the problem. After this Commission's report appeared the General Board of the National Council of Churches issued the following statement concerning the situation:

For thirty years the churches have co-operated through the Home Missions Council, now the Division of Home Missions, in providing a program of Christian service in thousands of migrant camps across the country. From this intimate contact with the situation we are convinced that the major problems include the following:

1. Migrant children have a limited opportunity for schooling due to the lack of adequate school facilities available to them; the interruptions of schooling by work in the field and frequent migrations, and often the exclusion of migrant children from local schools.

2. The lack of provision for the care of preschool children while parents are working causes neglect of many children.

3. Health problems are created by crowded and unsanitary housing; the ignorance of good health habits; the inability to pay for medical care; and the ineligibility of non-residents for public health services in the community where they are temporarily employed.

4. The low economic status and insecurity of migratory farm workers is a basic problem. The primary causes are the irregularity of employment due to an inadequate plan for the effective recruitment, fair employment and equitable distribution of seasonal farm labor by manpower agencies; the taking advantage of migrants by some employers and labor contractors; and the exclusion of migratory farm workers from legislation covering minimum wage, unemployment insurance and old age and survivors insurance.

5. Migrant people do not have an opportunity to participate in the life of the communities they touch because of mobility; the hostile attitudes of many communities; the inability of transients to establish legal residence and qualify for welfare assistance; the loss of the vote.

6. Migrant people are unable to be a part of established church life because of mobility.

7. Migrant people face discrimination based on race, color or national origin in employment, the use of housing, community facilities and public services furnished by the state and local governments.

Because of the problems enumerated above, we are sensitive as Americans to the fact that a million migratory farm workers and their families, citizens of our own land, do not enjoy the human rights and privileges which the General Assembly of the United Nations has agreed should be a "common standard of achievement for all peoples and all nations." The "Universal Declaration of Human Rights insists that everyone is entitled to all the rights and freedom . . . without the distinction of race, religion, origin or status. Everyone has the right to work, to free choice of employment, to just and favorable conditions of work and to protection against unemployment; to join trade unions and to a standard of living adequate for the health and well being of himself and his family." [3]

After receiving the Commission's report the President said "The public acknowledges the existence of migrants, yet declines to accept them as full members of the community. As crops ripen, farmers anxiously await their coming; as the harvest closes, the community, with equal anxiety, awaits their going." [4]

INDUSTRIAL VILLAGES

With the rapid growth of metropolitan areas, interest in recreation, and the decentralization of industry, it is imperative that more attention be given to the rural non-farm population. One such group is found in the industrial village.

About one out of four American villages may now be counted as an industrial village, in which the residents have no direct occupational connection with agriculture and so are not dependent upon it for their livelihood. To the surprise of some, it has been noted that the laborer is more content in the village or small town, where he may own his home with adequate living space, and where he is known and recognized by his neighbors, than in the larger cities. The matter of the social status which is possible in a small town means much. If for some reason the factory must close for a month, it probably will not be too serious a matter, for there are things about his home he would like to do, and he may have income or food from a small acreage. Such closing of the factory for a short while may, indeed, turn out to be a very welcome interval in the year's activities.

[3] "The Church and the Agricultural Migrant" (New York: NCCC, 1951) pamphlet.

[4] President's Commission on Migratory Labor, *Migratory Labor in American Agriculture* (Washington, D.C.: U.S. Government Printing Office, Supt. of Documents, 1951) .

The industrial village, according to John Kolb, has been with us long enough for us to know that it is a distinct type. In some four ways it differs from the agricultural village: The population is younger and has more males and children and fewer widows; one finds less contact with the land, the average trade area being only four square miles; the village will have only half as many stores as the agricultural village; there will be fewer farmers in the churches. While the agricultural chores, according to the seasons or the ages of the children, regulate and order life in the agricultural village, life in the industrial village is ordered by the factory whistle and the decisions of an often distant executive unknown to the villagers. Industry, not agriculture, dominates the social organization of the community bringing a high degree of paternalism.

The structure of industrial villages differs with their origin and growth. Where an agricultural village has had in it a small industry which has grown slowly, utilizing for labor the young people from the village and surrounding farms, there is no great clash in mores. The transition from agriculture to industry takes place in an orderly and not particularly unpleasant way. Where a manufacturing concern moves its factory and employees into a rural community there may be a clash of cultural values. Those who have lived in the village for years and gained status thereby resent the intrusion of "factory trash." When they find they have to pay higher taxes, in order to educate the children of the newcomers, their indignation boils over. They may find the positions that gave them status in the community being filled or threatened by the energetic new people who have come with the factory. In the church, if the newcomers attend, they may want to introduce a new type of worship, sing hymns unknown in the community, and introduce strange organizational forms for the church. Such "newfangled ideas" are often resented by older members.

Finding themselves not warmly welcomed in the churches, the new people may suggest the organization of another church, or worse still, they may absent themselves from all religious services. In any case, there is a clash between the "old-timers" and the "interlopers," and the once solid community is divided. To minister to old and new, to preserve the spiritual values of the agricultural community while adding the economic values of the industrial, would tax the patience of Job and the wisdom of Solomon.

MINING COMMUNITIES

A second type of rural-non farm community is the mining village. Most mining communities have populations numbering less than 10,000, thus placing them in the town and country category. While agriculture is a repetitive process and properly handled does not exhaust the soil, mining is exhaustive, taking from the earth without replenishing the storehouse. For this reason alone, mining communities are haunted with the idea that sooner or later they will become ghost towns . . . as many already have.

While some miners' sons plan to follow their father's vocation, probably a far greater number look elsewhere for work on completing high school. Thus the population, as in so much of rural America, is short on young adults, but long on elders and children.

Coal mining communities have been hard hit by unemployment since their peak production in the days of World War I. This decline has come about from a slackening in demand for coal with the introduction of the diesel-electric railroad locomotive, the increased use of oil and gas in homes and factories, and the mechanization of the coal mining industry.

In the peak days, when many miners came from Europe with much initiative but little formal education, they easily fell the victims of unscrupulous mine operators. Although their status has improved, "long years of control and paternalism have almost completely atrophied their sense of responsibility as citizens. They have slipped into the easy status of social wards."[5]

During the Great Depression, the Quakers launched a self-help program among the miners of Pennsylvania, which they named Penncroft. Securing a large tract of land, they divided it into small acreages. They then organized the miners so that they helped one another build simple structures in which they lived while they built their own homes. Then they converted the original buildings into chicken houses. They also interested

[5] Medical Survey of the Bituminous Coal Industry, p. XXIV—Report of the Coal Miners Administration, 1947.

a textile mill in coming into the village, and in general stimulated business and industry, thus greatly improving the lot of the miners.

At about the same time Msgr. Luigi G. Liguitte launched a similar program with the miners in and around Granger, Iowa.[6] Here he developed to a fine point, as did the Quakers, the techniques of the Productive Home (see page 244). The Productive Home fits the needs of mining people, for many of them live on small land holdings, but many must be shown how to get the most from their projects with a minimum of expenditure.

Mark Rich in his study of the coal mining communities of West Virginia, writes of the churches:

"As a whole, churches in the coal mining communities are not highly formalized in organization, staff, orders of worship, pattern of program, building or outlook. An atmosphere of other-worldliness is quite common. Hymns and songs are replete with references to heaven. Some come nearer to being folk songs than hymns. The Gospel is usually preached in personal terms, and within rather narrow limits. One receives the impression that here are genuinely devout and good people aiming to live good Christian lives within the mores and within their immediate area of personal association, with little awareness of the implications of their faith for the larger circle of human association."[7]

EDUCATIONAL VILLAGES

America is well sprinkled with villages and towns in which an academy or college holds a prominent place. The presence in these towns of active and retired professors, and other resources of the schools, offers the citizenry and the churches a powerful potential for cultural development.

Instead of gladly receiving this cultural potential, however, many such communities seem to have resented it. In many college towns there is a great gulf fixed between the town folk and

[6] Liguitte and Rowe, *Rural Roads to Security*, Milwaukee, Bruce Publishing Co., 1946, chap. 2.

[7] Rich, Mark, *Some Churches in Coal Mining Communities of West Virginia*, West Virginia Council of Churches, and the Committee for Co-operative Field Research: 297 Fourth Ave., New York 10, N. Y.; p. 27.

the school. Which group is at fault, we are not in a position to discuss. There are exceptions, however. One such place is Lindsborg, Kan., where the music department of Bethel College draws scores of citizens into cooperative effort with the college community, and together they present "The Messiah" annually to large and appreciative audiences. With the increased interest in adult education through all America, we may hope for further examples of rapprochement between "town and gown," to the benefit of both.

RECREATIONAL AREAS

As the nation matures and the conservation of natural resources continues to press its demands upon the population, far-reaching steps will be taken to assure a good supply of water to the coming generations. Already new artificial lakes are appearing in remote places. While these lakes are primarily for flood control, irrigation, and water transportation, the secondary results are not insignificant. They make possible recreation, hunting, and fishing for thousands of people. In some areas when the dams were completed and the lakes filled, hamlets became villages and villages became towns, because vacationers flocked to them in pursuit of fun. The natives at first opposed the dams, but soon changed their minds as, with the rising water, they saw the silver flowing into their towns. New businesses had to be established; eating places, motels, and additional service stations were built; recreational projects, such as a "Water Carnival" or "Ozark Jubilee," were developed to help the vacationers part with their money and still say "It was worth it! I'm coming back next year."

During the vacation season, the rural village may find its population multiplied several times over, as at West Yellowstone, where the population may zoom to several thousand people. With the vacation season past, the population drops to a few hundred, and the quiet of inactivity settles again over the place.

Though we have had a limited number of recreational villages with us for many years we still do not know as much about them as we should. We may be reasonably sure that in the future we will have more, not fewer, of the recreation-type villages and towns, and they will be scattered over the whole nation. No area will be complete without its several recreational villages exploiting the natural resources thereabouts.

THE RURAL-URBAN FRINGE

Within two and three hours' travel of the larger cities are the commuter villages and towns forming the "rural-urban fringe." A few years ago families were moving to the outskirts of the cities, hoping for more space with a better way of life. Many saw in suburbia the opportunity to own their own homes, and believed their dollars would go farther there. The city's outskirts have continued to stretch out farther and farther as villages and towns are strung along highways and electric lines.

Early in the morning the men arise, have a hasty breakfast, and rush for their cars, the commuter-trains, or buses. In two hours, more or less, they will rush into their offices or other places of employment. In the evening they will reverse the rush pattern and at seven o'clock will sit down with their families for the one meal of the day which they can eat at home. This evening meal may well be the father's only contact with his family during the twenty-four hours, and if his children are of high school age, they may have eaten an early dinner before father reaches home, so as to attend some school activity. In this case the father may not see them for two or three days on end. However, this mode of living does not mean a breakdown of the home as might be supposed. Brunner and Hallenbeck say: "There is some evidence that commuting strengthens family ties. Families spend more evenings together at home. They tend to do more things together, including not only attendance at movies, listening to the radio, or viewing television but also participating in games and sports such as skiing, sailing, and swimming, and in the care of gardens and the upkeep of the property."

With the men gone during the day, the commuter village becomes a matriarchal society. Many a "community" problem is decided as the women talk over their coffee cups. Much of the organizational life in commuter villages and towns is in the hands of women and the achievements of women's clubs are highly significant.

The men, being home on Saturdays and Sundays only, will try to crowd into these two days all the house repairs, "do-it-yourself" projects, recreation, and other family affairs. Since they have little contact with other men, not much of a community spirit will prevail in the area, and there will be a minimum inducement to attend church. Churches have found it expedient to have services early on Sunday mornings, freeing the rest of the day for other activities. In the midst of old rural America, where Sunday was primarily a church centered day, worship becomes just one of several Sunday activities for this strange modern family.

Generally speaking, the existing churches are handicapped by the sudden increase of population in these areas. There are fewer churches per unit of population here than in other types of communities. The churches are not prepared to cope with the new situation. The pastors are seldom trained to know how even to recognize the needs of these people, much less how to minister to them. Hundreds of new churches of all denominations are being built in this rural-urban fringe in a frenzied effort to minister to the people, without knowing what the people need, want, and can support. In some planned residential suburbs there is a single Protestant church, either nondenominational or community denominational.

One observer has noted that in the rural-urban fringe there are all the makings of a rural slum of gigantic proportion, except that the housing is new. Unfortunately much of it is so constructed that it will not remain new very long. One may shudder to think what the condition will be if the nation is touched with an economic depression; or when the present residents have reared their families and desire to move farther out or back to the inner city. Then the slums, though far removed from the inner city, will be equally demoralizing.

This rural-urban fringe, now counted in the city column in the census figures, calls for a meeting of minds of urban and rural leaders. These areas can be adequately churched and the people served only when rural and urban leaders pool their resources to devise a strategy for ministering to these people.

V

PROMINENT RURAL ORGANIZATIONS

OUR SOCIAL ORDER OFFERS LITTLE or no hope for advance without the support of effective organizations. Members of the Committee on Country Life recommended an increase in the number of voluntary organizations as a way out of the country dilemma. Rural churchmen understood this need and moved accordingly.

However, the first noticeable changes in the church's programs were not new organizations, but a new emphasis and concern among the existing organizations. The home mission agencies of the denominations that had been thinking of work among rural people gained new insights into their responsibilities and began to institute new and vital programs. The Presbyterian Church in the United States of America pioneered by establishing a Department of Rural Work in 1910. From 1916 to 1925, five additional denominations made places in their programs for rural work. Considering the slowness with which changes are made in national organizations, these new departments in seven major denominations in sixteen years (1909-1925) would indicate considerable interest in rural work on their part.

It was inevitable that, in time, the major denominations with headquarters in the East would devise some method of collaboration. The first evidence of any such movement was the Country Work Department of the International Committee of the Young Men's Christian Association, New York. The YMCA held the National Rural Church Conference in New

York in 1910. From 1910-1923 it published a periodical, *Rural Manhood*.

In 1912 the Commission on the Church and Social Service of the Federal Council of the Churches of Christ in America and the Home Missions Council (organized in 1908) focused their attention on rural work. There were many "ups and downs" in their endeavors during the following years.

In December, 1950, the National Council of the Churches of Christ in the United States of America came into being through the merger of the Federal Council of Churches, the Home Missions Council, and other interdenominational agencies. In this new organization there is a Division of Home Missions, and in this Division there is a Department of Town and Country Church. The Department has a full-time executive director, and a small office staff. The town and country work directors of the co-operating denominations work with the executive director as the Committee on Management. It is their custom to have an annual three-day meeting during which they study town and country needs and correlate their denominational programs. In this annual meeting the executive director seeks the counsel of the denominational directors. They also meet monthly, or as need demands, for short business meetings. The personnel of the Department is available, as time permits, to state councils of churches for the making of rural surveys and studies.

Ten times a year, the Department issues a sixteen-page journal, *Town and Country Church*. The paper is filled with articles of interest to town and country pastors and, to a lesser degree, to the rural laity. The purpose of the journal is stated on the masthead:

A. To encourage co-operation among rural churches.

B. To improve the administration of the local church, this to include organization of the church, finance, religious education, community relationships, and the training of lay leadership.

C. To stimulate the development of a Christian philosophy of rural life, this to embrace ethical issues in agriculture, social reconstruction, and government programs; and the content of the minister's message.

Each fall since 1943, the Department has called a three-day Convocation on Church in Town and Country, characterized by platform speakers of outstanding ability. The registration has averaged near the one thousand mark. Twenty to thirty seminars, workshops, and discussion groups are made available to all who attend. This Convocation, because of its interdenominational structure and its ability to command the highest type of talent, becomes a Protestant town and country sounding board for the nation. It can be a strong factor in building a Christian rural America.

In addition to developing and promoting the annual Convocation, the Department actively promotes the observance of Rural Life Sunday and the Harvest Festival. The first is observed on the fifth Sunday after Easter and the latter some time in the fall harvest season. Programs of worship are prepared and circulated for both services, and it appears that both days are gaining in popularity. The aims of the Department have been set forth in six points:

Discovering and developing the personal potentialities of the farmer and his family;
Building a strongly integrated Christian community;
Awakening in farmers a sense of responsibility for preservation of the soil;
Encouraging the maintenance of the family-sized farm;
Improving living conditions on the farms; and
Promoting co-operation and co-operatives.

A second rural organization is The Christian Rural Fellowship, which is defined in its recent bulletin thus:

The Christian Rural Fellowship is a voluntary membership organization composed of ordained and lay people interested in the quality of rural life around the world. It is nondenominational and international.

It is the only religious organization that attempts to tie together the rural leaders in all lands in the interests of a Christian rural civilization. It is in every sense a fellowship. This fellowship is provided mainly through the *Christian Rural Fellowship Bulletin,* news letters, the quarterly *Rural Missions,* and conferences.

The Christian Rural Fellowship serves in the following ways:
It promotes Christian ideals for agriculture and rural life.
It magnifies and dignifies the rural church and the rural pastorates.
It interprets the spiritual and religious values which inhere in the process of agriculture and the relationships of rural life.
It emphasizes man's moral and ethical responsibility as keeper of the Holy Earth.

It appeals to lay as well as professional people related to agriculture, rural life, and the rural church.

It fosters a spiritual fellowship among people in many lands and unites them in the common cause of a better rural life based on religious foundations.

It interprets the role of rural people in world unity and peace.

It provides a means of fellowship and co-operation among rural agencies.

Through its bulletin and other published materials it provides creative literature which stimulates and challenges the rural church and the religious leadership of rural life to a new appreciation of the vital significance of the rural church to the world-wide church and, indeed, to Christian civilization.

This Fellowship is doing the rural Christian cause an excellent service through its bulletins, which present some of the best and most up-to-date thinking in the town and country fields. Their accumulation over the years makes an invaluable addition to a minister's library.

While this book is devoted to Protestant churchmanship it would be unwise to ignore the interest of Roman Catholics in American rural life. The National Catholic Rural Life Conference was founded in 1923 by Bishop Edward Vincent O'Hara, whose diocese at that time was Oregon. The Conference now claims 10,000 members. They are recruited from both clergy and laity.

The National Catholic Rural Life Conference has developed a 200-year program for rural America, with excellent leadership. The Roman Catholic Church means business. The four-point program is simple; and it is as effective as it is simple:

Care for underprivileged Catholics living on the land.
Keep on the land Catholics who now live there.
Increase the number of Catholics who live on the land.
Convert the non-Catholics who live on the land.

Several Protestant denominations have rural fellowships within their organizational structures, such as the Presbyterian Town and Country Fellowship, or the Baptist Town and Country Fellowship. These fellowships are composed of interested pastors and a few laymen. The programs, although varied, usually consist of holding one or more meetings each year when rural work is discussed. Several of the fellowships issue quarterly bulletins which report the activities of members, promote denominational town and country projects, and, to a limited degree, carry inspirational articles. Some fellowships are tied in with the Department of Town and Country Church of the National Council of Churches in such a manner that members receive not only the denominational rural bulletin, but also the *Town and Country Church* at a financial saving.

The work of the rural churchman is much more than that of ministering to the spiritual needs of his congregation. In rural America he is a community man with a threefold task: co-ordinating community organizations, motivating individuals and organizations with the Spirit of Christ, and recruiting leaders. *In short, the truly effective churchman is a Christian statesman who holds the vision of a Christian community and directs the community's leaders along the right paths to its accomplishment.*

This leads us to consider the several rural organizations with which pastors may work. The first of these, and probably the one of greatest importance in town and country, is the public school. This institution is sometimes referred to as the child of the Protestant Church. It is supported by taxing all the people of the community. For better or worse the public school exerts a tremendous influence in the lives of children. The teachers are before their pupils for six hours a day, five days a week, for as much as nine months a year. They have equipment for teaching. They maintain discipline. Through their attitudes, the teachers give a constant witness of their faith, or lack of faith, in God and his Christ. Their influence can hardly be overemphasized.

A highly effective youth organization associated with the schools, is the Future Farmers of America. High school students enrolled in vocational agricultural classes are privileged to belong to it. The national organization was set up in 1928. The FFA program is designed to supplement school classwork in helping boys become efficient farmers. At the annual meeting outstanding achievements in agriculture are recognized, and the Junior All-American Farmer award is made.

While the Parent-Teachers Association is not peculiar to rural life, it is a factor in developing the American culture in town and country areas. The Association came into being as public school teachers and parents of the pupils felt a need for collaboration in school matters. From a humble beginning it has grown to national proportions.

Another organization, or service that should concern every town and country minister is the Extension Service of the State Colleges of Agriculture and the United States Department of Agriculture. Each agricultural county in the nation has a county agricultural agent. He is a specialist in agriculture and is available at the call of any person in the county. In some cases there is an assistant who has charge of the 4-H club work. These agents are paid from federal funds to lift rural life to a higher and more efficient level by its production of better crops, better homes, and better children. In most counties there is also a home demonstration agent who works out of the same office toward the improvement of rural homes. For the women, this agent frequently organizes study clubs which are so planned as to improve the rural homes. There are seven divisions in the home demonstration work: health, clothing, food, home management, home furnishing, family relations, and recreation. Home demonstration agents have been co-operative and helpful wherever they have had a chance. The tragedy is that they have not been better known and their work encouraged by the churches.

The county agricultural agent, or his assistant, is responsible for the organization and maintenance of 4-H clubs. The initials stand for things which the church has been trying to develop in the lives of young people for many decades. The pledge reads:

I Pledge
  My Head—to clearer thinking,
  My Heart—to greater loyalty,
  My Hands—to larger service,
  My Health—to better living
      For my Club, my Community, and my Country.

The system of 4-H club teaching represents the soundest pedagogy we have known, learning by doing.

The Soil Conservation Service has now organized most of rural America into soil conservation districts, with one or more conservationists to work with the farmers.

Usually, the minister does not need to tell his farmers how to do their work. There is available an army of men who know techniques better than the minister can ever know them. The rural pastor's job is to bring his men into contact with these workers and to inspire them, in the name of Christ, to be stewards of the natural resources.

Of farmers' organizations there have been many. At present there are three which are making themselves felt in American rural life in a definite, constructive way. They are known as the Grange, the Farm Bureau, and the Farmers' Educational and Cooperative Union.

For over 90 years the Grange has been active in American rural life. It was organized in 1867 as a fraternal organization under the name of "The Patrons of Husbandry." Shortly after its organization it entered into political and economic activities. This did not interfere with its growth, for in 1875 it had grown from four subordinate groups in three states to 21,697 subordinate groups in thirty-three states with an estimated membership of 858,000. It finally entered every state of the Union except Rhode Island.

A subordinate grange is a local community fraternal organization that concerns itself with many of the affairs of rural life. It is a family organization because families, rather than only heads of families, join and participate in its activities.

Three or more subordinate granges may form a "Pomona Grange," which is usually county-wide. Where there are fifteen or more subordinate granges in a state, a state grange may be organized. Masters (head officials) of the state grange and their wives are always official delegates to the National Grange, a national farm fraternity.

The American Farm Bureau Federation has become an important influence in rural life. The first local farm bureau was organized in 1911, in Broome County, N. Y. In 1913, when a county-wide mass meeting of the farmers of Broome County took over this organization, the Farm Bureau had its real beginning. In 1915, the first state farm bureau was organized in West Virginia. In 1920, a federation of state farm bureaus organized the American Farm Bureau Federation. Unlike the Grange, the Farm Bureau is not a fraternal organization, but like the Grange it is a local association of rural people with the family the unit of membership. Its activities include all phases of agriculture and rural life.

In 1902 Texas gave birth to a militant organization called The Farmers' Educational and Cooperative Union. The name has been unofficially shortened to *The Farmers' Union*. The organization spread rapidly in Texas, Arkansas, Georgia, Louisiana, and Oklahoma. It reached a maximum membership in 1918-1919 when it had twenty-six state organizations as well as locals in five other states. Although it declares that it is non-partisan, it does exercise considerable political influence. In a few states political issues and activities have been its chief concern.

The co-operatives, too, play a large part in American rural life. For years, the three farm organizations discussed above have been active in encouraging, organizing, and operating co-operatives. Today most farmers belong to a local business co-op or farm organization. Both economically and socially these associations serve the farmer's needs and those of his family, affording a means through which they can express themselves and take needed action. The co-ops are represented by, and get action through, national organizations with which their local associations are affiliated. There are three kinds of co-operatives, each serving a definite need in rural life, The Producers Co-operative, The Consumers Cooperative and The Credit Union.

The single co-operative venture that has made the greatest change in rural America in recent years is the Rural Electrification Administration, an agency of the Federal Government. Local groups organize and receive endorsement and financial backing from the government and then proceed with co-operative techniques to build power lines and buy electricity for their members. It was through this agency that rural America belatedly received electric power for its farms and homes.

From the very beginning of our nation the Federal Government has been interested in the welfare of the farmers. Repeatedly legislation has been enacted to make them more proficient producers of food and fibre. In 1937 the Bankhead-Jones Farm Tenant Act created a program to help farm people who had no land of their own to become farm owners. The law provides forty-year loans at low interest rates for the purchase of farms by those who cannot obtain suitable credit from other sources. In 1946 Congress broadened the program by providing for loans to farm owners to enlarge and improve farms that are too small or undeveloped. The enlarged program is called the Farmer's Home Administration. This legislation is of inestimable value to the rural church that would help its young people buy farms and settle in the home community.

In addition to the above listed organizations supported by government and/or economic interests there are philanthropic and cultural movements active in rural life. Recent years have seen a healthy growth of the Boy Scout movement in rural areas. Recognizing that there is a difference between urban and rural life, this excellent organization has adopted the Lone Scout plan and has developed rural scouting. There seems to be hardly a rural community in all America without some kind of woman's club. In addition to the clubs started by home demonstration agents there are other clubs whose emphases range from recreation through civic improvement, to classical music, and to church work. These clubs should not be overlooked by church leadership, for each club, properly directed, can make a valuable contribution to the development of a Christian spirit in the community.

There are other organizations in American rural life, of course, but those mentioned above seem to be the more influential ones. The rural pastor should know and co-operate with all of these in building a Christian rural America.

VI

AN ECOLOGY

THE RURAL CHURCH does not stand alone. It is not something separate from and foreign to all the other phases of a people's being. It is a part of man's existence. Attempt to separate it from the other parts of community life, as has frequently been done, and it dies. Revive it without relating it to these other things and it will promptly perish.

The ultimate success of any town-country church program hinges upon how its leaders and members operate in all areas of life. Sociologists speak of the interplay between the land, the home, the community, and the church as an ecology. The dead churches of the past years have resulted from the failure to recognize an ecology of town-country life and use it to Christian advantage. Christians often seem to feel that any area outside the church doors is of no concern to them. They should have learned by now that no good thing is outside the legitimate interests of the church, but rather should be considered as a part of its life. Not only are all good things a part of the mission of the church, but they are also tools which the church may use for advancing its work.

THE CHURCH

There are four areas in the ecology of town and country life. First in the ecology is the church itself. Chronologically it is last, but for convenience' sake we shall begin with it. The church must, first of all, work with itself. It is at one and the same time our hope and our despair. It is our hope because it alone has the words of eternal life; it alone has the message of salvation; it alone is divinely commissioned to proclaim the gospel truth to all mankind.

But the church is our despair, in that it often sinks to low ebbs of inefficiency and unconcern. It holds the sacred words of salvation, but again and again it makes little or no effort to share them with the world. It has even been known to exist amidst poverty, disease, and cultural retrogression and never lift its voice or stir a hand to relieve the sufferings. Such behavior is not unknown even today.

A great actor was once asked why his profession was so effective in fascinating and holding the attention of the people, while the activities of churchmen seemed so unattractive. The actor replied, "We of the stage handle fiction as if it were the truth—I fear you of the church handle truth as if it were fiction." Too often the church has uttered a great truth through its prophets, only to pull back when definite action was needed. Racial segregation is but one example. Many churches speak of the equality of men while labor unions, the military, the Federal Government, and some organized sports actually practice integration. In too many communities the church is the most segregated of all institutions.

Often a church is a class church, complacently ministering to one group and neglecting the others. In one rural area, it may cater to farm owners and neglect the tenants. In another, it may concentrate on the town people and shun the farmers. Another may neglect migrant laborers, sharecroppers, and people of other races, feeling smugly satisfied in ministering to the white middle class. Rural America will be saved to the extent that town and country churches find themselves the instruments of God for every man's total salvation.

This means that the church must have a program which is directed to meeting the needs of not only its members but every individual in the community. The church is the spiritual nucleus with which we begin our work.

THE LAND

The second element with which the rural church must deal is the land, although chronologically the land existed before the church. Unless stated to the contrary the definition of agricultural economists for land will be used; that is, all natural resources outside of man himself. This includes the soil, water, air, plant life, fowls, animals, and fish, as well as the minerals, oils, and gases below the earth's surface. The most apparent of these, though none can be eliminated, are air, soil, and water. It is directly from these that we have food, fibre, and fuel. Yet without the others we would not long survive, for they determine the fertility of the soil.

Since people cannot live without land, neither can church and civilization endure, much less prosper, without the land. The face of the earth is marked with examples of the decline and destruction of great civilizations that died because they had little or no concern for the land. Dr. W. C. Lowdermilk, in a 1942 brochure published by the United States Government Printing Office, called attention to the Mesopotamian Valley. Once it nourished a thriving civilization of between seventeen and twenty-five million people. It had, materially speaking at least, an abundant civilization. Today only about three and a half million people roam the deserts and eke out a meager existence. Dr. Lowdermilk declares that soil erosion was the cause of their decline. Silt filled their irrigation channels and eventually choked the streams of life. Mexico, Yucatan, and other parts of Central America show remains attesting that cities and fields once flourished there. The civilizations are gone, and the jungle covers the proud creations of these forgotten people. Some students think the Roman Empire collapsed for a similar reason. There were other contributing factors, of course, but we must not minimize the loss of the land as one of the chief contributors to Rome's decline and fall.

God has given man dominion and control, but never the right to destroy His earth. The expression of Liberty Hyde Bailey, "The Holy Earth," is a pertinent one. As God's handiwork and our home the earth is holy. It should at all times be treated as a holy thing.

As goes the land, so goes the church. If there is to be a Christian civilization in rural America, the churches must recognize the place that the land has occupied in history and teach men what the Scriptures say in regard to it. Men must know assuredly that God has made them stewards of the land.

THE HOME

A third part of the ecology is the home on the land. In past years the church has had more to say about the home than the land, but even so it has said and done altogether too little.

In rural America there are about four million farm homes and many more than that of rural nonfarm and town homes. Over 50 per cent of the children of the nation are born into these homes and continue to live in them for an average of about sixteen years, receiving from them their spiritual, moral, social, and physical nourishment. The home in its quiet way is a powerful teacher. It is the natural, primary, and God-planned teaching institution. It was so considered by the Hebrews. By divine command each family indoctrinated its children in the faith of the fathers. Their system worked! People never fully erase from their beings the attitudes received in their homes. Day and night, without ceasing, homes teach by word and example. The Christian strategy dares not any longer overlook the rural homes of the nation. To do so would be to invite ruin. Everything involved in home life, then, is the concern of the church, and the church's future lies in the home.

Rural people are a home-loving people. There is more familism in rural than in urban life. It is natural to think in terms of Christianizing the homes of rural America. They must receive special attention and study by religious planners.

The familism found in farm homes is in no sense artificial. It comes out of the necessity that each member of the family bear his share of the responsibility for a good home. Inside and outside the house there are chores to be done that will not be done unless the children do them. As the children perform these acts of helpfulness the economic level of the family rises, and the entire family profits. This same idea is carried into the hamlet, village, and town homes as each home attempts to produce a high percentage of its food, clothing, recreation, and cultural needs. To encourage and permeate with the spirit of Christ this familism in rural life is to strengthen an important part of town and country life.

THE COMMUNITY

The fourth and final area for consideration in this ecology of rural life is the community. Here again Christians have been shamefully negligent. They have concentrated so much on the individual that they have almost forgotten that one cannot be an effective individual without a community in which to exist. Human beings are gregarious. They like to, and of necessity must, dwell in communities and work together.

The community is a teacher that exerts no little influence on the lives of people. Dr. Kenneth Latourette in his *History of the Expansion of Christianity*, closes the first volume by saying in effect: Now in summary let us see what the church did to its environment, and then let us see what the environment did to the church. In his masterful way he goes on to show how the church did influence and change its environment and how also in the struggle the environment altered the church.

Reformers, preachers, and magazine writers accuse the homes of gross negligence when teen-age delinquents appear in police courts, and they praise the homes when children turn out well. Surely no one will minimize the effect of home training in character building, but let all recognize that the community also has something to do with character training. Always in a rural community there are many forces and movements that have come into being because the people needed and desired them. There are commerce, industry, and the professions. Powerful forces never cease to mold the character of young and old through schools, clubs, market places, radio, television, magazines, recreational activities, and informal contacts. While the homes and churches hold up one standard of conduct other forces in the community may be teaching another standard which is not at all in harmony with them. Christian leaders dare not leave out of their planning the community built upon the land and embracing homes and the church, for to do so would be to abrogate their noblest efforts.

USING THE INTERPLAY

As we draw together the threads of thought in this chapter we may observe that when some young ministers take their first churches they assume that they are going to win individual men and women to Jesus Christ and his way of life. But they are not in their churches long until they find that there is more to being a minister of Jesus Christ than winning an individual's avowal of faith. They find that individuals have their roots sunk deep in the ideologies and habits of the community, and that although a man may give lip service to Christ while he is in the church, his motives and actions are determined by the location of his roots. The minister may then become aware that he is dealing with tremendous forces outside the church, such as LAND, HOMES, and COMMUNITY. He needs to learn that these can be made into allies of the church. When the church wins on these fronts, it has won everything. It is the business of town-country Christians to work in these areas and so to bring all things into subjection to Jesus Christ.

This, then, is the ecology of town-country life: land, home, community, and church. The failure of any one jeopardizes the effectiveness of the other three. If this ecology is recognized and a proper program built, then churches once closed may be reopened, and caused to prosper. If this ecology is observed in existing churches, they will surely prosper.

PROTESTANT CHURCHMANSHIP

for RURAL AMERICA

PART TWO

TOWN-COUNTRY
CHURCH
ADMINISTRATION

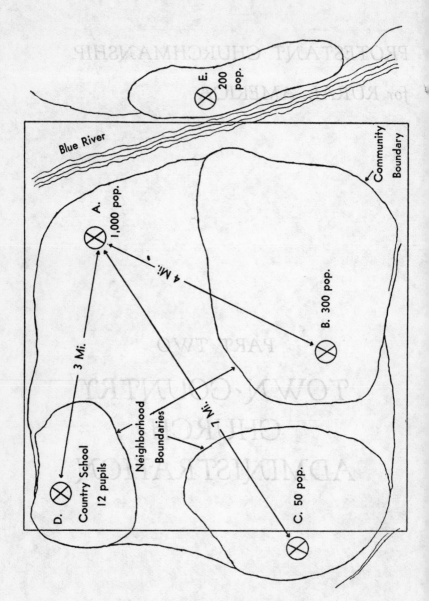

A Midwestern Town-Country Community

VII

THE CHURCH'S AREA OF RESPONSIBILITY

FOR SOME CHRISTIANS IT IS EASY to see needs which are far away while they remain blind to equal or greater needs at home. The writer of the Book of Proverbs commented on a like condition, saying "The eyes of the fool are in the ends of the earth" (Prov. 17:24b). A weakness, if not the tragedy, of Protestant strategy has often been its little concern for the welfare of local communities. Some observers believe that the high mortality of town-country churches is due to a failure to render significant service to individuals, neighborhoods, and communities.

Some churches assume an attitude of withdrawal from community life. Others express an antagonistic interest in the community by condemning and berating it and its leaders. Still other Christians live by a double standard which requires religious life only on Sunday, but conforms to community mores during the remainder of the time. Too seldom does a church say "We, as a church, are responsible for the well-being of this community." Yet that is the attitude which Christians should have, for the church exists for its community.

By the very nature of Christianity a struggle is inherent between a living church and the community wherein it works. Either the church will change the community or the community will change the church. In some situations churches are impotent because the community has subtly induced the members to conform to the world's way of life. Such churches are only cultural institutions bearing religious labels.

The Emerging Town-Country Community

Significant changes have taken place in community structure and attitudes since 1909, when the Commission on Country Life made its report. In that day many people marked the limits of community by the distance which a team of horses, pulling a load, could go and return on the same day. The radius of a community could thus be less than eight miles. There was much ill will between the people on the farms and those living in the towns. The latter felt that they were superior to those who tilled the soil. On Saturday, when farm boys went to town there were frequent fights between them and the town boys. Today, for the most part, this is changed and we have what rural sociologists call "the emerging town-country community." The area of the community is greatly extended beyond the "team-haul" limits. There is increasing good will and a sense of interdependence between town and farm people. This is a thrilling development. Hereafter, in this text, we shall refer to the town-country community rather than the rural community.

Each town-country community has its own natural interests, such as business, industry, farms, homes, schools, churches, and cultural and recreational organizations. The citizens think in terms of these interests for they are their life. They attempt, unconsciously, to syncretize these interests so that the community appears to them to be a comfortably secure, harmonious, and pleasant place, for which they will offer their praise whenever possible.

If the church is actively identified with the institutions of the community it then gives a daily testimony of its faith through its members and pastor. Like a stream of water, the people of a community, with their daily interests, are flowing in one general direction. It is important that the church as an institution be with and a part of this flowing movement, giving it needed guidance, rather than to sit, as it were, upon the stream's bank and watch it flow by.

If the buildings, equipment, and primary organization of a church are in one town-country community, while half its members are in another the church will find itself working at a great disadvantage. For example, such a situation makes it difficult to plan a youth program. The reason is obvious; half of its young people live and attend school and other activities outside the area served by the church. The power and pride of community contacts bring them to support their school, while they neglect their church's youth program which is centered in another community. The result is that the church's youth program is soon abandoned.

For a while, a strong church with a popular preacher may draw members from outside the church's community. This influx of people from a distance feeds the ego of both the preacher and the congregation. This power to draw people from a distance may feed the egos of preacher and congregation and be a strong talking point, but in the long run, such members seldom mean much to the church. The usual outcome is that the people from outside the community attend only the preaching services and *limited* church activities. When they join the church they are feted for their strong convictions and denominational loyalties. But their interest in business, education, recreation and social activities are centered in another community. These interests apply their own subtle pressures upon them. After a while the popular preacher seems to be a little less divine; indeed, he seems quite earthy. Then they look for "greener pastures" where they can hear more scintillatingly pertinent messages which they term "more spiritual."

If these people have school-age children, the break with the church may come even sooner, for, in diverse manners, the children bring pressure to bear on their parents to attend church where their school chums attend. Church members who live in the community where the church building is located sometimes resent the presence of people from other communities. They refer to them as "outsiders." If an "outsider" takes part in the activities of the church, a "regular" member is likely to lose his status. Sometimes questions are whispered: "Why do they come to our church? Can't they get along at home?" To prevent such situations from arising a church should delimit its community and focus its full powers there by entering into and guiding the life of the people in fulfillment of the Christian ethic. This procedure, of course, is not meant to reduce the church's mission in the nation and abroad.

COMMUNITY AND NEIGHBORHOOD

It is not easy to define community. Usually a community is described as a body of people who have common interests and who share the same organizations and living area. Or a community may be described as a society at large, as the people in general, or in a restricted sense, as the people of a particular region. In this book the word community is used to denote the area and the people with which a church works; it is an aggregate of people with common living conditions, who are reasonably self-sufficient in the five basic human needs—employment, trading facilities, education, recreation, and worship services—who have a sense of interdependence, a "we" spirit.

It is in such an environment that people have almost daily face-to-face relations. In this type of living the people know one another by name rather than by category. There is a feeling of concern for one another, and the personal notes or gossip columns of the local papers are read and discussed thoroughly by the housewives. Here the play produced with local talent may be presented to a full house, not because of its excellence of production, but because the people are interested in one another. The absence of this "we" spirit in a city prevents it from qualifying as a community.

The opposite extreme from the urban attitude is found in the neighborhood. The neighborhood is characterized by a strong "we" spirit. Here everyone knows everyone else. The majority of the people were born of the parents who themselves were born in this same neighborhood. But a neighborhood is not a community, for the people are not reasonably self-sufficient in the five basic needs of employment, trading, education, recreation, and worship. In fact the people of a neighborhood are a part of a community that swings around a trading center, or a consolidated school building. Communities usually include several neighborhoods, and, to confuse the issue further, a neighborhood often persists in referring to itself as a community. It will hold tenaciously to its school or church, while it fails to recognize that it is now a part of a genuinely larger community, the emerging town-country community, in which it can have a much better way of life.

To illustrate this emerging town-country community let us take a segment of a map of a North Central state (see page —). This segment is a township, [1] six miles on each side, plus the parts of adjacent townships. A river cuts through the northeast corner of the central township. On the west bank of the river is village A with a population of about 1,000. The village is a modern trading center with well-stocked stores. A small industry employs both men and women from the surrounding area. It is to this village that the young people of the area go to high school and for recreation which they find in the motion-picture theaters, the poolrooms and bowling alleys, and the swimming pool during the summer months. Several denominations of Protestants are represented in the village by churches, as are the Roman Catholics. Four miles to the southwest of A is another village, B, with a population of three hundred. In addition to a few stores, not modern, a pool-hall-tavern, and a grade school, there are two struggling churches. A mile directly west of the township line is hamlet C, with a population of fifty persons. In addition to one church, where occasional worship services are held and a few devout women maintain a Sunday school, there is a service station-garage-grocery store, and a grade school. In the evening, a few young people loaf around the store. In the extreme northwest corner of the township, there is a crossroads where neighbors are still maintaining their grade school though the enrollment is only twelve and the prognosis for next year indicates a decrease of four, there being no first-graders to replace the eighth-grade graduating class.

Between these settlements there are as many as five hundred or more people living on farms. These people send their older children to the high school at A, where they also do much of their trading. Their younger children go to the nearest grade school. Some of the farm girls find employment in the small industry, shops, and business offices at A. The farmers may occasionally patronize the business places at B or C.

Across the river, east of the township is the hamlet E, with a population of two hundred. It remains out of touch with these other centers, for not many people cross the river for

[1] Township. This word is used as in surveys of U. S. public lands.

trade, employment, education, recreation, or worship. Moreover, the people at E are not interested in activities centering at A. Their interests lie directed toward another center.

People in villages B, C, and D and those living on farms look to A as their community center. They all have some similarity. They are reasonably self-sufficient in such basic functions as trading facilities, employment, schools, recreation, and worship. They number two thousand, counting all the people in villages A, B, C, and D and those that live on the farms. When the religious life of this community is properly organized, they can support churches of three different denominations.

The religious responsibilities of the Baptist church at A, for example, are now clear. According to our theory, this church must have an active interest in all the happenings within the encircled area, which is the *natural and real town-country community*. It must maintain a spiritual fellowship with Baptists at neighborhoods B and C, since these are integral parts of the community. This does not mean that the Baptist churches at B and C are to be eliminated. They are neighborhood churches and, though small, often have a vital ministry to perform. Indeed, it is to the interest of the community and the church that the Baptist church at A must do everything possible to help the Baptist churches at B and C to attain and remain in a healthy condition. As neighborhood organizations they can do something that can be accomplished in no other way. For instance, since they are too small to maintain full-time services alone, they may, and probably should, form a larger parish. It would be even better for them to form a larger parish with A, thus giving a united denominational impact on the entire community through three Baptist churches working in one program in and for the whole community. Trouble will come if the church at either B or C, or both, attempt to unite with a church at E, which is definitely outside their community. Yet such a thing is a common practice where churches are not aware of the importance and power of a community.

DETERMINING BOUNDARIES

How does one determine a town-country community's limits? How does one determine a neighborhood? An excellent technique, *for its day,* was developed by Charles J. Galpin in his Wisconsin studies. From his center at Delavan, he drove along the roads and observed which way the farmers' lanes curved onto the highway. He reasoned that as long as the lanes pointed toward Delavan the people living along them were a part of the Delavan community. Farther along the main road the farm lanes seemed to indicate that the traffic went both to the right and to the left. This, reasoned Mr. Galpin, was the dividing line between Delavan and the next community. Shortly thereafter the lanes regularly curved away from Delavan, which indicated that the people belonged to another community. This graphic method is now replaced by a more detailed method for determining community boundaries. Today a large map of the area is marked to show the area served by business establishments, schools, etc. This information may be obtained with the help of community leaders. A study of the markings will indicate an overlapping of areas served by different institutions. It will be seen that they are very much alike, though not necessarily identical. One heavy line may now be drawn generally following the other lines (excepting for some extreme loops and corners). The heavy line is now a reasonably accurate boundary of the area encompassed by the town-country community. The people within this area, having the "we" spirit, are reasonably self-supporting in employment, trading, education, recreation, and worship.

Within the area of the town-country community there are islands of people, such as at the crossroads D and the hamlets C and B (see map on page 96). These are neighborhoods. In determining the boundaries of neighborhoods it is almost necessary to live with the people to become acquainted with the visiting and shopping habits which reveal their sense of neighborhood.

If a church is dominant in a hamlet such as B the membership roll of the church may be studied for neighborhood boundaries. This is done by spotting the membership on a map. Then a circle is drawn which includes the members farthest out from the church. This circle, with a few alterations, may be considered the boundaries of the neighborhood. Within its limit there will be a high degree of the "we" spirit, but the people will not be reasonably self-sufficient in employment, trade, education, recreation, and worship. They may be self-sufficient in one or two of the five areas, but not in all five. For reasonable self-sufficiency the people must continue to look to the community.

By an application of the technique of determining community and neighborhood boundaries, we find that the village B and hamlets C and D are a part of the A community, as are the enclosed farm people. The hamlet C, although it is outside the township line (which might be a county or state line), is a definite part of community A. Hamlet E, only a few miles from A, is not considered a part of the community because a river, like an impassable barrier, separates it from community A. Mountains, hills, streams, swamps, and sometimes highways frequently make such separations.

It has been the purpose of this chapter to determine the area of that community and/or neighborhood that is the immediate responsibility of a church or churches. It is within the limits of neighborhood or community that a church must come to grips with reality. Sometimes a church finds itself overlapping one or more communities, but in the end this usually leads to tension and problems, so that eventually the church is likely to become identified with one or the other of the communities.

The church must seek to give the community the leadership needed to become a Christian community. Only as a pastor sees clearly the area the church is to serve, with all of its good and bad characteristics, can he and his people formulate lines of procedure by which the church can change the community. Therefore, delineating the community is a necessary first step in drawing up a program for a church.

VIII

SURVEYING THE FIELD

AFTER DELIMITING THE AREA of a church's responsibility, now referred to as the church's community, the next step is to survey it. It is doubtful if any other single activity will yield so rich a harvest as a good survey. Surveying may be likened to analyzing the soil before plowing and planting, or to diagnosing a patient's ailment before writing the prescription.

There are three reasons for making a religious survey of the church's community. One is to secure information for building an adequate church program; the second, to acquaint members of the church with their community; and the third, to acquaint the community, to a small degree, with the church. Regarding the last two of these reasons, the present high mobility of American people makes this two-way nonacquaintance more widespread than it was a generation ago. People move into towncountry and out again, while 90 per cent of the church people know nothing of their presence.

A good survey will reveal the exact number of people in the area. It will indicate exactly the number of people for which the church has a responsibility. It will reveal the age groups to be served by the church program. It will show the citizens' church affiliations and how often they attend the church services. It will show their occupations and property ownership as well as other items useful to the earnest pastor and his church people.

As church members call in homes in making the survey, they gather first-hand information about the living conditions of

105

RELIGIOUS SURVEY BY FAMILIES

Survey Team _____ House No. _____ Date _____

1. Family Name _____
2. Street or Road _____
3. P. O. Address _____
4. Township _____
5. Neighborhood _____
6. Village _____
7. County _____
8. Phone number _____

9. Resident of this community since? _____
10. Resident of this farm since? _____
11. Owner? _____ Tenant? _____
12. Distance from Church: Miles: _____ Blocks: _____
13. Nationality: Husband _____ Wife _____
14. Race: White _____ Negro _____ Other _____

Given Name	Birthday	Occupation	Church Affiliation		Attendance		Last Time in		See Key*		
			Denominational Preference	Present Membership	Name Church	Name S. S.	Church	S. S.	I	II	III
15. F.											
16. M.											
17. Children											
1.											
2.											
3.											
4.											
5.											
6.											
18. Others in Household		and Relationship									
1.											
2.											
3.											

* Key: Enter appropriate letters in columns.
I. (a) Officer in Church. (b) Church School officer-teacher. (c) Desires to unite with church. (d) Willing to work. (e) Not interested.
II. (a) Grade School — 1 — 2 — 3 — 4 — 5 — 6 — 7 — 8. (b) High School — 1 — 2 — 3 — 4. (c) College — 1 — 2 — 3 — 4. (d) Name other schools and years attended.
III. Veteran — Mark X.

Canvassers: _____

19. Community and farm organizations to which family members belong (check X if they belong)

4H Club	Farm Bureau	Labor Union	PTA
FFA	Farmers Union	Producers Coop	Service Clubs
FHA	Grange	Credit Union	Patriotic Organizations
Boy Scouts	Consumers Coop	Women's Clubs	Fraternal Organizations
Girl Scouts			

20. Schools Which Children Attend

Grade School

High School

College

21. RECORD PASTORAL CALLS

Date | Brief Pertinent Data

the people. They become aware of the great number of lonely, frustrated and lost people in a town-country community. They uncover unfortunate moral conditions which they did not dream could ever exist in their community. In short, they are aroused to new endeavors for their community and the kingdom of God.

Planning a Survey

There is a variety of worthwhile survey approaches. One is the Religious Survey by Families. It stands midway between a religious census and a comprehensive sociological survey. For this reason a card entitled "Religious Survey by Families," is recommended and can be printed by a local printer (see pages 106-107).

If the survey is to be of the entire community, and there are several churches in the community, it is best to enlist as many of them as possible in the project. Advantages gained thereby are that there will be more workers, less accusation of proselyting, and a greater spirit of co-operation on the part of the people who are visited.

A single church conducting a survey can often secure help from town-country or sociological staff workers of the denomination concerned. A federated church or group of churches can usually secure similar aid from the council of churches.

It may seem advisable for a survey to be made not of the entire community, but of that area most closely related to the church. It might be expedient for the church at B to confine its survey to village B and its own neighborhood as encircled (see map, page 96). However, it would be more valuable if all the churches, or even all the churches of one denomination in the entire town-country community joined in a community survey. Such a survey would show the several denominational potentials for this community. It would reveal resources that all could use, yet which might be of little value to a single church. It would also indicate the need for the churches of a given denomination to form a larger parish to serve their community better.

The poorest way to make a survey is for the pastor to make it. This method deprives the people of the blessing of becoming acquainted with their community. Moreover, they are left unprepared to join the pastor in a program that the survey shows to be necessary. It is better to enlist lay participation.

At the outset, it is important and informing to make a map of the area under study. This should be accurate, artistic, and so neatly done that it will be a welcome addition to the wall of the pastor's study or the library of the church. It may be drawn upon a 22-inch by 28-inch piece of heavy cardboard. If the entire town-country community is to be studied a scale of one inch to the mile will be found practical; if a smaller area, such as a neighborhood, is to be studied a scale of two inches to the mile offers opportunity for more meaningful detail.

Where there is a large village (1,000 population or more) and/or town in the area to be studied a main map should be prepared and additional detailed maps should be made of each village and town, showing all streets, residences, highways, railroads, factories, schools, parks, and the business district. The map of the area outside the hamlets, villages, and towns should show and number every residence, all the roads, railroads, forests, swamps, mountains, and the rivers and streams. Where there are out-of-town businesses (and many are springing up in town- country areas), they should be clearly indicated on the area map.

It is usually possible to procure at no cost a county map from the state highway department. These maps have been prepared in much detail and show every farm residence, as well as other pertinent information. If a map cannot be secured from this source, inexpensive maps may be secured from the office of the Postmaster General, Washington, D. C. These maps have been prepared to show the rural mail routes and farm residences where mail is delivered. Of course, plate maps of the county can be studied at the surveyor's office in the county court house. A local chamber of commerce may also have maps available for study.

With these maps, a ruler, pencil, and drawing pen, the map maker is ready to go to work. From here on map making is a matter of accurately measuring and drawing. It is best to put all lines in with pencil, then to measure, and check again, before drawing them in with ink.

After a map has been prepared, if there is space for proper display, a relief model of the community may be built by an energetic group of young people or young adults. Such a model should probably be about four feet by eight feet, and should be built to scale and in considerable detail. This model displayed in a church, school, or community building will draw much attention and help focus the eyes of all citizens upon the area in which they live. An alert newspaper editor will give space in his paper to a story about such an undertaking. This is the kind of project that might be worked out by the high school class in social studies, a method which usually draws some outsiders into the orbit of the church's concern.

The area to be surveyed should be marked out in divisions of about twelve homes each. A team of visitors will be chosen to cover each division. Rough, but accurate maps should be drawn of each division on letter-size typing paper and given to the respective teams. Each house should be numbered, and the number should appear on both the team's map and the master map. As the visitors cover the area, they will mark each card in the upper left-hand corner with their team number and the number of the house in which they call. Thus a card marked 8/12 means that the work was done by team number 8 in division 8 and the card is for house number 12 on the map.

In case a house is not shown on the map the surveyors will call notwithstanding. They may then use the alphabet to indicate the location, showing it both on the map and the card by indicating that team number 8 called at a new house which follows call number 12 and is marked "a." The marking in the upper left corner of the card would then read 8/12/a.

The map of the area showing the church's responsibility should be displayed at regular meetings of the diaconate, the church council, or any other responsible administrative groups within the church. After the map has been examined, the pastor may suggest that a survey be made of this area. He should then lead them to recommend the authorizing and underwriting of the cost of a survey, which will be but a few dollars.

The next step is to select carefully the surveyors, preferably attractive young adults. Except in rare circumstances teenagers should not be used. As soon as possible, a supper meeting should be planned for the deacons and/or church council and the selected surveyors. Again the community map should be displayed prominently. After the supper and devotional meeting it should be explained in detail why a survey is needed and what it is expected to accomplish. The group should be divided into teams of two callers each and each team assigned to its division. Each team should trace its route on the map, making sure every house is covered. The callers should be carefully instructed as to how to mark their cards.

The following instructions, mimeographed, may now be placed in the hands of the surveyors and each point thoroughly discussed. The surveyors' questions should be invited and patiently answered. (This is worded for a co-operative survey by two or more churches. If only one church conducts the survey, change the wording to fit.)

INSTRUCTIONS FOR MAKING THE RELIGIOUS SURVEY BY FAMILIES

1. The purpose of this survey is to obtain information about the community in general and people in particular, in order to develop an adequate church program. It is necessary that the people of the area become acquainted with the churches, but more important still for the churches to become acquainted with the field of responsibility.

2. You are going into the homes of the community as a representative of its churches. At all times be courteous, kind, and considerate. *Never argue.* It is your purpose to make a pleasant contact between each home you visit and the churches. Begin each visit by calling the family by name. Introduce yourself and teammate by giving your names, where you are from, and your business on this occasion. If invited to enter the house, do so after carefully cleaning your shoes.

3. Always speak of "our community."

4. You have a small map of the area you are to survey and a supply of cards, as well as two sharpened pencils. Follow this procedure with them:

    a. Number on your map all calls as they are made or attempted.

    b. Number your card in the upper left-hand corner with your team number and the house number.

    c. If no one is home, number the card and map—also the family name on the card if it is known. Go back later.

    d. If the house where you call is not shown on the map, then give it a letter of the alphabet preceded by the number of the previous house, thus 2/16/a

5. Be sure to get all facts asked for on the cards, but do not allow your record keeping to be a prominent part of your visit. Some blanks may be filled in after you leave the house or before you call. One surveyor may ask questions while the other records the information.

6. Get information directly from each member of the family present.

7. If possible, get the exact birthdays of all the persons in the home.

8. If possible, get suggestions from those visited as to what *they think* the churches should do to make the community more Christian. Note on cards facts which show special needs, such as poor housing or lack of transportation.

9. Before closing the interview invite the people to attend religious services *next* Sunday.

10. Close interview with brief but sincere words of prayer for God's blessing upon this home and the community, unless prayer is unwelcome.

11. Keep on until the survey is completed. You have been given a division to survey. It is your responsibility. See it through.

12. Return to the survey director all cards and your map, properly numbered, as soon as your work is completed.

The alert pastor will not only keep his church informed of the progress being made in the survey, but he will also inform the general public. To do this he may use the newspapers, radio, and the public schools. In all publicity releases it is wise to state clearly that the purpose of the survey is to help the church do its work better. Tell the public when the survey will start and give names of surveyors. Such publicity will prepare the people so that they will receive the surveyors in friendly fashion.

After thorough instruction of both the surveyors and the public, the survey may be started. It would be advantageous (but not necessary) for all surveyors to meet at the church for dinner on the day the survey is to be taken. After the meal final but brief instructions may be given, a prayer of dedication may be offered, and the surveyors sent forth. They will work all afternoon, or until finished, then report back to the church with their cards. They may come back for supper if dinner was not provided. After supper, each team may report on some of its experiences. These reports may prove very interesting and be the highlight of the day's work.

STUDYING THE FINDINGS

When the survey is completed, the findings should be tabulated and studied carefully. Each participating church should have a complete set of the cards, if it desires them. The pastor of each co-operating church and a small committee should be responsible for tabulating the findings of the survey and the making of illustrative charts. The following is a partial list of tabulations that may be used.

1. Total number of people by age groups in area served by church.
2. Denominational responsibility by age groups such as:
   a. Denomination, member of local church
   b. Denomination, but member elsewhere
   c. Denominational preference
   d. Member of a church whose denomination is not represented by a church in the community
   e. No preference
   f. Roman Catholic
   g. Other evangelical denomination in the community
   h. Jew

The figures under items 2a to 2e, when added together, indicate exactly the number of people for whom the church of a particular denomination is responsible. A church cannot be built or maintained without people. Here are the people by name, age, and occupation. A pastor and his church have this number, no more and no less, with which to work. If the number is small, it may point to the need for a larger parish, or some other means of sharing work with another church, preferably of the same denomination.

Other tabulations may be made of the farm population, the rural nonfarm population, farm owners, tenants, other than farm occupations, distance of residence from church, participation in community organizations, etc. The census cards will yield a wealth of helpful information to those who study them patiently and record their message.

In tabulating the survey cards, a series of tally sheets should be prepared. By arranging these in proper sequence, one may take a survey card and distribute its contents to the proper columns in one operation. The columns may then be tallied and the results placed on a master talley sheet. Two or more master sheets may be prepared so that they will be available for the pastor and other responsible leaders in church and community.

From the master tally sheet tables, graphs, and charts may be prepared in order to interpret the figures to members of the church and its auxiliaries. The illustrative charts may be drawn on cards 16 inches by 18 inches. They may then be used to drive home the points that should be made.

By placing colored pins on the map, one pin for each person, the location and density of the domination's members and responsibility may be observed at a glance. An orange-colored pin may be used to denote a member of the denomination's local church; a green-colored pin to denote a member of the denomination's church elsewhere, denominational preference, or belonging to denomination not represented in the community by a church; and a red-colored pin to denote no church preference. The red pins will locate moral danger spots in the community.

USING THE FACTS

Now that the survey has been completed, the findings carefully tabulated and studied, and illustrative charts made, it is time to inform the church of consequent responsibility. This may be done at a supper meeting of the church, or it may be done by the pastor meeting separately with the different groups in the church, beginning with the deacons and surveyors, and showing each group the part on which it might well concentrate some special efforts. The pastor may ask each group separately, and also the church as a whole: "In the light of the facts revealed in our survey, what should we do to advance the kingdom?" He should seek answers from the people and encourage discussion of the church program. If he despises no suggestion, however trivial it may seem to be, helpful suggestions eventually will come. When the information is fully shared and suggestions have been made, the pastor, the church council, and the church will build a program.

With pins in their proper places on his map it may be in order for the pastor to ask: "What is the relationship of our present building to the density of denominational opportunity?" This is especially necessary if the church expects to rebuild or remodel its plant in the near future. As the people themselves answer this question it may occur to them that a building at another place would serve kingdom interests better.

A typical survey was made of a village which had a population of 390. It was chosen as the center for a neighborhood survey. Four churches, two of the same denomination, co-operated in making the survey. We shall designate them as churches A, B, B2, and C. The survey cards indicated that 702 people lived in the neighborhood and that 184 of these were without church membership anywhere. Church A had a membership of seventy-one, but 131 people claimed it as their church. Thus the membership of church A could have been almost doubled if its professing and preference people had been enlisted. If A could also win one third of the 184 who were not members anywhere it certainly could have doubled its membership. However if A could win only its ratio as compared to the other denominations in the community it would add only thirty-five new members. Thus the most optimistic membership figure for church A would be 192. A more realistic figure would be 166. It appears that church A, with first class pastoral leadership would do well to plan in terms of a future church of 150 members. But this church was building for a membership of well over 200!

This survey indicated that in the community organizations church A was represented by twenty-six memberships, churches B and B2 with sixty-three and church C with forty-nine. Interestingly enough there were also forty-nine who were not members of a church anywhere. Thus the non-membership group was bringing twice as much pressure on community affairs as the members of church A.

This would seem to illustrate that an analysis of survey figures brings forth many interesting and useful facts about community life which will enlighten the church membership and point them to the activities in which they should engage to advance the kingdom of God in their community.

OTHER USEFUL INFORMATION

Many other items of information which offer hints for the improvement of the church's present and future existence as well as for specific pastoral care and advice may be gleaned from the survey cards. The following are some typical examples.

Line 9: "Resident in this community since. . . ." If this reveals new residents, they probably are not acquainted with others in the neighborhood, and may be lonely. If they are old residents they may feel that they have certain prerogatives which are denied to newer residents. These older residents are a source of rich information on the community's history. Tactful conversation with them will reveal unsuspected stresses and strains in community life. A pastor, knowing of these problems, may be able to escape many damaging experiences.

Line 10: "Resident of this farm since. . . ." If the card reveals that these people have lived on a farm for several years, and the pastor in his calls should find gullies on the farm, he would immediately sense the need for stewardship teaching. But if the resident is new on the farm he probably needs friendly contacts or even help from Christian neighbors. The farmer may or may not need to have the stewardship of land more carefully explained to him. The same principle would prevail with regard to the condition of non-farm property.

Line 11: "Owner." Suppose the subject is the owner of this farm. What about his age? If he is sixty or over, how long can the church expect him to remain on the farm? Then what? A good pastor would want to know if the family is aware of the importance of keeping this farm in Christian hands. Do they know of the various Christian methods of transferring the ownership of the farm to other members of their family or to others in the Christian household?

Line 11: "Tenant." Here again we need to know the age of the tenant. If the tenant is young he may be a good prospect for the ownership of some farm that will be vacant soon. He may be the very person whom the elderly owner referred to in the previous paragraph needs to take over his farm on some Christian basis.

Line 12: "Distance from church." The answer to this question, by even a small percentage of the community, may help fix the hour and frequency of church services. It may call for church-sponsored transportation. Again, it may show that the church building needs to be relocated if the present building is old and the people have any idea of rebuilding. Church buildings should be near the center of the area they expect to serve and on good roads.

Line 15: "Occupation." The answer here furnishes clues to the time the family may be at home. It indicates probably the greatest interest of the worker — his job. Not all people of town-country are employed in agriculture. The demands of self-employment and factory jobs must be considered in planning church work and scheduling its activities.

Line 15: "Last time in church." This item calls for a definite answer instead of, "Quite some time now." Some people are surprised and chagrined when they count back and find it has been very long since they attended a church service.

Line 15: "Key:" Responsible offices held, educational attainment, and military service. This information is valuable to an active minister. One minister found from this questioning that his adult congregation averaged only a fifth grade schooling. He had been preaching to them as if they were high school graduates!

Line 19: "Membership in community and farm organizations." This information enables a pastor to know the social and business interests of the people, and indicates which organizations he should join in order to have nonchurch fellowship with people of his parish. It may very well show that a few people are engaged in many activities, and many people in none. It may show that the church members belong to too few civic organizations and so the church's influence is not felt there. Surely a church will affect the life of its community in direct ratio to the participation of its members in community activities.

Line 21: "Pastor's record." A faithful pastor records all the calls he makes, with useful notations. He checks his cards regularly to avoid missing any of the people.

IX

ORGANIZING FOR EFFECTIVE SERVICE

THE ORGANIZATIONAL PATTERN of Protestant churches is not uniform. For example, the Protestant Episcopal, Presbyterian, Lutheran, and Methodist churches have well-defined patterns. The congregational type of church, such as the Congregational, the Disciples, and the Baptists, whose local churches are completely self-regulating, provides great latitude in the forms of local church organization within a single denomination. In brief, congregational church structure may vary from a church having a pastor, a clerk, a treasurer, and two or three inactive deacons, to a highly effective organization with several boards and a multiplicity of committees. In some congregational-type churches the Sunday school and some societies may be separate organizations which feel no responsibility to the church in whose building they meet. The cleavage may be carried so far that these organizations actually are required to pay a rental to the church for the use of its building. In some New England states, the property-holding *society* is distinct from the congregation. Each individual who contributes financially to the society's expense is a voting member. Under these circumstances trustees are elected from the membership of the society and may or may not be Christians.

All churches seek to reproduce aspects of the primitive church pictured in The Book of Acts and the Pauline Epistles. The difficulty which this intention meets is the lack of any clear picture of those primitive congregations which grew so rapidly in New Testament times. Christians must remember

118

that the church under the leadership of the Holy Spirit is never static, but that it necessarily changes its outward form to serve each day, generation, and culture. Even those churches that talk most of being like the New Testament Church, have Sunday schools, mission societies, brotherhoods, youth fellowships, and other organizations to serve the present day, none of which are mentioned in the New Testament.

IMPORTANCE OF ORGANIZATION

Leaving then the primitive church we turn to our own day and the organization of churches to meet its challenge. It is important that every local congregation be organized, in keeping with the pattern of its denomination, to meet the opportunities of its community to advance kingdom interests. If a congregation is serious in its desire to advance the kingdom the Holy Spirit undoubtedly will lead it in perfecting the proper organization. Against this background, the reason for ecclesiastical organization may well be examined. If one desired to be scriptural at this point it could be said that through many examples, the Scriptures teach the need for organization. This argument carries much weight with some people.

Efficiency is the basic reason for organizing congregations. Christian people have the largest and the most important task in the world to perform. It is embodied in the Great Commission which our Lord gave to his disciples.

The world is too large and the number of potential Christian workers is too great to attempt to proceed without thorough organization. To organize is simply to put each part (person) into its proper place of service so that it may perform the task it has to do, and thereby accomplish all needful works. When thinking of organization, sooner or later one will turn to the human body which is probably the most efficient organization to be found anywhere on earth. Is it not significant that Paul referred to the church as "the body of Christ"? If "the body of Christ" were properly organized, there is little doubt that it could in one generation take its community for Christ. If town-country Christians would properly organize themselves, they might remake town-country America in a single generation.

Here a warning must be sounded. A perfect organization will give no assurance that Christians will do their work in this world. More than organization is required. For a body to function there must also be that mystical, ethereal thing called "life." In the church this is called Spirit. The most perfect organization of unregenerate people will perform the holy mission of the church no sooner than a perfect automobile without a "spark" will run. The church's dependence is never upon organization alone. It must be upon the Spirit of the living God who may and should dwell in its organization. Churches organize so that the Spirit can do his work.

Amid the multiplicity of church organizations the question rightfully arises as to where to begin. It seems reasonable to assume that the best place to begin is with a workable *Church Constitution* that will outline objectives and provide working channels.

The following constitution has been prepared for use in American Baptist churches of one hundred to three hundred fifty members. It is simple but adequate for a church that would be effectively organized. Where the membership is less than one hundred it may be further simplified by omitting some boards and committees. This constitution provides that offices be held by a large number of church members. The purpose is to spread responsibility, create variety, and use as much of the available talent as possible.

The constitution given here is merely a sample. Every line in it should be carefully appraised, not only by the ministerial student, but by each member, as any local church prepares to write its own constitution. It is hardly to be expected that any church could adopt this constitution as written. For churches of some denominations, great changes would be needed.

A SUGGESTED CONSTITUTION
FOR THE CONSIDERATION OF TOWN-COUNTRY CHURCHES

ARTICLE I.

NAME AND INCORPORATION

The name of this church shall be the _____ _____ of _____. The church shall be incorporated according to the laws of the state of _____.

ARTICLE II.

PURPOSE

The purpose of this church shall be to maintain public services for the worship of God and for the teaching and preaching of the gospel, and in general to promote the interests of the kingdom of God according to the teachings of the Scriptures.

ARTICLE III.

DENOMINATIONAL AFFILIATIONS

Section 1. Co-operation with Other Bodies.

The church's government is vested in the body which composes its membership; but because its parish is worldwide it recognizes its obligation and privilege to co-operate with other religious bodies having the same general objectives. It shall therefore be affiliated with the American Baptist Convention, _____ State Baptist Convention, and _____ Baptist Association.

Section 2. Declaration of Doctrine and Principles.

This church receives the New Testament as an all-sufficient basis of doctrine and practice. As a summary of principles for Christian conduct among its members it adopts the following church covenant.

CHURCH COVENANT

Having been led, as we believe, by the Spirit of God, to receive the Lord Jesus Christ as our Saviour, and on the profession of our faith, having been baptized in the name of the Father, and of the Son, and of the Holy Spirit, we do now in the presence of God, angels, and this assembly, most solemnly and joyfully enter into covenant with one another, as one body in Christ.

We engage therefore, by the aid of the Holy Spirit, to walk together in Christian love; to strive for the advancement of this church, in knowledge, holiness, and comfort; to promote its prosperity and spirituality; to sustain its worship, ordinances, discipline, and doctrines; to contribute cheerfully and regularly to the support of the ministry, the expenses of the church, the relief of the poor, and the spread of the gospel through all nations.

We also engage to maintain family and secret devotion; to religiously educate our children; to seek the salvation of our kindred and acquaintances; to walk circumspectly in the world; to be just in our dealings, faithful in our engagements, and exemplary in our deportment; to avoid all tattling, backbiting, and excessive anger; to abstain from the sale and use of intoxicating drinks as a beverage, and to be zealous in our efforts to advance the kingdom of our Saviour.

We further engage to watch over one another in brotherly love; to remember each other in prayer; to aid each other in sickness and distress; to cultivate Christian sympathy in feeling and courtesy in speech;

to be slow to take offense, but always ready for reconciliation, and mindful of the rules of our Saviour to secure it without delay.

We moreover engage that when we remove from this place, we will as soon as possible unite with some other church, where we can carry out the spirit of this covenant and the principles of God's word.

ARTICLE IV.
MEMBERSHIP

Section 1. The members of this church shall be:

a. Such persons as confess Jesus Christ to be their Lord and Saviour, and promise to live a Christian life, and have been baptized by immersion.

b. Such persons who present letters of dismission and recommendation from other churches of the denomination and are in harmony with the teachings and practices of this church.

c. Such persons who for good reasons cannot secure a letter, but who by their statement assure the church of their Christian faith and baptism.

Section 2. Dismission from this church shall be:

a. By death.

b. By letter. Any member who desires a letter of dismission and recommendation to any other church is entitled to receive it upon request. The name of the church to which membership is to be transferred must be indicated in the request, and the letter shall be sent to the pastor or clerk of that church. The letter will state clearly the record of the individual as to his attendance at worship, participation in church activities, and discharge of his stewardship obligations.

c. By exclusion. In all cases involving immorality, and in case of delinquency through failure to comply with covenant obligations, members may be excluded when, after the disciplinary process described in Matthew 18:15-17 is followed, it is recommended by the deacons and approved by vote of the church.

Section 3. Those members residing within (geographical area), plus any others attending regularly, shall be deemed resident members, and all others non-resident members.

ARTICLE V.
OFFICERS

Section 1. Church officers as listed below shall be elected or appointed as provided for in this article.

a. Except as otherwise provided all officers shall be elected at the annual meeting of the church for a period of one year, and after serving for three consecutive years shall not be eligible for re-election for at least one year. At least three months before the annual meeting of the church the church council shall appoint a nominating committee to nominate all officers and committees to be elected at the annual meeting. The committee's report shall be published at one or more public meetings of the church at least two weeks in advance of the annual meeting.

b. The pastor shall be called for an indefinite period by the church membership upon the recommendation of a pulpit committee. His election shall be by secret ballot at a regular or special meeting of the church, provided notice of intention to vote on the calling of a pastor at such a meeting has been given at all regular church meetings during the two preceding weeks. Three-fourths of all votes cast shall be necessary for an election.

c. The pastor's contract may be terminated by six-months notice from the church; or by three-months notice by the pastor, unless by mutual agreement of church and pastor a longer or shorter period is deemed best.

Section 2. Officers and Their Duties.

a. Pastor.

The pastor shall be the chief executive and spiritual leader of the congregation. He shall be an ex-officio member of all boards and committees. He shall preside at church meetings when the moderator is absent.

b. Moderator.

The moderator shall preside at the business meetings of the church.

c. Church Clerk.

The church clerk shall keep a correct and permanent record of all the business meetings of the church, sign all letters of dismission, take charge of all church records, and maintain a register of members in which shall be noted such changes as may occur.

The clerk shall enter upon the records of the church current events in the life of the church that are likely to be of historical value.

The clerk will make regular reports to denominational officers relative to the condition of the church.

The clerk shall be elected annually, and shall be eligible for re-election regardless of the number of terms previously served.

d. Treasurer.

The treasurer shall be the custodian of all funds belonging to the church, except the fellowship fund which shall be handled by the deacons. He shall disburse money only after he receives a voucher signed by the chairman of the board of trustees. He shall make a monthly report to the church council and quarterly and annual reports to the church. All money for benevolent purposes contributed through the church channels shall be held by the treasurer, who shall disburse it strictly for the items within the budget toward which those contributions have been made. All contributions for the missionary budget of the denomination shall be forwarded to the proper collecting agency at least once each month, to reach that office not later than the fifteenth of the month.

e. Financial Secretary.

The financial secretary shall receive all money given to the church for local expenses, benevolences, and missions through the regular channels and in special offerings, and shall keep a complete and detailed record of all individual pledges and payments on same. On Monday of each week, as nearly as possible, he shall turn over to the treasurer all money on hand. He shall send financial statements every three months to all contributing members, showing their individual financial standings.

f. Church School Officers.

A church school superintendent, assistant superintendent, secretary, and treasurer shall be elected by the church to have general supervision of the entire church school.

g. Chorister and Organist.

The chorister and organist, in co-operation with the pastor and board of education, will plan and lead the music for the public worship of the church, and be responsible for training the choirs of the church.

ARTICLE VI.
BOARDS AND COMMITTEES

Section 1. Unless otherwise provided, each board and committee of the church shall elect its own chairman.

Section 2. Church Council [or Advisory Board].

There shall be a church council composed of the pastor, the elected officers of the church, chairmen of the boards, the superintendent of the church school, the heads of the men's, women's and young people's organizations, and the chairmen of all standing committees responsible to the church council, thus forming a group representing the entire scope of the church's program and activities. The pastor shall preside at the meetings of the council. He shall be responsible for introducing matters of interest that should be presented to the council meeting, and shall arrange an agenda for each meeting. This council shall be the general planning body of the church. It shall constantly study the needs of the church and the needs of its community, and shall suggest the ways and means by which the policies and programs of the church shall be carried forward. It shall seek to correlate the programs of all the departments and groups in the church. It shall conduct an annual every member enlistment for the underwriting of the church budget. The council shall meet regularly at intervals of not more than three months on specified dates fixed by the council. Such fixed dates shall remain in effect until changed by the council.

If there is no board of Christian education, the church council shall function temporarily in this capacity.

Special meetings of the church council may be called by the pastor or by the chairman of the diaconate.

Section 3. Diaconate.

There shall be a diaconate consisting of ——— members, one-third of whom shall be women. [There should be approximately one deacon or deaconess for every twenty members, and not less than three.] The term of office shall be so arranged as to provide that there shall be an equal number elected each year to serve for a term of three years. No deacon or deaconess who has served a full term of three years shall be eligible for re-election until a period of at least one year has elapsed.

The diaconate shall have general oversight of the spiritual life of the church, aid the pastor in the performance of his duties, advise with the applicants for church membership and recommend those who are deemed suitable for church fellowship, have full charge of the fellowship fund, and serve the Lord's table whenever this ordinance is observed. It shall report at regular intervals to the church council.

Section 4. Board of Trustees.

There shall be a board of trustees, consisting of a minimum of three members. Their term of office shall be so arranged that one-third of their number will be elected each year to serve for a term of three years. No member of the board who has served a full term of three years shall be eligible for re-election until a period of at least one year has elapsed.

The trustees shall hold in trust all property of the church, and shall be responsible for the upkeep of the same. They shall not sell or encumber the real estate or other property of the church unless authorized to do so by a two-thirds vote of the members present at a meeting of the church called for the purpose of considering such a transaction. Such a meeting of the church must be called in accordance with the provisions of the laws of the state of _____ which govern the selling or encumbering of church property. The trustees shall recommend to the church, annually, a proposed budget of anticipated receipts and expenditures, covering all the regular work of the church for the coming year.

Section 5. Board of Christian Education.

There shall be a board of Christian education, consisting of not less than three nor more than six elected members, as the church shall determine. Their terms shall be so arranged that insofar as possible one-third of their number will be elected each year to serve for a period of three years. In addition to the elected members, the pastor and the church school superintendent shall be ex-officio members. The board shall be responsible for studying the educational needs of the church, and leading the church in the fulfillment of these needs. Its work shall be organized under the following functions, and each shall be under the direction of a board member selected for his interest and qualifications in the respective field: (1) Children's work, (2) youth work, (3) adult work, (4) leadership education, and (5) missionary and stewardship education.

Section 6. Land and Business Opportunities Committee.

There shall be a land and business opportunities committee composed of nine people, one-third of whom shall be elected each year to serve for a period of three years. The purpose of the committee will be to help the young people and young adults of the church to settle in the community by becoming owners of farms, industries, businesses, and by practicing the professions. The duties of the committee shall be fourfold:

a. To know the opportunities in the community for farm, industry, and business ownership, and the need for various professions.

b. To know the capabilities and resources of all the young people and young adults of the church.

c. To know the various sources of finance open to reliable Christians.

d. To introduce the proper young people and young adults to opportunities and available financial resources at the proper time.

The committee will also co-operate with the board of Christian education in supplying materials to members on such subjects as father-son partnerships, family farm-transfer arrangements, and vocational subjects that will be helpful in satisfactorily locating a large percentage of their young people in the community.

Section 7. Pulpit Committee.

When the church is in need of a pastor a pulpit committee shall be appointed by the church council and approved by the church for the purpose of recommending to the church a desirable candidate for the pulpit. This committee shall examine thoroughly a candidate's record, scholastic and otherwise, and, only after assuring itself that he is God's man for the field, shall recommend him for the church. It shall have a clear understanding with the candidate relative to the church's financial and other obligations to him, and report this to the church when the recommendation is made.

No consideration shall be given by the church to any candidate who is not first recommended by the pulpit committee.

Section 8. Auditing Committee.

There shall be an auditing committee composed of three members elected annually by the council. It shall be the duty of this committee to audit the books of the financial secretary and the treasurer at the end of the fiscal year, and to make a report of the same to the church.

ARTICLE VII.
MEETINGS

Section 1. Fiscal Year.

The fiscal year of the church shall begin on _____ and close on _____ of each year.

Section 2. Annual Business Meeting.

The annual meeting of the church shall be held during the week following the first Monday in the first month of the church year. At this meeting the annual reports of all phases of the church work shall be made in writing. After acceptance by the church these reports shall be delivered to the church clerk and made a part of the permanent records of the church.

Section 3. Quarterly Business Meeting.

A meeting for the transaction of business shall be held at the close of the regular midweek prayer meeting during the first week in each quarter.

Section 4. Special Meetings.

Special meetings may be called by the pastor, moderator, the chairman of the diaconate, or by the chairman of the board of trustees by announcement at one or more regular meetings of the church. Any action taken at a special meeting must be reported at the next quarterly meeting of the church.

Section 5. Lord's Supper.

The Lord's Supper shall be commemorated on the second Sunday of January, April, July, and October, and, if desired, on the Thursday night before Easter.

Section 6. Quorum.

A minimum of _____[25% to 60%] resident members shall be a quorum for a special or regular business meeting of the church.

Section 7. Procedures.

The business meeting of the church shall be conducted according to Robert's Rules of Order.

ORDER OF BUSINESS

1. The meeting is called to order by the moderator.
2. The minutes of the preceding meeting are read by the church clerk.
    a. May be approved as read.
    b. May be approved after additions or correction.
3. Statement of treasurer, quarterly or annual, is received as read and filed for audit. Moderator so states.
4. Reports of standing committees are called for by the moderator.
5. Reports of special committees are called for by the moderator.
6. Unfinished business is next in order at the call of the meeting.
7. New business.
8. The program. The program is part of the meeting; the moderator presides throughout, but the program chairman makes report.
9. Adjournment.

ARTICLE VIII.

AMENDMENTS

This constitution may be amended at any business meeting of the church on the recommendation of the church council, provided two-weeks notice of such proposed amendment shall be given. A three-fourths vote is necessary to adopt an amendment.

A church constitution is a sacred instrument, for it is the members' working agreement on organization and procedures. Good or bad, it must be followed until the church sees fit to amend it. There is hardly a need in the town-country field that cannot be met by a thoughtfully-written church constitution.

Some ideas in the foregoing constitution need additional discussion. Article I indicates that the church shall be incorporated according to the laws of the state where it is located. This important item is frequently overlooked by the small church. Why incorporate? Usually it is impossible for a church to borrow money from a public institution or a mission society without first being incorporated. If an unincorporated church instructs its trustees to borrow money, or in any way to obligate the church, the trustees who sign the papers are personally responsible for the obligation and may be sued in case the church defaults. If the church is incorporated the church as a body is liable, and not the trustees individually. If a damage suit is brought against an unincorporated church each member may be sued. If the church is incorporated only the church as a body may be assessed damages. If the church is unincorporated it is possible for an unscrupulous person to gain possession of the church's building and equipment. For the protection of its members, property, and good name, a church should incorporate immediately after organizing.

Because of local conditions or denominational affiliation, some churches may find it desirable to include a creed or statement of faith. This can be inserted along with a covenant or instead of a covenant.

The church constitution is a map by which a pastor and the church he serves may harmoniously move together to accomplish the greatest amount of good with the minimum of effort. The pastor's first obligation to the church is to know the church's constitution and be governed by it. A pastor is not a dictator who can do with the church as he pleases. He is expected to use only the powers granted him in the discharge of his pastoral duties. He is a servant of the church and honor-bound to remain as one who serves.

If, after a year or so of service, a pastor finds that the church constitution is out of date or that it could be improved, then as a good leader he is both privileged and obliged to suggest that it be restudied by the church. In this study he is free to make suggestions. As a result of corporate study, amendments may then be proposed and adopted as provided in the existing constitution.

X

THE OVERCHURCHED COMMUNITY

THE RELIGIOUS LIFE OF TOWN-COUNTRY AMERICA has grown
without the help of an over-all plan. It is not at all unusual to
find a hamlet of one hundred people with two churches. Villages of four hundred to six hundred people may have as many
as six churches. Even with such an abundance the community
is not evangelized, for all the churches together are not doing
the work that needs to be done. In spite of the many churches
there are large segments of the population without churches
and pastors. Even around the small centers where so many
churches are found there are pockets of people, little neighborhoods, without the ministrations of any church. Here people
are growing up in paganism. This unwholesome situation is
on the conscience of Christian people. They know it is wrong.
With denominational loyalties, investments, programs, and
emphases being what they are, the answer to the multichurch
problem is not simple. Out of the efforts toward resolving this
puzzle have come several possible solutions. These are presented briefly in the order of their acceptability.

DENOMINATIONAL CHURCH

The most efficient solution is that of a strong, central, denominational church which ministers in a well-defined community or neighborhood to the needs of all the people. Such
a church should ideally have from 200 to 350 resident members.
A greater or lesser number than this is outside the range of
maximum efficiency for town-country work.

129

It should have a church building designed for worship and formal religious instruction, a separate hall for social, educational, and recreational purposes, and a modern parsonage with about five acres of land for the pastor's use. It should have a trained and deeply consecrated pastor who will minister to the needs of all the people.

There are many situations in which such a church could be developed, given adequate pastoral leadership over a twenty-year period, and if the church would think in terms of community boundaries, as explained in Chap. VII. The constitution previously offered is intended for the organizational framework of such a church.

COMMUNITY DENOMINATIONAL CHURCH

The second solution is that of the community denominational church which must not be confused with the community church. There is a difference. The community denominational church recognizes that there are Christian people in the community without a church home and who are not of the denomination's persuasion. In one small community a survey revealed that there were thirteen evangelical groups with 131 members, besides those people who belonged to the two churches in the community. What should these 131 people of thirteen denominations do? Should they organize thirteen more churches? Should they remain outside of the existing churches because they cannot accept all the doctrines of any one church in the community? Should the existing churches ignore them because they do not interpret the Scriptures as they do? Should the churches seek to change the minds of these people and withold Christian fellowship until they fully agree with the existing churches?

Many such questions are answered by the community denominational church. It opens its doors to all Christians, inviting them to worship and to serve without abandoning their denominational heritages. If they accept the invitation they are usually carried on the church books as associate members. Their contributions support the local church and its denominational program of missions. The church may, and usually does, limit the offices they may hold and the subjects on which they may vote. It seldom happens that the proportion of associate members is more than 10 or 15 per cent of the resident membership of a church. They are not in position to control the church; few of them would ever want to do so. Article IV on membership in the sample constitution may easily be worded to accommodate this feature.

Those who favor the community denominational church believe that it creates a more Christian attitude in the community and that it provides a needed church home for some people who would not otherwise have one. They point out that many Christians brought into the fellowship of the local church in this manner are later won to the denomination. Their children are brought up in the denomination and the denomination becomes the expression of their Christian faith. Opponents to this plan claim that it is liable to lead the church into strange policies, that it weakens denominational ties, and that it is a kind of compromise.

LARGER PARISH

The denominational larger parish is a third plan which is worthy of consideration when two or more churches of the same denomination are to be found in a plainly delimited community. Although much can be said for small neighborhood churches where fellowship is intense, such churches may be too small to serve the people adequately. Often they have been in the midst of a declining population wherein they too will decline until they cease to function, and the remaining people of the neighborhood will be denied the ministrations of a church. Whether or not it seems feasible to bring all the members into one central church, such a suggestion might be vigorously resisted, for people hold tenaciously to an institution even when its days of usefulness are over.

Under denominational leadership two or more adjacent neighborhood churches may be encouraged to reorganize under modified constitutions, then join in a parish-wide or community-wide denominational organization which could be named from the community, such as the former "The Devil's Tower Larger Parish," at Hulet, Wyo., or the Presbyterians' oldest parish, "Old Providence," in Virginia. These churches could work out a parish constitution which they would solemnly promise to follow. The constitution would provide for a larger parish council. This is a co-ordinating and planning group similar to the church council in a local church. It is composed of three or more persons from each of the churches, elected annually by each church. Representation of each church is thus assured. The constitution also may provide for other members on the Council.

One treasurer is provided for in the larger parish. Each church has a financial secretary, but no treasurer. The financial secretaries, on receiving money, make proper records thereof, then turn it over to the larger parish treasurer. He pays the pastor's salary and all other authorized bills. In financing, one budget is set up for the larger parish and one every-member canvass of the entire parish is made to cover it.

In order to call a pastor, an interchurch pulpit committee with representation from all churches involved serves the larger parish. When this committee finds a man, it presents his name to each church of the larger parish through the larger parish council. Each church votes separately either to call or not to call the candidate and reports its action to the larger parish council. The council in turn reports to the candidate. A candidate is not called unless all the churches of the parish agree.

It may be that the community to be served will be so large and the needs so great that the pastor will need an assistant. This assistant may be a youth worker, one specialized in music, or one who can meet the recreational needs of the people and guide community activities. He too should be chosen according to the needs of the community and the resources of the parish.

There is much to be said for the denominational larger parish, though some argue that it destroys the independence of the small neighborhood church. Others argue that small churches are most reluctant to co-operate in this manner. The number of larger parishes is still small in most denominations, although the United Presbyterians in the United States report more than six hundred of them.

The interdenominational larger parish differs from the denominational larger parish in that the co-operating churches are of more than one denomination. This system generally calls for a rotation of pastors from one denomination to another. If there are difficulties in organizing and maintaining a denominational larger parish, they are vastly increased if the parish is interdenominational. It can be expected that the mortality rate of interdenominational larger parishes will be rather high.

FEDERATED CHURCH

The federated church should in reality be called a federation of churches, for that is its true nature. Incidentally, it is in no way representative of, or the child of the old Federal Council of Churches of Christ in America, as some have erroneously thought. Two or more evangelical churches in the same community may feel that the community would be better served if they had the same pastor and worshiped and studied in the same building. They accordingly work out a plan by which *each denominational group is preserved intact* while they all worship together. They maintain as many church organizations as there are denominations in the federation. These churches meet as distinct bodies at least once a year, preferably once a quarter, to conduct denominational business. Each supports its own denominational missionary program.

The federation may agree upon an order of rotation by which pastors will be chosen from the denominations represented. Sometimes they agree that the pastor shall be from an evangelical denomination not represented in the federation. When a pastor is to be called, the pulpit committee is composed of a fair representation from each church. The candidate's name is presented to the federation, and he is accepted or rejected by the total group.

While there are some highly successful federations in America, denominational leaders usually feel that federation is not the final answer. If the population begins to increase the federation is in danger of failure. One denomination is on record as favoring the frequent re-examination of a federation, looking to the time when it will be replaced with a community denominational church or a denominational church. It has been observed that where a strong pastor remains with a federation for several years, the tendency is for the churches to accept his denomination as their own. The usual criticism of a federation is that no pastor can minister to Christians of different denominations without compromising on matters of principle.

Nevertheless, some pastors are succeeding without compromising. An example is the thriving federation at Green Lake, Wis., where in 1949 the Congregationalists, Methodists and American Baptists, each a struggling minority group, federated and called a Presbyterian as their first pastor. The churches have prospered under a succession of well trained and adequately supported full-time pastors, serving a field adequate in size for effective work.

COMMUNITY CHURCH

The idea of a community church is popular with many laymen and a few pastors. Laymen frequently say "What we need is one church. Let's cut out this denominational foolishness and have just our own church." In some places denominational ties have been severed and an independent community church appears to prosper. Although there are about two thousand community churches in the United States most of them are urban, not rural. The constitution for a community church would be similar to the one outlined in Chap. IX.

In cutting itself free from all denominations, a local church severs its ties with a world-wide missionary program and communion, the very genius of Christianity. It cuts itself loose from fellowship with like-minded churchmen in the same general area. It cuts its ties with Christian schools where its young may be trained and from which ministers are secured. If it is to secure leaders it must become part of an organization that will provide them, and that comes dangerously close to forming another denomination. The unhappy fact is that some denominational churches are community churches, except for name. They have already loosed themselves from support of the denominational mission program and schools. They have as pastors men from non-denominational schools.

YOKED FIELD

One of the earliest efforts at serving the small church was the forming of yoked fields or circuits, a plan still in use in some denominations. Under this plan, if one church is able to pay only half a minister's salary, it is reasoned that it should have only half of his services. Several miles away is a church that can afford to pay only one-fourth of a pastor's salary. Thus it receives one-fourth of his time. In still another direction there is another church which is able to pay one-fourth of the salary, and it, too, receives one-fourth of the pastor's time. This minister is present in the half-time church two Sundays each month, and in each quarter-time church one Sunday a month. Thus the pastor is paid a full time salary and, when he proves himself, he may have a better charge. What an easy solution!

About the only thing to commend the yoked field is that it makes the payment of the minister's salary possible. With the churches situated in three different communities little can be done to develop a vital program in each church. The pastor is too far removed from any of the churches to be an effective leader, and he is the only connecting link between the churches. Neither churches nor pastors seem to profit under the yoked ministry. It would be far better to develop larger parishes and place each of the three churches in its proper community-determined parish.

WORKING TOGETHER

Much good can be accomplished and Christ's cause advanced in town-country areas if Christians will permit themselves to share one another's burdens through co-operation. The present denominational structure, rooted in both culture and theology, will remain on the American scene for generations to come. Denominationalism is not necessarily evil. Through the denominations Christ's message has been carried across this continent and into foreign lands. The denominations have invested millions of dollars in properties and endowments. These will not, can not in fact, be easily liquidated in favor of a non-denominational agency. There is no evidence that the elimination of denominationalism would solve all problems of the Christian cause. It is no blot on the Christian flag to have denominations with their differences of emphases in the theological opinions, culture, and practice. The blot of disgrace appears when Christians dissipate their energies in fighting one another instead of fighting the entrenched evils of their communities. A village of fifteen hundred people with four or five full-time resident ministers can be better served than it could if it had but one minister. These ministers, while seeking to win the lost and care for their own church constituencies, can present an unbroken front in leading the community, through their respective churches, in better ways of living.

Dr. Rockwell C. Smith, in his book *Rural Church Administration*, makes the worthy suggestion that a Protestant church suite of offices be established in the county seat, or chief town of a community, and that a secretary-receptionist be employed. Each co-operating pastor, or church, would have a room in the suite, and people desiring to have his counsel would be directed to his office. The secretary would handle the correspondence and the usual office details for all the pastors. By maintaining regular office hours, and frequently counseling with one another, the ministers would present a united Christian front and be better able to lead their people in worthy community projects.

If so ambitious a program for the ministers as suggested by Dr. Smith is not immediately feasible, then at least the ministers may form a community ministerial association. By meeting regularly they can counsel with one another and co-operate in Christian projects.

The idea of the association can be carried even farther by the organization of a community council through which all religious and civic organizations of the community co-operate to build a better community.

It is imperative that both the church and church field be organized with the intent of reaching for Christ the last man, woman, and child in the most remote part of the parish. To do less is to make light of Christ's command to go into all the world.

XI

ENLISTING THE CHURCH MEMBERSHIP

CLEMENCEAU IS REPORTED to have said "War is too important to be left to the generals." Following this thought, Christianity is too important to be left to the ministers. Yet that is where much of it has been left. The National Council of American Baptist Men has said that laymen should constitute the real strength of the church in its ministry to the world. Its success, humanly speaking, lies in the extent to which it can mobilize its manpower for active and effective Christian service. Then, dolefully it laments that only a small proportion of men of the average church are now actively identified with its life and program. The condemnation of the women in the average church is not quite so severe. Many times the women have kept churches open and ministers paid by cash contributions from their pin money, the earnings of bake and rummage sales, dinners, and quilting parties. Women have expressed an interest in missions, and through their mission societies have studied, shared their funds, and inspired the male membership to make at least an annual contribution to missions. Even so, only a small percentage of the men and women of a church are actively engaged in, and dedicated to, the fulfillment of the Great Commission. What, then, should be expected of members of town-country churches?

THE MEMBER'S CHURCH WORK

Be it man or woman, the expectation is that when any individual becomes a member of a church he puts forth an earnest

137

effort to become a vital part of that fellowship. It also follows that every member of the church should make every reasonable effort to include a new member in the fellowship. This fellowship should transcend a cordial "Hello" at worship and the friendly drinking of a cup of coffee at the church supper. It should manifest itself in a deep and vital concern for one another so that there is a wise sharing of all things needful for a well-rounded Christian life.

Christians have need of corporate worship, not only for what it can do for them but as their offering to God. It can hardly be expected that a new Christian will be able to enter fully into the worship of the church without help. Members of a church, in one way or another, should carefully teach each new member the techniques of worship. They should also aid their pastor in creating a stimulating service of worship every Sunday. The minimum for any Christian should be attendance and participation in public worship at least once each week.

There are offices to be filled in the structure of the church. Not only should these positions be filled, but the offices should be passed around so that all members have opportunity to serve in the official life of the church. For a few men and women to monopolize the holding of offices defeats the purposes of good organization.

Moreover, there is the duty of men and women assuming, willingly and gladly, the financial responsibility for the work of the church, including the far-flung missionary program. Leaders of the past have asked too little, and all too little money has been made available for the work of the church. Is it too much to expect that each member of a church contribute a minimum of one-tenth of his net income to the church's work? Only about 2 or 3 per cent is now being given!

To this point we have been concerned with usual and routine expressions of church membership. The question now arises as to whether or not it is possible for a Christian to fulfill his responsibilities to God only through these channels. Clearly, there is more than this to do. To be sure, the things touched upon are valuable, *but less valuable* than some other things that churches have left unsaid and undone.

THE MEMBER'S VOCATION

In 1952, Mr. Charles J. Turck, in the opening address to the North American Lay Conference in Buffalo, said: "Two years ago the Detroit Conference on the Church and Economic Life, among other things, unanimously agreed and stated 'The Gospel is concerned with all the activities of man, individual and social. Therefore, the Christian faith is relevant to the economic order. The Church must proclaim anew the Christian concept of vocation. All work must be seen in terms of its spiritual significance as helping to make possible fullness of life for all men everywhere. The Reformation doctrine of the calling of the Christian man must be re-emphasized, and all work must be done "as unto God." The Lord is present not alone in the broken bread and sacred wine of Holy Communion, but is present, too, in the sacred labor that brings to man his daily bread. When a man thinks of himself as a priest of God, his work becomes a sacred calling.' "

A Christian's vocation can, and rightly should, be a holy thing. If by its nature it is not holy, then a Christian must leave it and find something that meets with God's approval. It is not unreasonable to believe that God has called people to render service in his kingdom in keeping with the talents he has given them. Let us then see how this stewardship of vocation will work in a number of situations.

Why do people farm? Perhaps it is because they must earn a living and, having been born on a farm, it is the handiest or easiest thing to do. Perhaps farming offers more security and financial return than some other occupations. These are the common reasons for farming, and if conditions should change there would be no objection to the farmer changing to another type of work.

Suppose, however, that through the church's teaching, a young man turns to farming because he is convinced that God has called him to help feed the earth's two and one-half billion people. Will this not make a difference in his attitude toward what he grows, how he markets it, and how he protects and maintains the fertility of the soil? Will it not make a difference to him as he shoulders the daily responsibilities that call for hours of drudgery? Will not such a view give meaning to his life? It will make the same difference to him that a clear call from God makes to the man who shoulders the responsibility of being a minister of the gospel. It should mean no less.

There are other fields related to agriculture to which the idea of Christian vocation should also apply, such as service as a county agricultural agent, 4-H club organizer, soil conservation service technician, or veterinarian. In all such ways a man may work with God, thus changing his vocation from a mere livelihood to a holy venture in fulfilling Christ's prayer, "Give us this day our daily bread."

The Federal Government, the American Medical Association, and some church leaders are disturbed by the poor health of rural people, especially those people who live in the towns. There is need for more doctors, hospitals, and medical services in rural areas. There is an even greater need for preventive medicine. Why do men and women become doctors? A respectable profession? Good pay? Prestige? In many cases, yes. Others become doctors because of the opportunity the profession provides for being of service to their fellow men. Suppose a young man hears the voice of God calling him to minister to the physical needs of his rural brethren through the practice of medicine. Would this not lighten his load as he sought training, and give meaning to the long, fatiguing hours of travel over the parish later? Would it not make a vast difference in the kind of service he rendered? There seems to be no way of meeting the health needs of rural Americans except by an appeal to young people to dedicate their lives to full-time Christian medical service for them.

The public school is still another full-time avenue through which men and women may serve Christ. It is one of the most powerful agencies in American life for it exerts great influence in the thinking of the people. It is a leveler and sustainer of democracy. The public schools must have teachers. By the very lives they live, teachers mold the thinking of youth and determine to a high degree the moral atmosphere of the nation. The public schools offer another significant opportunity for full-time Christian service.

In the same spirit, Christian service may be rendered in the fields of banking, merchandising, manufacturing, transportation, communication, entertainment, and politics. The Christian is called to glorify God so that His will might be done on earth as it is in heaven. All these vocations are needful to the maintenance of a Christian society, and even to the Christian church. If any man will enter, in the name of Christ, these vocational fields in order to serve his fellow men, he will be fulfilling a divine commission.

There is, however, a vocation that needs rethinking. It is that of serving one's denomination in some paid staff or administrative capacity. It is the custom to fill almost all paid positions in a denomination's structure with ministers. The reasoning seems to be that, since the Reverend Dr. John Jones is a fine preacher, has a good record, and is faithful to the denomination, he is the man to head the presbytery, state convention, or the national work. When this kind of thing is done, often a successful pastor is removed from the place where he may be of the most service to take over an administrative job for which he may or may not be qualified. Because of their training such men largely confine their contacts to ministers, thus building up a hierarchy in the very denominations that denounce such things. Surely Christian men and women trained in the field of administration and placed in such offices of responsibility would give a good account of themselves, develop a closer tie with the laity, and advance the kingdom generally. This change is long overdue.

THE MEMBER'S HOME

Not only is the Christian's place to be found in church work and in vocation, but also in his home. The home is basic to all social development. It is basic to the church's work. While many have glorified the Sunday school, the home has easily been overlooked as a teaching agent and the primary evangelizing force of the church. The home must be re-appraised and then made all that it ought to be. Christian parents' primary place of service is in the home. To maintain a home that is Christian, not merely in name and form, but in spirit, is one of the noblest services a Christian can render his church and the kingdom of God. If they succeed here it will not much matter how well they have served in other ways. If they fail, their being deacons, teachers, choir members, regular attendants at worship, and tithers, will not make amends for the failure: the kingdom loses.

THE MEMBER IN PUBLIC LIFE

The conscientious Christian, moreover, can serve Christ by taking an active, constructive part in the life of his community, the state, and the nation. Whatever may be the meaning of "come out from them and be separate" (2 Cor. 6:17), it does not mean that Christians are to be mentally or physically separated from the civic life of which they are a natural part. On the contrary, they are the salt, the light, the community's only hope of redemption. They are Christ's witnesses. Therefore Christians serve as they enter into the activities of their communities. They may serve through volunteer organizations such as a 4-H club, parent-teacher association, civic club, cooperative, or a political office.

But service must go beyond the local community. As Christian laymen are able they should enter the affairs of their government. They should seek political offices so that they might glorify God there too. If they have opportunity for leadership in fraternal organizations, service clubs, and co-operatives they should fulfill them with Christian purpose. The Christian layman is to be Christ's arms, eyes, and ears in the development of a Christ-like community. This is not something he is to do professionally but is a part of his witnessing for Christ. There is no good reason why he should not join with other members of the church to launch some constructive program for the community's good.

CHURCH WOMEN

It has been assumed that the women march side by side with the men in their service to their churches. This is as it should be. However, it ought to be recognized that the nature of a woman's contribution to the church is determined by her age and marital standing. Church women may be divided into five groups.

Group one is composed of married women from eighteen to forty-five years of age. This is the child-bearing age and the time when a woman's husband may need her help in getting established in his chosen vocation. For this reason she may be somewhat limited in the time and energy she can devote to the church other than participation in public and private worship, but she has a good share of youthful zest and vitality and willingly does as much as she can.

Group two is composed of single girls and women eighteen to forty-five. Of the younger in this group some will be in school, some working, and perhaps all anticipating marriage. The members of this group have more time and more need to serve Christ through the regular channels of the church than their married sisters. They need the social contacts which are to be found in the wide acquaintances provided by state and national church groups. The older members of this group, for whom marriage seems more remote, may be able to open businesses or enter wholeheartedly into professional life, where by their vocation they can honor and serve God.

Group three is composed of married women from forty-five to sixty-five. As the forty-fifth year of a woman's life arrives she enters another exciting stage of her development. The years of child-bearing are over. The oldest children are married, in college, or in the military forces. This can be a critical time for her, for suddenly it may seem that she no longer has a reason for living. No one seems to depend on her as in the past. On the other hand, her age provides her with new freedom and additional time for church and community work. She will need to make some careful reappraisals. She may want to work outside the home to take up the slack time, and some such opportunities will be available in the town-country area. If she has had college training, she may, with a minimum of schooling, teach in one of the schools near home and thereby give witness to her faith. With additional training, she may be employed as a home demonstration agent or a librarian.

Women in this group who have no need or desire to enter the business or professional world may use their time to advance the program of their churches. They can be useful as Sunday school teachers, choir members, social workers, visitors, leaders of adult discussion groups, counselors to young mothers, and can hold elective offices in the church with honor.

Constantly there are many people moving in and out of town-country communities. Often they move from community to community without being touched by a church. Women of group three, going two by two, could witness for Christ by frequent, friendly calling on the newcomers. They might call on a lonesome young mother, and leave with her a good book or a few interesting religious pamphlets. They might care for the children of some young harassed mother for an afternoon while she secures much-needed recreation. The possibilities for service of this kind are unlimited. By belonging to women's clubs which are devoted to cultural and civic improvement, the Christian woman can bring the force of her convictions to bear where they will count, and bring about helpful changes in the community. In the women of this third group the church has a supply of unused labor which, if properly directed, could make the church a dynamic force in the community.

In the midst of all these activities, these women may develop their own spiritual lives through Bible study, reading of religious literature, and prayer. By doing so they may become a part of a powerful spiritual core in their churches.

It is in this period of life that a woman is most likely to become a grandmother. Who can estimate the value of her service as she shares in the care, development, and inspiration of her grandchildren? This will test her skill as a Christian, too, for she must not dominate the home of her daughter or daughter-in-law. At this point many a Christian testimony breaks down. Nevertheless, as a grandmother she is in a unique position to help the children to develop along Christian lines. Paul praised the contribution Timothy's grandmother made to his spiritual development, saying "I am reminded of your sincere faith, a faith that dwelt first in your grandmother Lois and your mother Eunice and now, I am sure, dwells in you" (2 Tim. 1:5).

Group four consists of single women over forty-five, some of whom are widows. Not many single women reaching forty-five will marry. Many will become depressed with loneliness as their parents die and they find they have no home life. They will help not only the church, but themselves as well by Bible reading, prayer, public worship, and whatever service they can perform in the church. They can show Christian friendliness to all they meet, and witness for the Christian way of life in their encounters with younger women.

It is in this period that the number of widows will sharply increase. The accident and death rate among rural males is high, although not as high as it was a generation ago. The loss of her mate may throw a heavy burden upon the woman. She may find herself the manager of an extensive farming venture or business. Also, she may find herself in dire financial straits. Her children may still be young and in need of every educational opportunity. In the midst of this perplexity she should deepen her dependence upon the Father and renew her determination to keep her family together as a Christian unit. The burden she is called upon to bear will necessitate her belonging to one of the women's groups in the church and/or community. Without its fellowship and outlook on the world she would tend to become "family bound" and perhaps cynical, if not given to self-pity. To carry on as a Christian and rear the children as Christians is her opportunity and responsibility to Christ's church. Those widows who have enough of this world's goods may well follow the pattern of their married sisters of the same age, but they will be able to give more of time and talent in a ministry to others.

The fifth group for consideration is that which consists of women over 65 years of age. At this age they may be slower, but no one should think of them as being "on the shelf." In these women, as in the men of similar age, the church has a storehouse of power. The hurried pace to make a living is over, but with abundant energy still at their disposal they need direction in useful work. Because their children have become established in their homes and vocations, these years may be the golden time of life for study, Christian hobbies, and service to younger people. Now these women may sagaciously enter into the civic life of their communities through clubs and political organizations. If they have stayed alert mentally and socially, they make valuable contributions to community life. A good minister will encourage them to do so. In the church, through a vital prayer life, friendly Christian courtesy, and willingness to be of service in the kitchen, dining room, and sanctuary, they may lead many, both old and young to a more wholesome way of life.

Thus far in this chapter we have been thinking in terms of the home and volunteer work of women. There also are women serving as paid workers in the town-country church. When women serve as pastors, there are complications, but these are not insurmountable. Some nationally known women pastors such as Margaret Johnstone, of Groton, Mass. and Jeanie Sherman, of Timber Lake, S. D., have demonstrated that women can serve churches as ministers in an acceptable way. There should be more women leading the churches, and more opportunity should be provided them for the study of theology and church administration.

As larger parishes are developed there will be an increasing demand for women to serve as directors of Christian education and as youth workers. Frequently this will include serving as the pastor's secretary. A woman who is a director of Christian education has opportunity for correlating her work with that of the county agricultural agent and the home demonstration agent in serving the youth and women of the community.

In large fields women might serve as staff missionaries. The missionary's duty would be to visit homes which the pastor could not reach due to the time consumed in traveling great distances. She could make contact with the women in these homes, rendering valuable service, winning the households to Christ, and helping them to grow in the Christian tradition.

Some women can be of real service to the church as musicians and as religious journalists. The latter would not be employed by the church; as a self-employed person she would write for magazines, newspapers, and the denominational journals, never overlooking the possibility of writing books of a religious nature. A woman skilled in music can render a most valuable service by training choirs. A small town-country church could hardly pay a choir director for full-time service but a number of churches might support a full-time skilled choir leader.

The women, as of old, are in strategic places to advance the cause of Christ. No matter what their station or age in life, they hold in their hands the destiny of many. They witness for Christ, as do the men, through their vocations, in community activities, and in the immediate work of the church. In importance their work is second to none.

Young People

Not to be overlooked are the young people of the church and their service to Christ. When a child is old enough to become a Christian he is old enough to render some service to the Christian cause. To aid in this responsibility there are youth organizations in both church and community. There are two good reasons for these youth organizations. The first is to educate the young people in both doctrine and service. Organizations for this purpose include Sunday school classes, youth fellowships, 4-H clubs and other similar groupings. The second is to provide the young people with an opportunity to serve Christ now. The organizations for this purpose are the same as those listed for the first, plus the possible addition of youth choirs, and/or gospel teams.

Young people should understand that they should not try to serve Christ apart from the fellowship and worship of the church, for they too are a part of the church. They serve when they participate in worship and in the giving of their resources as they have received. Because so much of life is yet ahead of them they also serve as they diligently apply themselves to their school studies, 4-H club activities, and in other events where their clean, wholesome attitudes can be a constant witness of their faith in Christ.

As Christian men, women, and youth take seriously their Christian responsibilities in church, home, vocation, school and community life they serve Christ and advance the interests of the town-country churches.

XII

WORSHIP

IT IS DIFFICULT TO OVERESTIMATE man's need for public worship. Dr. Charles Heimsath in *The Genius of Public Worship* opens with the penetrating statement: "Why people stay away from church is not the riddle, but why they go." He goes on to explain that people go to church because of a deep hunger that can be satisfied only through the experiences of corporate worship, and he concludes that it is not the authority of the church but the want of the people that has created places of worship.

It is common agreement among psychologists and some anthropologists that the human race moves forward by way of three overwhelming desires or needs: the desire for food, the attention of the opposite sex, which in its highest form is called love, and communion or fellowship with the Supreme Being. The latter is obtained in part through worship, either corporate or private.

The town-country church, which usually ministers to a small and homogeneous group in which each individual knows and is known by all the participants, is ideally equipped to satisfy this third inherent drive. Even the smallest, poorest, and least-equipped church may join in the rediscovery of worship. Because the effects of Christian worship on people are so outstanding the cultivation of true worship is an opportunity that has been too often neglected.

A study of the effects of Christian worship on the people of a village in India was made by Jarrell Waskom Pickett. Making allowances for the peculiarities of Indian culture, the same results might be found wherever true worship is practiced. The survey revealed that where Christian worship existed there was a notable increase in self respect, greater occupational variation, increased unselfishness, new respect from other communities, cleanliness and appreciation of beauty, importance of women in church life, love for education, better marriage customs, and less participation in heathen festivals. The closing paragraph of the report is of special significance:

> It will be seen that these beneficial social changes are not the mere theorizing of someone with devout hopes nor the idle dream of wishful thinking but are the changes actually observed where a strong program of worship is now being carried on. These social changes may be called some of the by-products of Christian worship. It has been found that to produce these by-products it is not enough to have a strong program of religious teaching, nor to have high standards of admission to the church or to the communion. These changes came about largely through the instrumentality of Christian worship rather than through teacher or pastoral care or any other factor.[1]

Worship is too valuable to pass over lightly if it accomplishes all that this study indicates. Much that has been assumed to be Christian worship has not been worship at all. It has been a mere attendance at a preaching service which fell far short of serious and true worship. Although there has been no formal study of worship and its effects on people in American town-country churches, certain observations may be offered.

VARIETIES OF WORSHIP

The liturgical churches have their set forms of worship which vary little, whether practiced in the open country or in the metropolitan church. There is a question as to whether or not the content of the liturgy used in metropolitan churches is the best that can be used in open country churches. There might be a better use of environment than is commonly found in the country, hamlet, and village churches. These forms, nevertheless, are in keeping with the best thinking concerning worship. The services are couched in stately language which is often archaic in expression. In following a liturgy there is always the danger that the form will be maintained while the meaning is forgotten, and the spirit that first inspired the form

[1] *The Christian Mission Among Rural People.* (New York: Foreign Missions Conference of North America, 1945.)

is lost. This danger is not peculiar only to liturgical services, for often the nonliturgical churches too have a form from which meaning and spirit have departed.

In the nonliturgical churches of the congregational type there is little conformity to prepared forms of worship with rich content. In rural church institutes the town-country people have often said that they were dissatisfied with the worship services conducted in their churches. They complain of a lack of reverence on the part of those who attend and those who conduct the services; that "worshipers" are frequently engaged in conversation or reading the Sunday school papers during the service; that many ministers try to entertain their congregation rather than lead them into an awareness of God and devotion to his work. In what is perhaps an extreme case, one woman frankly stated that she often returned home from church in such bad humor that she would have felt better had she not gone. Usually, when conversation turns to the subject of worship people respond enthusiastically. They want to know how to have a more satisfying experience. Because many such people have not thought deeply enough about worship they do not understand it, and would resent the introduction of a genuinely helpful order of worship in their churches. Nonetheless they continue to feel that they are missing something. On the other hand, when people are instructed properly in worship they not only accept better forms of worship but rejoice in them. They may not want to go as far as their leader when making changes, but they are ready for more vital worship experiences.

Pastoral leadership is important to good worship. Among the congregational type of churches the picture in this respect is mixed and confused. A few ministers seem to understand the value of well-balanced services of worship and are successfully leading their people in them. There are others who resent any suggestion which indicates that they ought to rethink their worship service.

There are three forthright assets to worship in a town-country church: sincerity of the people, innate friendliness, and the handling of great truths. But there are no less than six factors that tend to neutralize the effectiveness of worship. These are

lack of meaningful order, lack of dignity in the service, absence
of appropriate music of high quality, lack of teaching in the art
of worship, a disproportionate emphasis on preaching, and symbolism and architecture which have but little meaning.

Church worship should be meaningful. Liturgical churches
have made it so. In some congregational-type churches worship
is meaningful, while in others it is not. Let us seek the principles underlying an order of worship so that they may be applied to any and all orders that may then be used.

One of the finest expressions of worship is found in Isa. 6:1-
8. This is the account of a disturbed man who, in his day of
trial, went into the house of God. As the man meditated he
saw God in his holiness and power, and himself in his sinful-
ness among sinful people. But the Lord purged his sin, then
called him into His service. As a cleansed man he gladly rose
up to do God's bidding. This sequence provides a pattern for
a formal service of worship which may be constructed in the
following manner:

1. PREPARATION
   PRELUDE
   PROCESSIONAL HYMN
   CALL TO WORSHIP
   INVOCATION
   LORD'S PRAYER (in unison)
   GREETINGS (if necessary. Very brief.)
2. PRAISE
   HYMN OF PRAISE
   CHILDREN'S OR YOUTH CHOIR
3. PRAYER
   SCRIPTURE READING
   MEDITATION — SILENT PRAYER
   HYMN OF PRAYER
   PASTORAL PRAYER
   CHORAL RESPONSE (One of the choirs or congregation)
4. INSTRUCTION
   ANTHEM — Adult Choir
   SERMON
5. CONSECRATION
   CONSECRATION THROUGH TITHES AND OFFERINGS

HYMN OF CONSECRATION AND INVITATION (if recessional is not used)

ANNOUNCEMENTS (only if absolutely necessary)

RECESSIONAL HYMN (if hymn of consecration and invitation is not used)

BENEDICTION

POSTLUDE

It is assumed that the people have come to the church from many walks of life. Some have had to hurry, some are worried, some have tried to teach a Sunday school class, and others are anxious that the service may be concluded promptly so that they may pursue some other activity. But regardless of their many moods as they come into the place of worship the minister attempts to start them on the high road of worship with a period of preparation. This will aid the worshiper in gaining the right perspective, the quietness of heart, and the openness of mind necessary for true worship. Each item has its own significance.

PREPARATION. *Prelude.* Potential worshipers should "Be still, and know that I am God" (Ps. 46:10). If they are comfortably seated in a building conducive to worship, a few minutes of soft music may inspire a devotional mood. The organist or pianist plays the prelude, frequently a medley of old familiar hymns, to focus attention on God. Many town-country churches do not have skilled pianists. This handicap is not insurmountable, for recordings of religious music suitable for preludes made by great artists may prove a quite satisfactory opening for the service.

Processional. Before entering the chancel to lead in worship, it is appropriate for the minister and choir to meet in the back of the one-room building, or in a separate room if one is available, for a few moments of prayer. During the latter portion of the prelude they may quietly walk to the places they will occupy during the worship. This is the simplest kind of processional. A well-trained choir may, with the congregation, sing a processional hymn as it enters the sanctuary. The minister, following the choir, will go to the pulpit or lectern and reverently open the pulpit Bible to the reading for the day. This he has found and marked before the start of the service.

Call to Worship. The minister signals the congregation to stand and calls them to worship with an appropriate verse of Scripture, such as "Behold, I stand at the door and knock; if any one hears my voice and opens the door, I will come in to him and eat with him, and he with me (Rev. 3:20). The purpose of a call to worship is to invite the people to worship God. It sets the tone for the day's service.

Invocation. The worship leader, by use of a prayer, now invokes God's presence and the leading of the Holy Spirit throughout the service. This prayer should be brief and to the point, beseeching God to enter every heart. It can very well be done by a layman, provided he is well coached and offers the prayer without announcement. The congregation may now join, as part of the invocation, in offering to God the Lord's Prayer, or in singing the Gloria Patri, or both. This invocation should be sufficient to attract the attention of the assembled people and focus their thoughts on God. The few minds that continue to wander may be captured in the next portion of the worship.

Greetings. On some occasions the leader may desire to recognize strangers or visitors in the congregation and assure them that they are welcome in the church's worship. Unless this is done very briefly and carefully it will destroy the atmosphere of worship.

PRAISE. It is impossible to worship God without praise and adoration. Therefore the minister should make it possible for each member of the congregation to express his praise of the Holy One of Israel. This he does through the order of service and the selection of the proper hymns.

Hymn of Praise. A hymn of this type is a particular asset to effective worship. Every good hymnal has a large selection of praise hymns. At this place in the service a hymn of praise which expresses the experience of the people should be selected and sung from beginning to end. To omit a verse is to break the continuity of the author's thought and frequently leave the rest of the hymn without meaning. In order to help the people more intelligently to praise God, the leader may occasionally read one or more verses before the congregation sings them. This is not to be done on the spur of the moment, but after careful examination of the words. Occasionally the congregation may read in unison one or more verses of the hymn, and sing the others. A large repertoire of praise hymns should be learned in the church school so that the worship of the whole church might be enriched.

Hymns should be the best the congregation can comprehend. They should be selected for the vital message they convey to the worshipers. Moreover, they should be in keeping with the mood of the part of the service where they are sung. For example, a hymn of prayer, however fine it may be, is out of place if it is sung during the praise section of the service.

A church of more than a hundred resident members should have both a children's and a youth choir. One of these choirs, through the spirited singing of a well-prepared praise hymn, may lift the entire congregation to a new height of adoration of the heavenly Father. Of course, this will be done without an introduction and the pastor will not ordinarily thank them publicly for their contribution. This is their offering to God, and God will reward them in his own way.

PRAYER. The third phase of an order of worship is prayer. After praising God the people should be ready to enter into a season of prayer from which they will emerge cleansed and refreshed in spirit. It is not enough that the pastor pray; the people too must pray if the service is to accomplish its desired ends. It is reasonable to hope that every person present will offer a sincere prayer to God for himself and his fellow men.

Scripture Reading. The season of prayer begins with the reading of a selection of Scripture. It may or may not be the context of the sermon text. The Scripture should be such as to incite the hearer to prayer. It may itself be a prayer, such as Psalms 51, for forgiveness; Psalms 9, thanksgiving; 1 Kings 3:6-9, wisdom; or Ephesians 1:15-23 or 3:14-21 for churches.

The Scriptures are the Word of God and are said to be "sharper than any two-edged sword" (Heb. 4:12). Therefore, like a sharp sword, they should be used skillfully. The best calls to worship, offertory sentences, and benedictions are those which are Scripture passages.

The Scriptures deserve respect from minister and congregation alike. The passage to be read should be studied and rehearsed, and perhaps memorized. It should then be read aloud in such a manner as to carry its meaning unfalteringly into the minds of the listeners. There is no place for mumbling or stumbling. Paul wrote to his disciple, Timothy: "Devote yourself to the public reading of the Scriptures" (1 Tim. 4:13, Williams). A commendable practice in some churches is that of having the congregation to stand with bowed heads while the Scripture lesson is read.

Meditation—Silent Prayer. At the close of the Scripture reading the reader makes no comment or any such statement as "may God add His blessing to the reading of His Word." Rather, the pianist or organist softly plays one of the familiar hymns of the church, the words of which are in harmony with the Scripture reading. Or a good recording may be played. Two or three minutes of calm music will give the congregation time and opportunity to reflect on the Scripture reading and to offer silent prayers.

Hymn of Prayer. Good hymnals contain a number of hymns which, like some of the Psalms, are prayers. Such a hymn should be selected for this part of the service and the people invited to offer it to God as their prayer. Attention may be called to the words in order that the congregation may pray more intelligently. The congregation stands while offering this hymn-prayer and remains standing for the pastoral prayer.

Pastoral Prayer. The pastor, thoroughly acquainted with the hopes, needs, frustrations, ambitions, and sins of his people, is now ready to offer on their behalf the pastoral prayer. This should be so *carefully prepared* that it will, as much as is humanly possible, lift the people to the throne of God. It should be grammatically correct, yet in the vernacular of the people. It is not a composition to be read but a supplication to be offered from the depth of the heart.

Choral Response. As the pastor closes the pastoral prayer, the organist gently sounds a chord, and the choir offers a brief prayer response.

INSTRUCTION. The fourth phase in the order of worship is instruction. The people have assembled not only to praise God and to pray but to be instructed in his word. This instruction may take two forms.

Anthem. The choir sings an anthem whose text is revelant to the sermon subject.

Sermon. The pastor reads the Scripture from which he is to speak and without further preamble delivers a carefully-prepared sermon. At the close of the sermon the pastor offers a brief prayer asking God to use the message for the salvation and strengthening of souls.

CONSECRATION. The fourth aspect of worship is consecration. No service provides true worship for any individual unless it encourages the surrender to God of the worshiper's whole being. Supposedly the worshiper has come to the house of God to praise him, to pray, to be instructed; now he must act through a consecration of his possessions. Ample opportunity for consecration should be provided, both symbolically and in active living. Psychologically, then, this is the time for the offering. The worshiper can give expression thereby to the impulse to serve that has been building up within him.

The Offering. The ushers or deacons come to the chancel, take up the offering plates, and pause while the pastor recites a verse of Scripture. They then pass the plates among the people while the organist plays. When they return with the offerings, the pastor offers a prayer of dedication, setting this money and the lives it represents aside to the work of the church at home and abroad. The ushers return to their seats.

Hymn of Consecration. A hymn in harmony with the sermon and prayers, and one that gives the people a chance to speak forth their consecration to the Lord, is now in order. Because the Christian people have already reconsecrated themselves to the Lord through tithes and offerings the unconverted may now be invited to accept Christ, church membership, and their responsibilities in his kingdom, by coming forward. Later they will be examined and instructed by the proper group in the church.

Announcements. The congregation stands for the singing of the hymn and remains standing while the pastor makes the announcements of the church's activities for the week ahead. Needless to say, with the congregation standing these must be brief. Another viewpoint holds that it is not inappropriate to have the congregation seated after the hymn and remain so until the postlude is completed. This gives the people an added moment for reflection and avoids the appearance of haste in leaving the House of God.

Benediction. After the hymn of consecration and whatever announcements are deemed necessary, the minister closes the pulpit Bible and pronounces the benediction, preferably from the Scriptures.

Alternate Conclusion of the Service. As soon as the offering has been taken the minister may proceed to the announcements. Then a recessional hymn may be sung, during which the choir may march out. The minister may either remain in the pulpit or follow the choir. After the recessional hymn has been sung, he pronounces the benediction.

Postlude. After the benediction the organist plays a postlude. During this, the pastor stands at the main exit of the church to speak to the people as they leave the House of God conscious that they have been in communion with Him. The Christian will leave "rejoicing in the Lord," and sinners will be converted and added to the church.

The first objection raised to such an order of worship is "We do not have the choirs, so we cannot do these things." The answer to this objection is "Get them!" As the leader of the congregation, it is the pastor's responsibility to begin a program of musical training so that choirs will be available after a few years. The development of musical abilities in the church will bring a rich reward.

Better music is needed in most town-country churches. It can be secured by having the church's board of education or music committee arrange for the musical training of the children and young people of the church. The boys and girls of the Sunday church school may be organized into a junior choir. This choir could include all from nine years of age through the eighth grade of school. As a part of their regular Sunday school training, they are taught the great hymns of the church, the responses, and the musical calls to worship. Choir rehearsals as such should be held outside of the hour which is designated for the Sunday church school. Weekly rehearsals are desirable. If these are not possible, the musical selections to be sung as anthems may be frequently used in church school worship services, and a monthly rehearsal held, perhaps in conjunction with a party, on the day before the Sunday on which the choir is to sing in the church's worship service.

Plans should be made for more advanced musical training, so that when children have finished with their choir they will be passed on to the youth choir in which they will study and sing until they are through high school. Their training also should be a regular part of the Sunday church school work. They, too, may take their place once a month as the choir for that service.

On graduating from high school, or shortly thereafter, the young people may be promoted into the adult choir of the church. By this time they should be able to participate in the singing of music of medium difficulty. If this procedure is followed there will be an abundance of good singers in the church in a few years and only the best will be accepted into the church choir. Those not accepted will be a welcome asset to the congregational singing.

PHYSICAL AIDS

In an effort to improve town-country worship there are a few things which churchmen ought to do. One is to maintain cleanliness and tidiness in the place of worship. A start must be made somewhere, and it should be made where the most visible good can come with the least opposition. The congregation should begin by making their building and grounds as clean and neat as possible. At an annual "cleaning bee" the building may be thoroughly swept, dusted, mopped; wires for stage curtains taken down, and strung up again only when needed, soiled flags and pennants removed, and useless accumulations of periodicals sold. This may be a good time to redecorate the interior and perhaps paint the exterior of the church buildings. Interior decorating, however, should be done only after consulting a competent decorator.

Cleaning and painting should not be confined to the interior of the church buildings, for even before a person enters the church building his mind is being conditioned for worship. If, as he approaches the church, he observes the neatness and cleanliness of the premises, he is in a better psychological condition for worship than he could be if he had to struggle through unmowed weeds and rubbish, and then push through unpainted front doors partly off their hinges. Are these to be considered but little things compared to the greatness of worship? Then remember the Arabian proverb, "It is not the mountain, but the grain of sand in the sandal, that tires one."

After the building has been cleaned, pastor and people may want to plan how their building can be remodeled to provide for more adequate worship. All changes in the architecture of the building should make use of the experience and have the approval of a church architect. Many atrocious things called church buildings are the result, in part at least, of having ignored this elementary precaution. Lesser changes can be made at the annual cleaning bee according to an overall plan that has previously been approved by a church architect.

As rapidly as the people are brought up in the understanding of worship, they will make places for meaningful symbols of the Christian faith. Church symbolism, differing somewhat according to the faith and practices of the denominations, usually consists of the cross, the baptistry or baptismal font, the communion table or altar, the pulpit, and the Bible. Good taste suggests that none of these, especially the cross, should be gaudy, lighted affairs. These minimum symbols have Christian meaning and when properly placed and used, teach silently but effectively the great truths of the Christian faith. To neglect them is to cast aside one of the church's best aids in changing the minds and hearts of people.

Air is an important factor in worship. There is no evidence that sitting in a wrong temperature and breathing the same stale air week after week makes people religious. Windows should be opened for fresh air before every service. On the other hand, some rural churches are so airy that the most urgent ventilation problem is to stop the drafts. Heating and cooling systems are necessities. They should be installed in as modern a fashion as possible and kept in working order. In the end, good equipment is not as expensive as a makeshift contraption which some church member volunteers to install.

As to seating, the least that can be done is to make it comfortable. Pews are generally preferable to individual seats, but they need not be as uncomfortable as many of them are. Pews or seats should be arranged so that no one will be looking into a strong light, and everyone will be able to see and hear what takes place in the chancel.

Flooring, too, is important. The floors may be cleaned, sanded if necessary, and treated with a floor sealer. Well-padded carpets should be placed in the aisles. A tile type of linoleum or similar modern floor covering may be cemented to the vestibule floor, thus making a pleasing and easily-cleaned entrance and a quiet, colorful interior.

If the foregoing suggestions are followed the people will soon become justly proud of their church building. This may even suggest to them what their own houses should be. In time the homes will be neater and cleaner, and a better community will result.

PAINSTAKING PREPARATION

Throughout this chapter our thoughts have been directed toward the mechanics of worship, architecture, and symbolism. All are important if worship services are to be a medium through which the Holy Spirit brings about a new creation in Christ Jesus. But the content of each item of each service should be carefully selected, down to the last word. Extemporaneous speaking should be reduced to a minimum so as not to draw the worshipers' attention from the worship of God. The act of worship is not an entertainment, recital, debate, or oratorical contest. It is an effort by all the participants to find the will of God, each for himself.

In town-country worship, pastor and people should be aware of the seasons as they come and go. For example, in the springtime, churches should take advantage of the planting season, with its prospects of new life, to call attention to the wonders of God, the laws of growth, and the necessity of planting good seed of all kinds if a fruitful harvest is desired. Rural Life Sunday, the fifth Sunday after Easter, is observed at this time of the year. "Go to Church Sunday," a 4-H club emphasis, comes at this season too, and offers the church an opportunity to touch the youth of the community in a meaningful way. The pastor should make good use of such occasions.

In the fall it is well for worship to be couched in terms of the harvest. There is a harvest of the soul as well as of corn and pumpkins. The season is ideal for a Harvest Festival Service, wherein the people bring in the proceeds from their Lord's Acres, if such a project has been promoted. Ministers have had excellent responses to services of this kind, and evidences point to a wholesome growth of this type of service in the future.

Helpful material for planning the Rural Life Sunday and Harvest Festival observances is available from the National Council of Churches.

Many nonliturgical church members have shied away from the idea of the "Church Year." However, it is gaining in favor. Perhaps there is a need to build another kind of church year that expresses our evangelical ideals. Until this is done let us examine, and use as best we can, some features of the traditional Church Year.

Since all Protestants observe Christmas in their churches and homes, why not the Advent season? That is, use the four Sundays before Christmas as a period of preparation for Christmas. It seems better to lead people to an intelligent and spiritual celebration of Christmas through the use of Advent services than suddenly to thrust before them the announcement: "Next Sunday is Christmas Sunday, and we will have a special sermon, and music by the choir if they can get it ready." Instead of such a travesty it is much more effective to plan a preaching program and worship services that cover all four Sundays of Advent, plus the Sunday after Christmas, so that when the day comes and passes it will leave an indelible mark on the souls of the worshipers. This practice will help to counteract the trend toward commercializing Christmas.

All that has been said of Christmas holds true for Easter and the Lenten season. Why not take the seven weeks preceding Easter to prepare the people for Easter? This is an ideal time to hold evangelistic services, study groups, and special prayer meetings. Each night of the week before Easter may be used to good advantage for deeply devotional worship services in the church. A celebration of the Lord's Supper is appropriate on Thursday night before Easter and may be the highest point in the church's worship for the year. Lent can be a spiritually rich season of the church year if the pastor will wisely lead his people through it.

Because mimeographed or printed bulletins are almost universally used let us consider again their use in the worship service. They can and should be an asset to the worship services. All announcements of the church can be included in the bulletins rather than call attention to them during worship.

If a bulletin is an aid to the worship service it should be distributed at the beginning of the service. If it is only for the promotion of program activities it should be distributed at the close of the service. There should be a quality about bulletins which will dignify the worship services. It is possible to secure good art cover bulletins weekly through denominational channels and church supply houses. If these are too expensive to provide a new one for each Sunday, then only a few different covers may be used during the entire year. They may be distributed in this manner:

      Advent and Christmas, four or five Sundays
      Lent, six Sundays
      Easter, one Sunday
      Summer Services, five or six Sundays
      Rural Life Sunday, one Sunday
      Harvest Festival, one Sunday
      Lord's Supper, four Sundays

Bulletins so planned are within the financial reach of most town-country churches. Although the printing bill seems to be a sizeable item, the bulletins are worth all they cost and pay for themselves in various ways. These bulletins cover 22 to 24 Sundays. For the other 30 Sundays of the year, an order of worship may be printed and pasted in the front of the hymnal. The congregation will understand that, if there is no bulletin, the order of worship as pasted in the hymnal will be used. Several orders of worship may be printed and pasted in the hymnal. The leader merely announces at the beginning of the service which one will be used that day.

The public worship of God is a fine art. It does not come naturally; it is achieved only after much painstaking. Even the Disciples, after having been with Jesus for nearly three years, felt their inadequacy in worship. They requested Jesus to teach them to pray. How much more then does the harassed congregation of today need to be taught to worship God!

The board of Christian education should institute courses of such study until every member of the church knows how and why Christians should worship God in public services. It may be that the pastor will find it necessary to teach the prospective teachers of worship.

In a village church a pastor preached on worship. He did not use his time telling people that they should worship, or scolding them for not attending more frequently. Instead he talked for thirty minutes on how to worship. It was one of many good sermons on worship and the congregation has profited thereby, for the building is filled with worshipers each Sunday morning, whereas a few years ago a mere handful of elderly saints attended.

XIII

EVANGELISM

THERE IS NO GREATER CHALLENGE to town-country churches
than the making of true Christian converts. To meet this challenge the lordship of Christ must be central in all presentations
of the gospel. Christian evangelism points to Christ as Lord
and his way of living as the only acceptable way. But although
evangelism has the first claim on a church's resources it is not
the last claim. As parents bring a new life into the world in
the consciousness that they have only begun to discharge their
responsibilities, so a church must nourish a new member until
he comes into the fullness of Christian maturity and takes on
the very likeness of Christ.

No environment seems more suited for the conversion and
development of people into Christian maturity than that of
the town-country area. Here prospects, converts, and mature
Christians have close contact with nature, which constantly
holds before questioning minds the glory, majesty, wisdom, and
power of God the Creator. Here the home has a pre-eminence
that gives it great power in molding character. Here the community is a reality that in its own way strengthens and forms
character. The town-country churches are, potentially, at the
center of the rural communities. They may, if they will, inspire, comfort, strengthen, and instruct every member of their
respective communities. In this kind of environment it is possible for spiritual giants to be born and reared, giants of whom
it may be said, as of those of another generation, "These men
. . . have turned the world upside down" (Acts 17:6).

164

EVANGELISTIC PREACHING

How can we win converts and develop Christian character in the town-country environment? One of the most popular ways to win converts is by way of the revival. In many churches the revival is an annual procedure. Some churches hold two or more revivals a year, with a week or ten days set aside for each. Usually the church secures a visiting preacher as the evangelist. Sometimes a music leader is also engaged. The services are publicized and it is hoped the whole community will turn out to hear the evangelist denounce sin, exalt righteousness, extend God's invitation to eternal life, and defend the faith of his particular denomination.

While revival meetings have been popular, it is becoming increasingly difficult to reach the unconverted by this method. Some evangelists say their audiences today are 90 per cent Christian. The greater portion of unchurched people are not being reached by revivals, and a discouragingly small percentage of the church members have come to attend these services. Sometimes less than a third or even a fourth of the resident members of the church can be induced to attend the revivals with any regularity.

It is becoming more evident each year that town-country churches cannot do their evangelistic work through revivals alone. If revivals are held they must be greatly fortified with other implements. There is a growing feeling that the New Testament method of going into the market place with the gospel must be adopted. Christians have no right to assume that they can erect church buildings, announce services, and expect the unconverted to come. The commission is "Go . . .!"

The value of revivals varies with the Christian experience of the evangelist. Some meetings are of great value while others take the hearers on an emotional spree that leaves them worse than they were before. However, there is a place for the protracted preaching of the gospel. The preaching should be of the highest quality and avoid the cheap, sentimental exhortations with reference to mother, home, and flag that have characterized too many revivals. Thoughtful preaching missions can do much to win people to Christ and to confirm those who are weak in the faith.

Some of the best evangelistic preaching may be done not by an outside speaker, but by the pastor of the church, who week by week, in a variety of different ways, reminds his people that Christ offers them forgiveness and salvation, and calls them to a new way of life in which every act bears witness to him.

CLASSES IN DISCIPLESHIP AND CHURCH MEMBERSHIP

In place of or in addition to revivals some churches find the church school (Sunday, week day, and vacation) a rich lode for evangelistic endeavor. In addition to the church schools some pastors plan to have an annual instruction class for the older boys and girls of the church school who have not previously made a profession of faith in Christ. Their non-Christian friends also may attend. With the consent and co-operation of the parents, they meet with the pastor from six to ten times over a period of as many weeks. Using study materials prepared by his denomination, he carefully discusses with them what it means to be a Christian, how to become a Christian, the ordinances, prayer, and church membership. He deals with each youngster in a quiet, friendly, and reasonable fashion. The Sunday following the close of this class is designated as Decision Day. On this day, they are invited to accept Christ publicly as their Lord and Savior. If they have been properly instructed, a large number of them will intelligently accept him and go on to live Christian lives.

Because of the different levels of understanding possible at different ages, it is good to have separate classes for juniors, junior highs, and senior highs. Often it is better even to instruct a person individually than to put him in a group so much older or younger that he feels lost.

Such classes, slightly modified, may be used for winning adults. It is usually well to enlist married couples, with as many Christian couples of the church as non-Christians in each group. The group meets weekly at first, going from home to home. The meetings are kept informal and a constant effort is made to create a lively sense of fellowship. The discussions on being a Christian should be about an hour in length, and should be discussions — not sermons — led by the pastor. A textbook should be given to each couple, that they may read before coming to the discussion. At least an hour should be allowed after the discussion for conversation and refreshments. Sometimes these informal discussions over coffee prove more pertinent than those during the preceding formal hour.

After a series of several adult discussions has been held the pastor should visit the non-Christian couples and talk with them of their relationship to Christ and his church. Thus he may lead them to accept Christ and become active members in the church.

In many cases this type of meeting can be continued for the further training of church members. Such a close fellowship may develop that no one will want to drop out, and the group may become a strong spiritual nucleus in the church. Those who have not accepted Christ during the first weeks will be urged to continue in the group, for no one knows when the Holy Spirit will bring about their conversion. The meetings, after the original series, should preferably be held every second week because once a week is too frequent and once a month too seldom to maintain good fellowship.

It is in such study groups that the pastor is brought face to face with unconverted people under conditions that prompt them to ask questions and to talk back. The experience is profitable for both pastor and people for too long there has been a chasm between pulpit and pew, neither properly understanding the other. Study groups have the additional advantage of creating a sense of fellowship before the non-Christian joins the church. This Christian fellowship in itself may be the instrument for winning men and women to Christ. Certainly it will be a means of holding and developing those who do make a profession of faith. Group discussion also has the advantage of putting Christian couples in a favorable position to witness for Christ by telling of their experiences.

From time to time it is necessary for the church to go beyond its immediate list of prospects in its search for converts, like a farmer breaking a new field. In almost every community there are pockets of people untouched by the church. These pockets are usually small neighborhoods in the community. It has been estimated that there are ten thousand such neighborhoods in rural America without religious services of any kind.

The pastor, through an adequate survey, will find the pockets in his community and thoroughly explore them. He may find it profitable to put an extension of the church school in some of them. In others, an adult study group may be the means of attracting and winning people. The pitching of a tent and the holding of Vacation Church School during the day, with preaching in the evening, may also provide means of interesting these people. Another variation would be a vacation church school for all ages held at night. The very novelty of this device may make it successful. Such pockets challenge a good pastor to digress from his usual pastoral calls and become, through visitation, the pastor of all the people. Because of economic or cultural reasons, it may take some time to win people in the pockets to attendance at the central church, but the cost in time does not excuse the pastor from a vigorous ministry among them.

Many churches have small, limited fields of service because they are not aware of, or do not care for, the people in the pockets scattered over the town-country community.

THE PRINTED PAGE

Still another means of evangelism is the parish paper. Many churches issue a weekly mimeographed bulletin. It may have an attractive cover and back, but inside it carries the same order of worship the church has used for the past fifteen years. There are a few lines of personal news, a feeble effort at a joke, and an exhortation to attend church. The mimeographing is smudged, streaked, and irregular. Such a bulletin is a waste of time and money, and an affront to good taste.

The same money, time, and effort could more profitably be used to issue a monthly eight-page, well-mimeographed paper which would be distributed to all families of the constituency whether they attend church or not. As an example of one such paper we mention the *Newsette*. Late in August or early in September a cover is designed which will be used for the entire year. One year the cover carried the picture of the cross, another year the picture of the pulpit of the church, and another year Mark Rich's "The Christian Farmer." The layout for the cover is given to a reliable printer who is asked to print sufficient copies, using five different colors of paper, with an equal number of copies of each color, for the year's distribution. A different color is used each month for five months and the sequence is repeated for the second five months.

One purpose of the paper is to relate such incidents as will keep the community or church constituency informed about itself. For this purpose the pastor who edits the bulletin carries a pocket notebook and jots down items of community interest wherever he finds them. Weddings, funerals, births, graduations, and so on through the whole gamut of community life, are noted and published as soon as possible.

The paper has other purposes, too. There are community projects to be championed. For example, for three years, *Newsette* advocated a consolidated school for the children of the parish. As a result, five schools merged into a state graded school with profit to all concerned. Through such a paper, the public or constituency is kept fully informed of church activities and plans, news of the denomination, and of Christian work at large. The last page of the bulletin carries a three-hundred word evangelistic sermon. In this manner six or seven mimeographed pages are filled with news and propaganda that is calculated to turn those who read it toward Christ and his church.

After the pastor has prepared the copy and mimeographed and stapled the pages together under their printed cover, he finds that his next chore is distribution. On the Sunday when the paper is issued it is taken to the church and each family present receives a copy. Some people take two or three copies to mail to friends and former members of the community. The next day the papers are taken to the public school and given by the teachers to the children. Suitable holders are made and placed in the village stores. These are also filled on Monday morning, and in a few days all the papers have been taken. Such a paper with its friendly news of the community and church and its carefully prepared evangelistic message goes into practically every home of the constituency. It prepares the way for adding people to the Sunday school and to adult and youth study groups wherein they may be won to Christ and held in the activities of the church.

It has been said that no periodical is more thoroughly read

than the country newspaper. If this is true, the average town-country church is losing an opportunity for winning and holding people if it does not tell its story in the country press. Newspapers deal in news. They are interested in keeping the community informed of what is happening. If a pastor will go and see or write to the proper representative of the press, and give him a newsworthy story, it will almost certainly find a place in the next issue of the paper.

Many rural newspapers print "standing type" which gives in identical form each week the announcement of services. If this is used, it should be complete and accurate. The enterprising pastor, though, will send in specific items each week, thus offering the editor material for fresher and newsier treatment.

There is, however, little value to the church in telling the public of bean suppers, bazaars, and all such things that are not the church's distinctive work. In the end such publicity may do the church more harm than good. But if the church has an aggressive program, if it features an unusual worship or service project, if the people take part in state and national functions, that is news, and the public should know it. The press will tell it to the world, and new evangelistic doors will be opened.

Another most helpful and far-reaching project is the weekly newspaper sermon or religious essay. The minister prepares four or five one-page, double-spaced sermons or essays under under such a heading as, for instance, "Old Thoughts from a Country Manse." Each essay should carry a release date for one of the four Fridays of the month. The minister sends them to the editor with a covering letter to say that the writer is contributing these essays to his newspaper as a service to the larger community served by the church, and that he has so planned them that they will deal with the pertinent, constructive interests of town-country life. Usually editors are glad to accept such contributions from local pastors and give them prominent places in the papers. In this manner, with no more cost than that of preparing the copy, the church's power to win and hold people is extended over the entire community and sometimes far beyond its boundaries.

AUDIO-VISUAL MEDIA

In recent years God has provided three new media, radio, television, and films, for the use of his church. They can be powerful instruments for winning people in town-country areas, for through them the church may reach into areas where a pastor rarely goes. Of the three, radio seems to offer the town-country church the best opportunity, for it is an established part of American rural life.

Leroy Willard, in "The Rural Church's Use of Press and Radio," [1] found that all the radio stations he interviewed (twenty-two) were broadcasting four kinds of religious programs. They offered local news and bulletin board broadcasts which provided for religious news and announcements; spot announcements, at very low cost; devotional programs, popular with preachers but not effective; and church worship services, the least acceptable by the public. On the whole, Mr. Willard found that the churches were not using more than 50 per cent of the available time.

Good radio programs, dealing with problems and opportunities of the town-country church, can be developed with a little imagination as was done by a Colorado church with their "Rural Churchman." The program opened with their theme song "The Church in the Wildwood," followed by the station announcer's 20-second identifying paragraph. The pastor gave greetings and an account of some phase of the church's program for the near future. Then came inspiration in verse, the careful reading of an inspirational poem, followed by inspiration in music, often a recording of exceptionally fine music. A "word from the Word" followed in the form of one verse of scripture. The pastor then gave a brief and well-thought-out meditation, concluding with the words, "After the brief prayer I will give the parting thought." This thought would be a pithy sentence, often from non-biblical literature but always pertinent.

Television, the latest medium of mass communication, though valuable, does not lend itself so readily to town-country church use, due to the expense of producing the programs and the smaller number of stations. However it must not be over-

[1] Willard, Leroy, *The Rural Church's Use of Press and Radio.* Unpublished Bachelor of Divinity thesis, Central Baptist Theological Seminary, Kansas City, Kansas, 1953, p. 33.

looked. If the pastor takes the trouble and time to cultivate the acquaintance of the news and special feature departments of the stations serving his area, he will find them more than willing to film occasional newsworthy events of the church and show them on their evening and night newscasts where they receive a good viewing.

A certain amount of free time for religious use is provided by most stations as part of their public service. Films of interest to rural churches can often be shown during such time, perhaps with a plug for the church that provides them. If the County Council of Churches sponsors a film, a special series of messages by local pastors, or a dramatic or panel show, a wider viewing may be obtained with comparatively less cost and effort on the part of the participating churches.

UNSELFISH SERVICE

One evangelistic endeavor that has consistently been overlooked is service to communities and individuals. Town-country people are practical. They see the church members holding meetings to sing, to pray, to talk; but if nothing more comes of these efforts they question the value of the church. The service motive of church and missionary in overseas areas is not thought strange. There the missionaries establish schools and hospitals, and even model farms to teach better agricultural practices, that the hungry might be fed. Through these various services many are won to Christ. It should not be strange to think of the church in the home community also as the body of Christ. Is it then unreasonable to expect it to do what Christ did when he was on earth?

In every American town-country community there is at least one unselfish service which the Christians can render. It may be in the field of adult education, in a ministry to public health, the teaching of better agricultural practices, or in the establishing of a small factory, so that men might work and thereby eat. Let the church do such things and people will have a new respect for the gospel it represents and men will be won to Christ!

In winning men for Christ there is no greater instrument than loving pastoral care. It was said of David that he came in and went out before the people. The people loved him, and because he knew the people and had their confidence, he could do the things which he did. A minister will not go far in winning men to Christ if he remains in his study and garden. Winning men is accomplished by living with the people until they think of the pastor as being one of them. He will then know them and be able to minister to their needs. There is no substitute for pastoral care. It is the tiring, unglamorous leg-work that gets the job done!

It is one thing to win people to Christ, baptize them, and add them to the church rolls. It is another equally difficult problem to hold them in the church until they have developed into well-rounded, mature Christians. But there seems to be little point in winning people unless they can be held and developed. In the final analysis, people are held in the church in direct ratio to the spiritual interest which is developed in them through its fellowship.

In recent years, the high mobility of families in America accentuates the problem of nonresident members. A change of employment, a desire to live in another part of the nation, or early retirement may uproot a family and send church members to the other end of the continent. When people attend a church which is new to them, they do not see a single familiar face. The order of worship may be even stranger. Probably no one except the pastor speaks to them. In their loneliness, they return home feeling that this church has failed them.

They do not go back. Others find themselves very busy getting settled in their new home. So, during the first month in their new residence they do not go to church. By then the worship habit is weakened and they have made friends with non-churchgoing people. They are likely to join the company of Christians who attend church only on Easter Sunday.

By the very nature of American life, it is inevitable that the churches in town-country areas will lose many of their younger members as they go away to school or employment in the cities. Time and money would be well spent in giving young people and young adults periodical instruction on what to expect when they move to the city, and how to get acquainted in a city church. From time to time a city pastor or a denominational worker may visit a town-country church and discuss some features of city life with the view to helping those who shall move to the city.

If a church fellowship is what it should be, nonresident members who have moved away will not be forgotten. When an individual or family moves, a letter should be sent to the pastor of the church where they are moving. The letter should tell of the life of the people, so that the pastor may call and talk freely to them about the church. The home church should feel a responsibility for all nonresident members until they are secure in the fellowship of another church.

CULTIVATING A FELLOWSHIP

To win and hold people, a church must be a fellowship. This means that it must have a living, vital concern for all members. The first-century Christians were so convinced that Jesus had risen from the dead, and thus was the long-anticipated Messiah, that they were drawn together in a fellowship that could be broken by nothing but death. The goal, today, is to reproduce a fellowship such as existed in the churches of the first century. It will not be produced by the preacher offering one more sermon on "Love the Brethren." It may be reproduced, however, by a sharing of Christian experiences so that the faith of each is enriched by the experiences of others.

The fellowship may be further enriched by age groups or cultural groups within the church banding together in the interest of tithing, prayer, settling of a dispute, soul winning, Bible study, or some other vital experience. Through such sharing there will come to each member of the group a new awareness of the power of Jesus Christ. In this manner he will become the focal point in the lives of the members of the church. The church then has a living cause.

The fellowship may be further advanced by a deliberate and determined effort on the part of the members to help one another, that is, to live together in such a way as to share resources as well as experiences. Why should not the older members help the younger folks to become owners of farms and businesses, and become established in certain professions? One of the easiest and most satisfactory ways of sharing resources is by way of a church credit union. It can be used to teach the younger members to save. Older members with capital find in it a useful investment of their funds. Those in need of cash can draw from it at a reasonable rate of interest. With few exceptions, every town-country church should have a credit union. With some thought many other activities may be devised to develop a vital fellowship.

DOCTRINAL INSTRUCTION

A second means of holding new converts is by a careful, thorough teaching of the fundamental doctrines of the church. In many churches there is unseemly haste in baptizing new converts so that their names may be accounted for on the statistical tables of the denomination. Nothing in the Scriptures is contrary to the idea of thorough training of candidates in the Christian faith before they are baptized. Before baptizing a candidate it is not enough for the pastor to ask him a few questions to which the answers are obvious. All those who confess Christ should be thoroughly instructed in the fundamentals of the Christian faith, worship, church history, missions, and church polity for a period of six to twelve months. During this period they should demonstrate by their living that they are Christians. Only then should they be subjects for baptism.

At first this practice may reduce the number of baptisms, but it has been demonstrated on the mission fields that after a while it greatly increases their number. There, outsiders notice that there is a difference between Christians and non-Christians. The Christian way of life appears so superior that the non-Christians begin to desire it, and are led to make inquiry of the missionaries. The same thing can happen in America when the Christian ethic is taken seriously.

ENLISTMENT

The effort to hold or to build new converts into the body of the church must not stop with teaching. God calls men and women to serve in his kingdom. It should be the business of the church to help each and every member find a place of significant service. When the idea of Christian service is carried into the realms of home, vocation, and community, it is necessary for the church to give more definite instruction in these areas of life. In the case of vocation it may be necessary to help some converts to leave unchristian vocations and enter those that are in keeping with the Christian life, as in the case of a tavern keeper or one who works for a printing establishment that produces pornographic literature in slack work seasons. According to their ages and talents, members should be given tasks to perform in the church, such as teachers, visitors, writers, and singers. The church, by utilizing all its resources, may become the power of God in the community.

The greatest loss in the church membership of town-country churches comes as members move away from the community. Many babies are born in the rural area. There they are nurtured, educated, and won to Christ. Beginning at the age of about sixteen, however, many of them leave the home area. Some are taken by the military, some go away to school, and some leave in search of employment. Only a few remain on the farms or find employment in the home community. If there are to be town-country churches of the optimum size of about 350 resident members we must devise methods for helping young people to establish themselves in the area served by the church. The Roman Catholics and several Protestant groups are giving serious thought to methods for settling their church members on the land. These churches are growing and are showing evidence of a new stability.

Protestants need to do two things to hold their people in the town-country areas. The first of these is the transfer of farm ownership within a church family. If farms and businesses cannot pass from father to son or daughter they should pass to members within the denomination or to Christians of another evangelical denomination. The second means of holding people in the area is by the establishment of suitable industries in the community. With the advent of the Rural Electrification Administration a new day came to rural America. Power lines mean that industries may now be established near the origin of the resources with which they work. Industries located in town-country areas will help town-country youth to remain at home or to return home after college and their day in the armed forces. For further discussion of this problem the reader is referred to his state industrial commission.

XIV

CHRISTIAN EDUCATION

By Jane Bennett[1]

CHRISTIAN EDUCATION IS ONE of the principal tasks of the church. Through it, children and youth are guided toward the attainment of a vital faith, and helped to express this faith in Christian living. Also through it, adults may find understanding of the Bible and may grow in their ability to meet life bravely. Yet many of our smaller churches approach the task of Christian education with something of an inferiority complex. "We are too small, too limited in all our resources, to do as others do," they reason. Therefore they settle down to a mediocre program which satisfies nobody.

But a small church, whether in town and country or in a difficult urban area, can have an excellent program of Christian education if those in charge are truly dedicated to their tasks, and the congregation gives loyal support. Countless examples could be cited.

ADMINISTRATION

Christian education must be planned carefully and administered efficiently, and to do this it is important that the program does not become top-heavy with organization and ad-

[1] Rev. Jane Bennett, who has prepared this chapter at the request of the author, is assistant professor in the department of religion and Christian education at Keuka College, Penn Yan, N. Y. For eight years she was a rural missionary of the Woman's American Baptist Home Mission Society, serving over 40 churches of various denominations, specifically in the field of Christian education. She holds a B.A. degree in Christian education and sociology from Keuka College and an M.A. degree from the school of religious education at Hartford Theological Seminary. She has also studied rural sociology at Cornell University.

ministration. The people who are essential to the administration of Christian education are:

Members of the Board of Christian Education (see p. 179).

The Minister: In the rural church he will often be the one trained person responsible for supervising the program on a professional level.

The Church School Superintendent: He will be the lay person responsible for the administration of the Sunday church school program. Some of his duties will include (1) acting as liaison between the church school teachers and officers and the board of Christian education, (2) planning church school workers' conferences, (3) supporting the church school teachers, (4) helping to prepare a climate in which they will be able to teach to the best of their ability, and (5) supervising the more technical aspects of the church school such as scheduling, records, and finances.

The Church School Secretary: He will be responsible for keeping adequate records.

The Church School Treasurer: If the church school has a treasury of its own, he will be its custodian; if church school funds are handled through the church treasury, he will cooperate with the church treasurer, by maintaining a record of church school offerings and expenditures.

Other people might be added as the need arises, such as a librarian or an audio-visual co-ordinator, depending upon the church and its facilities.

There is a part of administration which is sometimes overlooked in the small church—records. Too often people in a rural community feel that they do not need records because their church school is small or "they know everyone anyway." Records are far more vital than one would imagine: (1) They help the leaders to know what has happened in the past. (2) They help them to become aware of the potential in the present. (3) They offer important information for planning the answers to future needs.

If the church is just beginning to develop a system of records, the denomination might be contacted to discover what suggestions are offered. It is not necessary for the small church to begin with a complicated system. Inexpensive stock forms can be purchased. The church could even have some forms mimeographed and/or printed to meet the needs of its situation. Some of the records which are essential are the following:

1. A record card for every church or church school family.

2. A separate card for each individual.

3. An enlistment or recruitment file for every young person and adult in the church which will include information concerning past experience, education, training, interests, etc. This would be helpful when, for example, a leader is needed to teach the nursery class, counsel the 4-H, direct the choir, make shelves, plant shrubbery or sew curtains.

4. A record card for each potential member.

There are excellent suggestions on the organization, administration, and supervision of the church school which will be helpful to churches regardless of their size or location in Paul H. Vieth's book *The Church School.*

THE BOARD OF CHRISTIAN EDUCATION

Every church should have a board (or committee) of Christian education. The number of members of the board will vary, however, according to the membership of the church. For instance, a church with 50-100 members would find a board of three people quite adequate and a church with a membership of 150 would be able to have a six-member board.

If a church has never had a board of Christian education (and sometimes even when it has!), several questions are raised: What areas of work are within the board's responsibility? Who should be members? How should it be organized? Some of the specific responsibilities of the board are:

1. Establishing the objectives for the program of Christian education in the church.

2. Studying the needs of the church and building a program in accordance with the needs.

3. Planning and co-ordinating the total program of Christian education in the church.

4. Recruiting and training leaders.

5. Choosing the curriculum materials, after careful study.

6. Planning for the best use of space and equipment and the purchasing of new equipment.

7. Scheduling the program for the Sunday church school.

8. Interpreting the program of Christian education to the total congregation.

9. Initiating new groups as they are needed.

10. Planning and administering the budget for Christian education.

Each church may add to this list. However, in a small church it is important to choose one or two areas where the need is greatest and to concentrate on these areas for the year. Although the emphasis will change from year to year, work in every area will need to be continued at all times. This means that each spring the members of the board will need to evaluate the past year's work and after analyzing their situation to the best of their ability, determine their goals for the year to come.

Who should be members of the board of Christian education? First of all, they should be individuals concerned with the total program of Christian education. They should be able to be objective in their thinking and planning and should be committed Christians who are willing to work. However, each will be freer to function impartially if he does not represent a specific group (women, youth, deacons, etc.), but rather represents the church as a whole. It is wise to have a good balance among workers with children, youth, and adults on the board.

These members should be elected for three years at a time. Rotation of members is desirable; life terms tend to stifle initiative and growth. It should be possible, however, for each member to serve two terms before having at least one or more years off the board. It is essential to allow enough time for members to become acquainted with their jobs and to administer them effectively. In addition to the elected members, there would be two ex-officio members, the pastor and the Sunday church school superintendent.

How should the board be organized? Very simply! In a small board, each of the three elected members should carry responsibility for one age group, as chairman of children's, youth or adult work. Three other responsibilities which might be divided among them are the chairmanship of the board, the chairmanship of leadership education, and the chairmanship of missionary and stewardship education.

The board of Christian education is one of the hardest working boards of the church, if it is doing its work properly. If the members feel they do not have enough to do to keep them busy at monthly meetings, then perhaps they need to take a long look at their responsibilities. One way to educate the members in their responsibilities is to have them read books or leaflets provided by the denomination concerning its concept of the board of Christian education. Copies should be available for each member. If read in preparation for a meeting, the information may be used as a point of departure for study and discussion.

The board members should take time as they begin each year (and this is especially true for a new board) to refresh their minds concerning the needs of their church in particular as well as the work expected of them in general. Time spent in this kind of preparation will be repaid a hundredfold. Perhaps a denominational representative, or a pastor or board chairman from a nearby church, could lead an evening's discussion and give the members some stimulation.

But we must always remember that the key to an effective program of Christian education in any church is good planning —both short term and long range. This is essentially what will be expected of every board, and it can be done as well with three members as with twelve.

Opportunities for Christian Education
in the Small Rural Church

There are many opportunities for Christian education in the rural area. The following suggestions may stimulate your imagination:

Sunday church school
Vacation church school
Weekday religious education classes
Youth groups
Small groups meeting in homes for study and discussions
Day camping (Many rural areas offer ideal settings for this type of program)
School of missions
Leadership training classes

Family activities—suppers, game nights, Christmas caroling

Weekday sessions for special activities for which there may not be time on Sunday morning

Seasonal activities—plays and programs geared to the specific season of the year

Meetings with parents and church school teachers

Sponsoring 4-H Clubs, Scouts or other worthwhile community groups

The program planned by the church should depend on the offering of other agencies within the community so there is no duplication of effort.

CHURCH SCHOOL WORKERS' CONFERENCE

One of the responsibilities of the church school superintendent is to plan for the church school workers' conference. This should not be "just another meeting," but should strive to fulfill the needs of the church school staff for training, inspiration and fellowship. Each teacher needs an opportunity to be aware of his place in relation to the total program of Christian education, and to be able to share his problems as well as his triumphs with those who can understand all that is involved. He also needs to continue to grow in his own knowledge of the Bible, his pupils and himself, and to worship and have fellowship with those who share his concerns.

Conferences planned around the needs of all the teachers might be held once a quarter, every two months, or every month. It is probably wise to begin such a plan with one general meeting a quarter. On other occasions, the children's, youth, and adult divisions might have conferences of their own to discuss curriculum and program. If the church school is so large that it has several classes in each department, the planning sessions could be on a departmental basis. The meetings should concentrate on training, fellowship and worship rather than "business." Too many church school workers' conferences have died a premature death because most of the time was spent in discussing lesser matters such as what refreshments should be planned for the next meeting.

GRADING IN THE CHURCH SCHOOL

Since the mark of a good program of Christian education is the ability to meet the people's needs adequately, it is vital that the children, youth, and adults be grouped according to age and ability. Many teachers who have complained that the curriculum materials were either too easy or too difficult for their particular group have, upon study, discovered that it was the age grouping of the individuals rather than the materials which caused the inadequacy.

Although there is a preferred way to group the members of the church school, there may need to be variations within individual churches. A survey of the congregation to determine the number of people within each age group will give the best pattern for deciding the specific grouping needed. This may vary from year to year. The Board should draw up a chart which will show the number in each age group over a five-year period. Rachel Swann Adams, in her book *The Small Church and Christian Education,* has some helpful suggestions concerning this on pages 38-42.

Grouping	Age	Grade
Nursery	Birth-3	
Kindergarten	4,5	Kindergarten
Primary	6,7,8	1,2,3
Junior	9,10,11	4,5,6
Junior High	12,13,14	7,8,9
Senior High	15,16,17	10,11,12
Older Youth	18-24	
Young Adults	25-34	
Adults	35—	

There are other possibilities. Some churches prefer to use the following in the children's division:

Grouping	Age	Grade
Primary	6,7	1,2
Middler	8,9	3,4
Junior	10,11	5,6

And quite often in the rural community the public school system of grouping will cause a difference in the church school.

If the local senior high school begins with the 9th grade instead of the 10th, then the church school departments might correspond.

Grouping	Age	Grade
Junior High	12,13	7,8
Senior High	14,15,16,17	9,10,11,12

Lack of space as well as small enrollment often affects the pre-school children. If the number of nursery and kindergarten children is small, they could be grouped together. However, it would be wise to have two teachers, so that the 2- and 3-year-olds could be separated at times from the 4- and 5-year-olds. Small babies should not be grouped with active, vigorous 2- and 3-year-olds, especially if the kindergarten children are also included. If there is no space for the babies in cribs and the toddlers in restricted play areas, they should be kept with their parents. In this case, a teacher in charge of the home department would meet the needs of these children through calling on the parents and sharing literature provided by the church. Many denominations have material to be taken periodically to the home from the time of a child's birth until he is two years old.

RECRUITING AND TRAINING LEADERSHIP

The recruitment and training of leaders cannot be accomplished well if it is done once a year and then forgotten until the next spring or fall or when a crisis occurs. And a church cannot expect to have an adequate educational ministry without good leadership. The cry for leaders is one of the loudest we hear within our churches, and the need increases as the church grows in size. Unfortunately, good leadership doesn't just "happen." Many hours of planning and work are essential in order to achieve a systematic approach to this particular phase of work.

The specific recruiting of teachers for the Sunday church school, for instance, should take place in the spring before the next church school year. This would allow time for the potential teachers to get some training and observe the classes they will have in the fall. Very often we lose good teachers by our approach in trying to recruit them. Here are a few suggestions to follow when recruiting teachers:

1. A committee—not an individual—should be responsible for recruiting teachers. Group thinking is preferable to the work of any one person, whether he be the pastor or the church school superintendent. The committee might well consist of these two persons plus the chairman of leadership training. Age-group chairmen might also work with this group.

2. The committee's first job is to determine the needs for teachers in the coming year. This means checking the present situation and determining the number of children, youth, and adults who should be in the classes.

3. The committee should list specifically what is to be expected of each teacher, including training, preparation, materials to be used, attendance at meetings and church school, and calling in the homes, so that there will be a clear understanding of responsibilities.

4. The next step is to list the qualifications for teachers in the church school. Then list the people available who come closest to meeting these qualifications.

5. Having two teachers for each class has often proved most effective. These would be co-teachers who would plan together and share responsibility.

6. Plan to make a personal call on each of these prospective leaders. Preferably two people should go together to make the call. Make an appointment. Do not apologize nor imply that this particular responsibility will not take long nor involve a great deal of work. Present rather the idea that this is an opportunity for this person to serve Christ and to grow in his own religious knowledge and faith. Be specific! Be enthusiastic! Be able to tell what training opportunities will be offered before he begins to teach as well as in service training and help. Make him aware of the fact that he is part of a team with the other teachers, the board of Christian education and especially with God.

7. Make it clear that the acceptance of this position is for one year only. Then it may be renewed if the committee and the teacher are both happy with the arrangement. Some people have refused to teach because they were afraid they were committing themselves for a lifetime!

All recruiting for Christian education should be channeled through this recruiting committee so the same people are not asked to do two or three unrelated jobs at the same time or even in the same year.

It is important that a record be kept of all the church members with an account of their interests, abilities, previous experience, and training. If such a record is kept up to date, it will be of tremendous value to the recruiting committee. Perhaps there will be one person in the church who cannot serve in any other way, but would be glad to take the responsibility of maintaining this file.

Potential leaders within the church need to be motivated to serve. Here are some suggestions for helping members of the congregation to become aware of the program of Christian education and its challenge for them:

1. A service of dedication for church school teachers and leaders on the Sunday before they are to begin a new church school year. This may be part of the regular morning worship service.

2. Some good Christian education sermons which will help the members of the congregation to know not only what is involved in Christian education but also what part each of them plays in it.

3. A good film or filmstrip about teaching, presented at a family night supper.

4. Invitations to parents to visit classes.

5. An "open house" at the church, at which parents and friends can see some of the activities that have been taking place in the classes or youth groups.

6. "Sharing programs" on Children's Day or at the close of the vacation church school, in which the children and young people actually tell and show some of the content of the courses they have been studying.

7. How often do we remember to express thanks publicly and privately to those who spend hours in teaching? We can use such methods as a spoken word from the pastor, parent or other church member to an individual, a public recognition from the pulpit, a brief mention in a bulletin or newsletter, or a bit of praise at a family night supper. All these help teachers

to know that the fellowship of which they are a part is aware of what they are trying to do within their classes or youth groups, and grateful for it.

A small church may feel that it is limited in its resources for training leaders. However, some of this feeling is due to the fact that we are too short-sighted. What opportunities are available to the small church?

One of the first is the church school workers' conference (page 182), which can provide the opportunity to study and develop skills in Bible study, worship and teaching methods.

Very often the curriculum materials themselves can be effective teacher training aids if they are read carefully and put into practice. They offer resource material for the teacher on the needs of the age group, methods of teaching, and Bible content. Too often their value is lost because the teacher reads only a small part of his "teacher's book" and does not really give it a chance to help him.

The wise use of a retired public school teacher or an exceptional teacher from the church school can be an excellent training method. Such a person could work closely with an individual teacher or with several who teach the same age group, helping them to plan, teach, and later evaluate the session.

Some churches have found that a Sunday morning leadership training class, held at the same time as the other church school classes for three months or longer, will often reach prospective teachers for training who would not be available for classes during the week.

Even when a small church may be too limited in personnel to conduct formal leadership training on its own, the churches of the community may cooperate in a denominational or interdenominational leadership training school. This would help to provide qualified leadership and an opportunity to share problems, concerns, and insights. Most of all it would develop an inter-church fellowship of workers which can add immeasurably to the joys of teaching. In developing plans and choosing courses for such a school it is wise to consult denominational and interdenominational Christian education leaders for suggestions. However, the teachers and leaders who will be students in the school should have an opportunity to indicate their interests at the start of the planning so that as many as possible of the desired courses can be provided. There needs to be a balanced diet of both content and method courses.

Take advantage of the opportunity to use area training meetings set up both denominationally and interdenominationally for Christian education workers. These might involve workshops, or demonstration days, when a team from other parts of the state would come into the area for a day. These teams would teach classes while the teachers from the area observe, and then all would together evaluate the session. One of the very best training methods is the laboratory school such as many denominations sponsor on a one-week or two-week basis, usually in the summer.

Discover what opportunities are offered within a reasonable distance. Then promote them and arrange for as many of the teachers as possible to attend. Once teachers have made the effort to attend one of these training sessions, it will not be difficult to get them to repeat the experience.

One can always find some time to read. Start a church library for the teachers and show them how to make use of it. Some books are suggested on p. 195.

Training, as well as recruiting, takes careful and systematic planning. It will pay for itself, however, as prospective teachers are trained for future work in the church school, and those already teaching have opportunities to grow.

WORSHIP IN THE CHURCH SCHOOL

Since it is often necessary in a one-room church for all ages to worship together, it is important for the minister, church school superintendent, or whoever is responsible for the service, to keep several things in mind. First of all, a service of worship should be planned that guides everyone into the presence of God. This should not be a passive, listening experience, but an active response to Him. One of the ways in which people respond is through the language of worship. Therefore the leader's words, as well as the language of the Scripture and hymns, are intended to express the thoughts and needs of the congregation. When all age groups are participating, their different understanding of words causes difficulty. When a service is geared primarily to the youth and adults, children cannot understand. They are often kept from worshiping, but (even worse) are taught by inference and experience that either worship is for adults only or it really is not important.

If children, young people and adults must worship together, the services must be very carefully planned. All age groups, with their differing vocabularies, needs, and experiences, should be kept in mind. Materials familiar to each of the age groups should be used. If the services are planned several weeks ahead, the children could study the meanings of hymns or portions of Scripture in advance and memorize them for future use. Juniors and young people might periodically (not too often) plan the worship service as the climax of a study unit, so that their thinking and experiences might be shared with the total group. The service should be dignified and short (not more than ten minutes). The superintendent, whose responsibility this service will be, must be aware of all that is taking place within the various classes if he is to make good use of it in planning worship. It may take him as long to prepare a ten-minute service of worship as it takes a church school teacher to prepare an hour's session.

When graded lessons are taught, one of the problems in conducting a period of worship for all ages is that all are studying different subject matter, and the worship cannot be made relevant to all. One way to meet this problem is through the use of general themes. There might be a theme for each month or two months or quarter. The superintendent will find help along this line in his denominational magazines or in *The International Journal of Religious Education.* He may be able only rarely to use the services of worship in the exact form suggested in these magazines, but he will find ideas and resource materials which will be most helpful.

If this is a one-room church, it means that the majority of these people either have worshiped together as a congregation prior to the church school or will be worshiping together afterwards. If such is the situation, it is not always necessary or vital to have a church school service of worship each Sunday. The extra ten minutes might be used once a quarter to learn new hymns and material for worship. This time might also be added to the class sessions on some Sundays with far more effective results than "just another worship period" which provides no real response of the soul to God.

Informal worship experiences within the class sessions are also important. These moments may or may not be planned. They may come as a result of a story, or of gaining new insight, or of a discussion upon the completion of an activity project. The alert and sensitive teacher will watch for opportunities to lead the pupils into this meaningful kind of worship.

SPACE AND EQUIPMENT

The space in which a particular church school class meets, as well as the equipment provided for its use, is an essential part of the program of Christian education. These factors may often "teach" more effectively than the formal curriculum materials which are used. Indeed, unsatisfactory rooms and equipment may teach ideas and attitudes directly opposite to those which we intend. Thus it is important for each board of Christian education to plan the use of the space within its building to the best possible advantage of the various age groups concerned. This is true whether the church has one, two, three, four or even more rooms. The congregation may not be able to build additional rooms, but with study and imagination they can make the most of what they have.

The board of Christian education, or a committee chosen especially for this purpose, should begin a space-and-equipment study in the following way:

1. Become aware of the objectives of the total program of Christian education.

2. Make a chart of the number of pupils in each age group within the church, and project this into the next five or ten years in order to forecast the potential growth in each of the departments.

3. Estimate the present and future needs of each of the various age groups (nursery through adults). This will include the amount of space needed per pupil, depending upon the age group. (Pre-school children need 30 to 35 square feet per child; primary and junior children need 25 to 30 square feet;

junior high and senior high youth, 15 to 18 square feet; and adults from 8 to 12 square feet, depending on the type of teaching.)

4. Draw a chart of the actual space available for use at the present time. Then try various rearrangements based on the actual space needs rather than upon such reasoning as "this class has *always* met at the back of the church." This kind of study might be made jointly by workers with adults, youth, and children, so everyone will understand at first hand the reasons for any changes that may be recommended.

There are some excellent charts dealing with the arrangement of space as well as the building of simple space-saving equipment on pp. 76-82 of *Building and Equipping for Christian Education* by C. Harry Atkinson.

A few practical suggestions toward making the most of available space and equipment are offered with the hope that they may stimulate the reader to think of additional ideas for space-saving and equipment-adapting:

1. Turn the back pews around and use the seats as tables for the pre-school children.

2. Use the piano as a divider, with one class being held behind it. The back of the piano makes an excellent place for bulletin board or pictures.

3. Make some shelves that will be hinged to the wall or back pews. These can be used for table space and then let down when not in use.

4. Wherever possible use chairs in a circle for discussion and story, rather than seating the children around a table.

5. Keep tables normally pushed against the wall, and use them only when necessary for writing or activities.

6. Use lap boards for youth and adults who sit in the pews for their class sessions, but have writing to do.

7. Make some portable dividers.

8. Instead of blackboards, use newsprint attached to the divider or to an easel or wall with masking tape, and write on it with a marker pen or marking pencil.

Equipment does not need to be expensive, even though it should be top quality. A great deal of the equipment could be made by skilled young people and adults. However, the committee needs to decide what equipment is necessary and then plan to add a little each year over a period of time. This means planning ahead for five to ten years, establishing priority year by year, and then buying good equipment in the order of need. In this way the church will in time become well equipped for its educational work.

In recent years many rural churches have added excellent educational wings to their buildings. Such a step is possible for the majority of rural congregations if they are aware of their needs and really want to do something about meeting them. A building program takes careful planning by a representative group of people (not just the pastor or church school superintendent), as well as sacrificial effort by all. Such planning should be done on a long range basis with the hope of seeing the results in two or three years or more, not rushed into in a matter of months.

Many churches feeling cramped for space have made use of buildings nearby. Grange halls and community halls of various kinds have been used on Sundays and sometimes during the week. If the parsonage is available and the pastor and his family are willing, a room might be used here, especially for pre-school children. And, of course, there is always the out-of-doors when the weather is suitable. Many stimulating discussions and thought-provoking dramas have taken place under a tree or in some other corner of the church yard. It would also be possible during the summer months to erect a tent to serve as a classroom in rainy weather.

Look around and use the resources at your fingertips!

CURRICULUM

Writers and editors of curriculum materials probably receive more than their share of criticism from the pastors and church school teachers of rural churches. Too often, the teachers have been quick to complain that the curriculum material just doesn't fit their situation, or it's too hard to teach. It has been the experience of this author that many of these church school teachers have not even read the material thoroughly. They were looking for some easy "lessons" that could be taught without effort.

It is not possible for the writers of curriculum to meet the specific needs of every section of the country and of every type of church. Thus materials are prepared which offer a broad base and more than enough resource materials for every session. Those concerned with Christian education in each church, whether it be in California or Maine, the prairies or the mountains, city or open country, 100 members or 1,000, must adapt the materials for their own particular situation. In order to do this, they must take into consideration their objectives and facilities, the knowledge they have of their community and the specific needs of the people they serve. This consideration will enable them to read the curriculum materials intelligently, choosing the resources and suggestions which will be particularly helpful to them. Work and time and effort will be required but good, creative teaching cannot be done without them.

Make good use of denominational bulletins, articles and books, as well as suggestions within the curriculum materials in the adaptation of materials to the needs of smaller churches. Denominational leaders are often available in person to help individual church teaching staffs learn how to use their materials effectively. Sometimes a group of churches in a given area will use this kind of help co-operatively.

The church school teacher's job is not one of merely transmitting knowledge into the minds of his pupils, but rather of guiding them to think, to know, to experience and to interpret life in the light of the Christian Gospel. The community and environment are vital in such learning. The teacher should be aware of the experiences of his pupils to such an extent that he can think of and use illustrations from everyday living in his teaching, supplementing those mentioned in his textbook. In other words, the teacher has the opportunity of making the Gospel relevant in the life of the child, youth or adult. Such teaching involves an advance reading of the quarter's or even the year's teaching materials so he is aware of the general goals and the posssible paths for reaching them. This cannot be done in an hour on Saturday night or Sunday morning and any program which proposes short-cut methods is cheating the teacher and the pupil.

Teaching is fun and exciting! Trying to fit together the Gospel, the pupils, the environment, and the curriculum materials into a meaningful whole can be tremendously challenging. It is not impossible.

It is wise to use denominational materials in all grades, since these have been planned with progression in mind which will be hindered or broken if extraneous material is used in even one of the departments or classes — particularly in the children or youth divisions.

There are opportunities to use materials based especially on the rural environment. The adults will find periodic use of elective courses concerning rural life stimulating and helpful. Plans should be made for weekday and youth fellowship groups to include this kind of material in their programs. Materials written over the past decade on the town and country church for home mission study themes could be used in all three age groups most effectively.

How wonderful it would be if each church school teacher could be handed a formula for success at the same time he received his curriculum materials for the year! There is none, of course, that can be guaranteed, but here is one which if conscientiously followed will help greatly:

COMMITMENT TO JESUS CHRIST

+

KNOWLEDGE OF PUPILS AND COMMUNITY

+

KNOWLEDGE OF ONE'S SELF

+

KNOWLEDGE OF CURRICULUM MATERIALS

+

WORK

+

PRAYER

+

SUCCESSFUL TEACHING

SOME SUGGESTIONS FOR A LIBRARY FOR THE RURAL CHURCH

Adair, Thelma, and McCort, Elizabeth, *How to Make Church School Equipment*. The Westminster Press, 1955.

Adams, Rachel Swann, *The Small Church and Christian Education*. The Westminster Press, 1961.

Atkinson, C. Harry, *Building and Equipping for Christian Education*. National Council of Churches in U.S.A., 1956.

Bowman, Clarice M., *Ways Youth Learn*. Harper and Brothers, 1952.

Brown, Jeannette Perkins, *The Storyteller in Religious Education*. Pilgrim Press, 1951.

Foster, Virgil E., *How a Small Church Can Have Good Christian Education*. Harper and Brothers, 1956.

Gable, Lee J. (Ed.), *Encyclopedia for Church Group Leaders*. Association Press, 1959.

How of Vacation Church School, The. Division of C. E. National Council of Churches, 1957.

Keiser, Armilda B., *Here's How and When*. Friendship Press, 1952.

Little, Sara, *Learning Together in the Christian Fellowship*. John Knox Press, 1957.

Methods books for each age group published by each denomination.

Perkins, Jeannette E., *Children's Worship in the Church School*. Harper and Brothers, 1939.

Smither, Ethel L., *Children and the Bible*. Abingdon Press, 1960.

Vieth, Paul H., *The Church School*. Christian Education Press, 1957.

Wyckoff, D. Campbell, *The Task of Christian Education*. The Westminster Press, 1955.

XV

BUILDINGS AND EQUIPMENT

IT WAS THE PRACTICE of the first century Christians to meet in their homes to study the Scriptures, sing songs of praise, pray, and generally encourage one another in Christian living (see Col. 4:15; Rom. 16:5). They may have invited neighbors and friends to join them and hear the gospel story. Often they were compelled by persecution to worship in secret meeting places. When, however, they won government recognition in A.D. 313 they turned to the erection of church buildings for public worship.

In the seventeen hundred years that have elapsed many types and forms of buildings have come into being. These range in style from elaborate cathedrals, such as St. Peter's at Rome, to the Midwest "cracker boxes" of the 1920's. From the most ornate cathedral filled with symbolism and relics, church buildings run the gamut of various forms to the simple, bare meeting houses of the Society of Friends. By 1950, new types of church architecture developed which had a modernistic-utility design. Whether or not the Christian movement is spiritually stronger with church buildings than the movement of the first 300 years without buildings is debatable.

American prosperity, plus unprecedented population growth, leads many authorities to prophesy that the boom in church building is merely getting under way. The next twenty years will see thousands of new church buildings go up, and thousands more remodeled for better or for worse. The interest in new buildings and the possibility of making costly mistakes are

196

all the more reason for Christian leaders to give much thought to the buildings of the church, lest they waste the Lord's money. "For what purpose is this building to be used?" is the first question to ask about any anticipated church building. Unless there is a clear answer the building may be of limited value and very expensive.

PURPOSE OF BUILDINGS

In planning a church building the first thought should be for the worship of God as revealed in Jesus Christ his Son. Let worship be the central theme and from it there will radiate all the good things the congregation desires and needs. Worship is basic. But to stop with worship is to stop short of adequacy.

There must also be desirable buildings for religious education. The vast majority of people who enter into the fellowship of a church come to it by way of the church's educational program. Great care, then, should be exercised in designing a building to provide rooms and equipment to handle an effective program of Christian education which will cultivate the well-rounded Christian character.

It is not enough that a church provide only for worship and the education of its members and prospective members. The New Testament churches were fellowships of people who believed in Jesus Christ, loved one another, and were seeking to do his will. Whenever the church has been a virile and worthwhile organization it has been a fellowship. It must continue to be a fellowship if it is to serve humanity as Christ intended.

Somewhere in the program of a church the members must come together in fellowship activities, so that they have a fair chance to appreciate one another and work together. It is bad for churches to be run by age groups, or any other cliques. Town-country churches must strive to cut across all dividing lines and serve all the people of the area. However, this does not eliminate the need for people of the church and community at times to meet exclusively with others of their own age groups and interest groups. Therefore, room for all kinds of social activities must be provided in church buildings.

The fourth purpose of church buildings is to provide adequate housing for the paid staff of the church. This staff usually consists of only the pastor. On some larger fields it may include the caretaker of the buildings and grounds. Housing for the pastor and his family is not provided as a convenience for the pastor or as an addition to his pay. Housing is provided that the work of the church may be done more effectively.

To accomplish the purposes of worship and education, fellowship, and staff housing, three buildings and a minimum of five acres of ground are needed. Whether a church is called an auditorium, a sanctuary, a meeting house, or church house, it should be "a house of prayer" (Is. 56:7). Because it should be set aside for a holy and sacred purpose, it should not be used for other meetings. It is not a gymnasium; it is not a public auditorium where the children run up and down the aisles between Sunday school and church and where lyceum courses, musicals, and commencement exercises are to held. God should be worshipped and honored there.

THE SANCTUARY

When one enters the door of the sanctuary (or call it by any other name) he should be so impressed by the appearance of the interior that he feels that this is the house of God. To produce this effect one may have to reconsider the use of the furniture and symbolism.

It is not unusual to go into a church building and find from one to a dozen crosses. Some of these crosses are lighted in gaudy fashion. They do not call the worshiper's attention to the meaning of the cross, but rather detract from that meaning. A cross should be kept in the right proportions, and it should be placed where it will attract the worshiper's attention and remind him of Jesus Christ who gave his life for sinful men.

In churches which practice immersion a baptistry should be provided. Sometimes the baptistry is so hidden from sight that it has little meaning to the congregation except at the time of a baptismal service. Sometimes it is an ugly permanent structure, always open to view. Sometimes it is decorated with a crude painting made by a local resident (though, of course, not all baptistry paintings are crude). The baptistry should be a place of beauty in a position of prominence. It should remind the worshiper that here he testified to the world that Jesus Christ died, was buried, and rose again from the dead. It should also remind him that those who have gone into this water have declared their death to the old life of sin and by the grace of God have been resurrected to a new life in Jesus Christ.

A third item of furniture and symbolism is the communion table. Most churches have a table which they use for this purpose, but sometimes it can hardly be found for the hymnals, Sunday school quarterlies, and ladies' hats and purses which have accumulated upon it since it was last used. Its significance is too great to be used as a storage area. This table is symbolic of the fellowship Christian people have with Christ and with one another. A worshiper is spiritually lifted when he sees this table properly covered with a clean cloth and recalls the words of the Master, "Do this, as often as you drink it, in remembrance of me." The table draws him closer to his fellow Christians and his Lord.

Whether the pulpit is on one side of the church, or in the middle front of the platform, it seems reasonable to place upon it a Bible, the Word of God. The value of keeping this Book in a prominent place is often overlooked, even in those churches which take pride in claiming to be churches of the open Bible.

Provision for Education

Much has been done by the experts in Christian education to awaken Christians to the need of satisfactory places for the study of the Word of God and its application to daily life. A particularly helpful book on this subject is C. Harry Atkinson's *Building and Equipping for Christian Education*.

Taking the only large room in the church, aside from the place of worship, and dividing it into small cubicles with permanent partitions usually proves to be unsatisfactory for the small church. The small church must use one large room for many different activities.

When classes are gathered around their teachers there is more economical use of space, and a satisfactory way of separating classes is to use curtains, stretched on frames. These can be stored when not in use. Some have experimented with an accordion type of curtain that pulls out from the wall. This is more expensive than others, but there is no reason they should not be used if the church has the money. Others have made more or less stable dividers from heavy cardboard such as is used in refrigerator packing cases. When the classes are not in session these are put back against the wall or into a closet, and the whole room is available for such other purposes as the church may desire. Portable room dividers can also be had.

Although Christian educators have warned against it, there is a tendency to put the educational plant in the basement of the church. As a general rule it is better to stay above ground. The amount of money expended in putting a hole in the ground will accomplish more pleasant and desirable results on top of the ground. If a church stays above ground it can be reasonably sure of having plenty of fresh air and light. The educational wing may well be placed at the rear of the sanctuary in either a "T" or "L" plan. Since less ceiling height is needed here than in the sanctuary, this wing may be two stories in height and still show pleasing architectural lines.

The best equipment could never be too good for teaching in Christian living. Every class should be equipped with a chalk board, chalk and erasers, and chairs and tables of appropriate height. Such equipment is basic and inexpensive, but often missing. From this beginning there may be added pictures which are available from the publication houses, projectors with small screens, and recordings of good hymns.

In the educational departments, pupils should be prepared for worship in the sanctuary. This will not be done by putting in their hands small, inferior song books and chorus sheets. Introducing them to the great music of the church through the use of good hymnals is the only safe procedure. As for musical instruments, the church should refuse to use castoffs from the homes of the congregation unless they are good in quality and serviceable in condition. Pianos and organs are to aid in the praise of God. They should be in tune at all times, and they are not to be used as catch-alls for books, papers, periodicals, faded scarves, torn raincoats, lost Bibles, or discarded handbags.

THE PASTOR'S HOME

For continuous leadership it is necessary for the church to provide a satisfactory living space for the pastor and his family. Many town-country churches have lost their pastors, not because God called them to other fields, but because of inferior living quarters. A church should construct a house for its pastor that will satisfy the needs of the pastor's wife and children. The minister's family has a right to live in a home that is at least on an equality with the homes of the church members, plus a little more, to serve as an example which may raise the living standards of some members.

The pastor's home should include at least three bedrooms, so as to provide a guest room for visiting church leaders. It should have a large living room for it is important that the town-country pastor accommodate in his home, from time to time, the official family of the church. Of course, there must be a room which he can call his study. This study should have an outside and an inside entrance and should be on the ground floor, so that people may have easy access to the pastor without disturbing the rest of the household.

SOCIAL HALL

The third building of the unit is some type of social hall. It is most useful when built adjacent to the church building and the parsonage with no physical connections between, although some prefer to have the buildings joined. It should be large enough to provide an auditorium where a large percentage of the community or neighborhood can be seated for such public meetings as the church may desire. It can be used for such adult educational features as a winter night college. It can be used for forum speakers who may come with a message for the community. In the heat of political campaigns, the church could do worse than have a spokesman for each party come and present his theories and ideas and let the people question him. Such a social hall should be open to the public from three to six days and nights each week. In the hall, rather than in the sanctuary, many a soul may catch the meaning of the gospel for the whole life.

This auditorium should be of such size and so constructed that the young people will feel free to hold their parties in it. Where it is an acceptable part of the culture they may have regular roller skating nights, folk games and folk dancing, in which the young people and the older folks come together for an evening of wholesome fun. The hall should include a dining room that will seat as many people as can be expected to come to a public dinner of the church, and, of course, a fully-equipped kitchen will be needed. It is good to have a completely-outfitted stage in order that the church may give dramatic presentations of both recreational and educational value. If the church owns a motion-picture projector it should be used frequently.

Creative thinking may suggest many ways of winning and developing people in the Christian way of life through social activities. A lounge with an open fireplace may be provided, where small groups meet for discussion; adjacent to this there could be a small pantry where hamburgers, hot dogs, pop, and hot chocolate are readily prepared. A library room may be included. The library books would be primarily religious in content, but if young people are to use the books vocations should be well represented in the collection. The best magazines should be on the shelves for all to see and use. Because men and boys like to make things, one room could be a workshop or hobby room. Let it be equipped with tools and materials so that any person may have a chance to express himself creatively. Women, too, like to make things, so another room could be devoted to hobbies and creative work for women. Let it be furnished with all kinds of items from sewing machines to a range for cooking. Surely a room could be devoted to fine arts. Here the embryo painter may blossom out into a significant painter of religious art. Who knows the beauty that may eventually result when a paintbrush is placed in the hands of a child? A room should also be devoted to music, and equipped with piano, record player, sheet music, hymnals, and records. Here duets, quartets, and choirs may sing as long and loud as they desire. Here an orchestra may practice, and here the young may make music just for the love of it. In a day when it is so difficult to keep abreast of scientific findings the church could do worse than have a room designed to help both young and old experiment and seek for undiscovered things of this life while they hold on to, and even increase, their faith in God.

These five or six rooms, in addition to the hall, stage, dining room, and kitchen, would provide the church with the equipment whereby it could make a considerable impact upon the life of the town-country community. If these ideas are incorporated in the early planning of the building, they are not prohibitive in cost. They can be furnished and equipped by different groups over a period of years, and there is great social value in the process of equipping them.

Over-All Planning

Much excellent literature on church buildings is available through denominational channels, or from the National Council of Churches. This material should be fully studied by the church and its building committee. Then a competent church architect should be employed and his advice followed in preparing the blueprints for the buildings. The money spent for a competent architect's services is the best money a church spends when building. When the time comes to landscape the church grounds advice and help can usually be obtained from the state college of agriculture at low cost. Sometimes this service is free.

The outlined plan calls for three buildings. Therefore the church should think in terms of a minimum of five acres of land on which to place its three buildings, a Christian compound in the midst of a town-country community. It may easily become the most popular and inspiring place in the community. Of the five acres three of them should be adjacent to the parsonage. Certainly the pastor in a farming community should have a garden, a berry patch, a small orchard, and a pasture for his cow or goats, and even the pastor in a non-farm area should consider having a garden. Not only is it to his advantage to have these things, but it is an advantage to the church to have a man of his standing and quality engaged in such mundane things as tilling the earth and growing his own "daily bread."

At least two acres should be reserved for the church building with its educational plant and social hall. Building a church close to a sidewalk or pavement in town-country areas looks a little strange and is not recommended. Instead a church should plan to have a spacious lawn in front of the building where the people can leisurely gather before they go into the house of God. As a place of beauty it will attract the attention of all who go by and compel some to turn into the house of prayer. Ample parking space is a modern necessity, even as a past generation found the hitching sheds necessary.

Back of the hall, and around it, there is need for recreational grounds for children, young people, and adults. This might include a softball diamond, a tennis court, pits for horseshoe pitching, croquet and badminton courts, and room for other games. These grounds should be lighted so that they may be used at night. Lighting has not proven to be expensive and such playgrounds are a great asset to the church and community. The grounds may be used also for outdoor pageants and vesper services.

RETHINKING THE LOCATION

For a location, many churches are no longer thinking of building on the public square or in the center of town. They recognize that people have cars. They know that public schools are being located on the outskirts of town-country communities. Therefore, in many cases it seems wise to locate church buildings at the edge of the town where ground is ample and transportation is no longer a problem.

Such land and buildings will cost a considerable sum of money. Therefore many churches cannot, or think they cannot, do all that is suggested here. On the other hand, the town-country church is here to stay. To be sure, many of them should be joined with other churches and some churches will close because of a change of population. But town-country people will remain. They need their own churches. If their churches are properly located, where there can be hope of reaching the optimum of 350 resident members, a realistic building program which is to take place over a period of several years can be planned.

The first thing for church people to do is to appraise their present location to see if their building is where it should be for the foreseeable future. If it is not, Christian common sense will lead them to find a proper location, although the traditions and prejudices of some members may make the task difficult. When the location has been determined, a *long-term building program* that will eventually provide the things needed should be planned. If there is no social hall or parsonage and the present sanctuary is acceptable with or without remodeling, it may be well to begin new construction with one of the needed buildings, preferably the parsonage. When a church has the right pastor settled, it can make rapid strides with the rest of its building program.

After the architect's plans have been adopted by the church, they can be given to an artist to paint a picture of the buildings as they will look when finished. Better still, a scale model may be made. This model or picture kept before the congregation will be an incentive to keep going. If it is true that it is more blessed to give than to receive, each generation should make some worthy contribution to the material possessions of the church. Every generation should have the blessing and responsibility of sharing in a building program. It may take ten, twenty, or even forty years to secure the full set of buildings. What does it matter? The town-country church is here to stay!

XVI

BUILDING A CHURCH PROGRAM

THE CHURCH IS GOD'S SERVICE AGENT for the people. Paul spoke of the church as being "the body of Christ." It should be doing for the people the things Christ did in the days of his flesh. Did he not say to his disciples . . . "he who believes in me will also do the works that I do; and greater works than these will he do . . ." (John 14:12)?

Even a casual study of the Four Gospels and the Book of Acts uncovers a long list of good deeds Jesus performed for the people. He healed the sick, opened the eyes of the blind, cast out evil spirits, raised the dead, fed hungry multitudes, received into his arms and blessed little children, preached, taught, visited, and ate with recognized sinners. He attended the wedding at Cana, and took such part in its activities as to ally himself with home life. He selected twelve men and directed them into a new vocation, and climaxed his service by dying for the people, while praying for his tormentors. In these deeds Jesus was revealing to the people his Father, the God of love, mercy, and forgiveness.

The church must give its life for the community in which it lives, thereby revealing God the Father. To do this, the New Testament churches overlooked but few of the things Jesus did. Their primary motive was to reveal to the world that Jesus of Nazareth was the Christ, that he had conquered death, and that he arose on the third day from the dead. They testified that they had seen him, touched him, and eaten with him. He was alive forevermore.

In their ministry of making the Christ known to the world they had fellowship, in so far as it was possible, with "sinners." They remained near the Temple until persecution drove them to the farthest parts of the Roman Empire. They taught, and although they may not have raised the dead, they were active in healing the sick. As for feeding the hungry that were outside the church membership, there is no New Testament record that they did so. However, there are other records which indicate that the early Christians were the Red Cross of their day, ministering even to their enemies. Did the author of Romans not write ". . . if your enemy is hungry, feed him . . ." (Rom. 12:20)? As the church became organized and persecution developed there was a greater need for Christians to help one another. We read that they sold their possessions and all lived from the proceeds, each receiving as he had need. Out of the attempts to meet one another's needs, there came into being a fellowship that could well be the envy of today's churches. It meant something to belong to a church in those early days.

DISCOVERING NEEDS

In every person there are three powerful drives that demand fulfillment. They have been identified as the drives to obtain food, love, and fellowship with the Supreme Being. If these drives are recognized as basic needs it is easy to fit all other needs into some phase of one or more of them.

In order to live and work out their earthly destiny, people must have food for their bodies. The better the body is nourished, the better tool it can be for the work of the Holy Spirit. The church is then in its rightful place when it casts its weight on the side of helping people to obtain their daily bread, even as Jesus fed the hungry.

Everyone wants to be loved and to love in turn. Love is God-given. One writer says "God is love" (1 John 4:8). People are never closer to God or happier than when they are in love. The church is in its rightful place when it helps its young to find acceptable mates, build and maintain their homes, and rear their children. This one need opens a great vista of work for the church. The returns to the church for the work done in this field are immense.

Planted deep in the heart of every human being there is the desire to know God. Some have stifled this urge and in others it seems to be dormant, but it is there as a seed, waiting to be awakened, that it may sprout and grow. Surely no one will argue that the church is not in its rightful place when through worship it seeks to bring people into fellowship with God and the surrender of all they have to the purposes of God.

Keeping in mind these three basic needs, the student may go now to finding the needs of the people and building the church's program upon those needs.

To discover the specific needs of a church and a community is not easy. A pastor must live much with his people to be able to sense their needs. If he moves among his people with ears open and mouth closed, he will, in time, be very much aware of their basic needs. If he lives as a part of the community he will sense certain underlying weaknesses, and thus will become equipped to minister to the people. But his findings cannot be exhaustive and he cannot adequately meet the needs he discovers in a ministry of only one, two, or three years.

Another means for discovering the needs of the people is the survey, as discussed in Chap. VIII. This survey shows some of the needs and hints at others. It also shows some of the resources available for meeting the needs. No long-term program building should ever be attempted before a survey of the church's community has been made and carefully analyzed. However, it should be pointed out that the Religious Survey by Families does not reveal all the needs of the people. Rather it only indicates clues that may be followed in searching for the real needs. There is no substitute for a pastor who lives close to his people and searches diligently to know their needs.

A CHURCH'S RESOURCES

While the church should spearhead all kinds of advance in a community, its program must be based largely upon the resources within its membership. These resources may be classified as spiritual, cultural, and material. Each resource should be carefully weighed before attempting to outline a program, lest the church attempt that which is impossible. The lack of resources, in one or more of the classifications, will limit the church's effectiveness. By using available resources to their limit they will multiply, and then the church can do more.

One church may be composed of people with so little spiritual power and understanding that it does not have the immediate spiritual resources to launch a great program of community service. Perhaps its members have little concept of depending upon God for the wisdom and strength needed to do a piece of kingdom work. Perhaps they have not learned to seek the will of God and then "launch out into the deep." Evangelistic, building, stewardship, and mission programs are all hindered by the church members' lack of ability to discern, and willingness to do, the will of God. Some church members think of religion as being so otherworldly that it cannot be concerned with the things of this life. To be interested in 4-H club work, the P.T.A., or soil conservation is, in their understanding, outside the interests of the church. To them religion is a segregated compartment of life from which all other activities must be kept. If such people have ever been born from above they certainly have remained babes in Christ.

On the other hand there may have been some who have learned what it means to wait upon the Lord. They have confidence because they know God. They understand the meaning of the gospel for the whole man. They are concerned to have the Spirit of Christ permeate the whole fabric of community life. They know that just a little faith, a little prayer, a little compassion used in the name of Christ has a way of multiplying a hundredfold in a very short time. Therefore a modest program should not be discarded because of a lack of spiritual resources. Probably more spiritual resources are available than are being used.

The cultural level of the church membership and community must be considered. If the level of school attainment for the average adult church member is the eighth grade, while that of the community is twelfth grade and higher, the church will probably not have the cultural resources to lead a large segment of the community. Even allowing for exceptional people in the congregation, for adult education, and knowledge gleaned from experience, it will still be difficult to overcome this barrier. This cultural disparity will be noticed in the worship service of the church, in the use of music, and in the demand for certain types of sermons. Cultural resources will reveal themselves even in the architecture of the church building. Sometimes the cultural level in the church is deep and broad and the people have a spiritual discernment that makes it possible for them to minister in many different ways to the needs of the whole community. When these people are blessed with a pastor of their own kind there seems to be no end to the good they can do.

Finally, there must be a consideration of the material resources in the control of the church membership. It sounds very devout to declare that if all the people will bring a tithe there will be plenty of money for the church. But if the people have no money, their tithe is zero. If the members' land is fertile but the seasons are unfavorable, or if the factory where they work shuts down there will be little money for the church. Likewise the number of people in the community who are members of the church and those who are not must be considered as material resources. If the membership is comparatively small, the variety of talents and of hands ready to work may also be meager. On the other hand, if 80 per cent of the people of the community are church members, the evangelistic potential is small. Thus, the balance between the number of members and nonmembers in a community will help determine the type of program the church should launch. Buildings also must be considered as a part of the material resources of a church and must be considered when making a program.

The purpose in appraising material resources is not to find excuses for failing to do what ought to be done, but to build a realistic, workable program. The very absence of certain resources will indicate the type of program that should be launched and vigorously prosecuted to the end in order to build a supply of these very resources. A wise leader will be careful lest he and his people dwell so long on the lack of resources that they fail to use those that are available.

Beside being based upon need and available resources, a program must be *the program of the church*. Building such a program is not easy, but it must be done if success is anticipated. A program must never be merely the program of the pastor, of a clique, or even of one of the boards. Success comes when a program is the program of the entire church. Only then is there hope for using the full resources of a church. When 85 per cent or more of the members of a church enthusiastically agree upon a project, after thorough exploration and discussion, its success is usually assured. Only then is there hope for using the full resources of a church.

Results are often slow in coming, both in building and executing a program. Therefore patience should be practiced. Every forward move is seed sown which in time will bear fruit. It is better to go slowly and keep a church unified than to rush forward and divide it. Learning to move at the people's pace is a hard lesson which often is learned only at the cost of many tears.

THE PASTOR'S PROGRAM

Thus far we have confined our discussion to the program which a church may launch and carry through. We need to keep in mind also the pastor's long-range program for the church. This must not be too prominent, lest it arouse opposition and thereby defeat its purpose. Nonetheless, it should not be overlooked. Let us assume that a minister has accepted the call to a church and has been duly installed as pastor. At once he begins to study the church and its field of service. The eyes of the church members may be closed to their responsibilities and opportunities. They are content with the *status quo*. For the pastor to call the church to launch the needed program at this time would probably be futile, and it might result in his resignation. The people are not evil or unconcerned, but their minds and hearts have not been cultivated and made responsive to the challenge. The duty of a pastor then is to build his preaching, his prayer services, and his visitation program so as to awaken the church people to their responsibilities. With great patience he follows through, one step at a time, until the church members themselves begin to raise questions as to why they are not ministering in this or that area. Through the pastor's leading, the church then moves to construct its program.

Another set of circumstances will serve to show how a pastor may lead. On his first Sunday as pastor he finds that the worship services are inadequate. The architecture, music, and order of service are not conducive to Christian worship. The subject could be brought up in a business meeting of the church, but this would probably result in a quarrel which would mar the fellowship for months to come. It would be better for the pastor to take inventory of all the assets at his disposal and quietly begin to use them. He can meet with the choir and request the use of certain hymns and anthems. He can help plan the worship service for a special occasion such as the harvest festival. He can organize a children's choir and introduce the children to the better music of the church. Through classes and sermons he can teach his people why and how to worship God "in spirit and in truth." By quietly doing these things, the pastor brings about necessary changes in worship with a minimum of friction, and the people are blessed.

A pastor must master the art of group dynamics so as to be able to lead his people into setting up and carrying on a program for their community. Too long Christians have talked about democracy only to practice rule by clique or dictatorship. If the pastor understands and uses the approved methods of group thinking, he will from the beginning encourage his people to think until they have the answers for their problems. Several good books on this subject have been written in recent years, including those by Bonner, Day, Douty, and Kuhn, which are listed in the bibliography.

With few exceptions, the pastor's program is concerned with the church's spiritual vision and health, and the church's program is concerned with its service to its community. There are, of course, no clear-cut lines of demarcation. The pastor's program blends into the church's program, and vice versa.

SERVING THE TOWN-COUNTRY AREA

In former chapters we have dwelt on the four phases of the ecology of the town-country area: land, home, community, and church. We have argued that to neglect any one of these is eventually to destroy the other three. Like the wheels of a car, the four must move together if there is to be progress. In building its program a church should consider these four phases in the same way as the pastor has previously considered them in his program. A comprehensive program can then be built according to the needs, and the resources for meeting those needs.

Under the headings of land, home, community, and church are now listed projects for the pastor's and church's consideration. This is a comprehensive list of suggestions and, of course, no church will attempt all of them at one time. Page references indicate locations in this book where further discussion of the item may be found.

SUGGESTED PROJECTS THAT MAY BE INCORPORATED INTO A CHURCH'S PROGRAM OF SERVICE

I. In the Realm of Land
   A. Study
      1. Adult education—"Winter-Night College" (p. 317)
   B. Projects
      1. Productive homes for minister and church members (p. 244)
      2. Lord's Acre project for supplemental funds (p. 227)
      3. 4-H Clubs, Future Farmers of America, Farmer's Home Administration, Rural Boy Scouts (pp. 83-87)
      4. Rural Life Sunday Harvest Festival observances (p. 160, 161)
      5. Co-operate with Home Demonstration Agent and County Agricultural Agent (p. 318)
      6. Co-operate with public schools in promoting vocational guidance conferences (p. 318)
      7. Distribute farm and home bulletins from state colleges of agriculture
      8. Organize credit unions and co-operatives when and where necessary (p. 319)
      9. Parish-wide plan of father-son partnership for farm, business, and industry ownership (p. 319)
      10. Placement committee to assist young people in professions
      11. Promote village industry or home crafts to reduce unemployment and increase income (p. 320)
      12. Encourage ownership of homes and family-sized farms

II. In the Realm of Christian Home Life
   A. Study
      1. Adult education—"Winter-Night College" (p. 317)
      2. Home study classes in addition to Sunday school classes on *The Christian Home in a Rural Setting* (p. 321)
      3. Preparation for marriage studies (in other than Sunday school classes)
      4. Sermons on the Christian home in the town-country area

B. Projects (other than study) that might be fostered
1. Christian home standards adopted by the church, such as grace at meals and breakfast devotions, Christian pictures on the walls, church papers in the homes, and religious music records
2. Christian book-reading clubs
3. Modern parsonage as a model for homes of the parish (p. 201)
4. Young married couples' club for study, fellowship, and service
5. Regular family night at church
6. Father-son, mother-daughter banquets
7. Co-operation with home demonstration agents
8. Home dedication and baby dedication services (p. 321)
9. Productive homes for members (p. 244)
10. Home ownership
11. Special day observances in the home (p. 321)
12. Observance of birthdays by each family for each member of the family
13. Publicize religious programs appropriate for family on radio and television (p. 171)

III. In the Realm of the Community
A. Study
1. Adult education—"Winter-Night College" (p. 317)
2. Responsible church group, alone or with other Christian bodies, make a thorough study of the community (pp. 105, 321)
3. Sermons on Christian's responsibility for community life
4. Study classes on community (other than Sunday school classes) (p. 321)
5. Circulate, read, and discuss books on community life

B. Projects (other than study) that might be fostered
1. Delimit, map, and survey the community, tabulating and charting the findings
2. With responsible persons, construct and then follow a community calendar of activities (p. 322)
3. Provide religious services for all groups in the community (p. 322)
4. Encourage and co-operate with needed health, educational, and recreational projects
5. Make adequate library facilities available to all citizens
6. Foster adult educational programs
7. Summer camps for all ages and both sexes
8. 4-H clubs and Boy and Girl Scouts made available for all boys and girls (pp. 83-87)
9. Seek adequate industry for community (p. 320)
10. Community Christmas program
11. Community and/or neighborhood fellowship meetings
12. Observe significant community anniversaries

13. Attractive signboards at entrances to community
14. Campaign to beautify community, including roads leading into community
15. Organize to provide economic opportunities for young people to remain in their home communities (p. 176)
16. Organize a community council (p. 322)

IV. In the Realm of the Church
  A. Study
    1. Church school, including Sunday school; discussion groups; vacation church school; weekday church school (p. 177)
    2. Sermons on the church and its work or the mission of Christ
    3. Membership training class covering Bible teaching on salvation, church history, missions, and church polity (p. 166, 175)

  B. Projects (other than study) that might be fostered
    1. Worship (p. 148)
      a. Public worship services at least once a week
      b. Adult, youth, and children's choirs for public worship
      c. Religious observance of special days such as harvest festival, Rural Life Sunday, baby and home dedication, consecration services for church teachers and officers
    2. Organization (p. 120)
      a. Adequate, up-to-date constitution which provides for the complete organization of the church
      b. Meetings held and duties performed as provided by the constitution
    3. Outreach (p. 164)
      a. Prayer cells
      b. Missionary endeavors at home, such as support of denominational missionary program; ministry to all groups in the community; Sunday bus service where needed; evangelistic campaign; friendly visitation
      c. Missionary endeavors through support of Heifers for Relief, Inc., Christian Rural Overseas Program, and student exchange
      d. Missionary endeavors abroad, such as support of denominational missionary program and study of mission fields through use of foreign students, retired missionaries, and mission literature
      e. Denominational literature used in Sunday schools, vacation church schools, and weekday church schools (p. 192)
      f. Church newspaper distributed regularly (ten times a year) to church members and constituency (p. 168)
      g. News items and religious essays in local papers (p. 169)
      h. Attractive bulletin board before the church building

4. Stewardship (p. 217)
   a. At least annual presentation of the stewardships of natural resources, cultural resources, abilities and skills, body, time, and money
   b. Annual presentation of tithing as the basic financial responsibility of the Christian
   c. Annual church budget and every member canvass
   d. Frequent fellowship meetings of the church

5. Land, Buildings, and Equipment (p. 196)
   a. Adequate land to provide space for buildings, lawns, parking, pastor's productive home, and recreation
   b. Sanctuary which is neat, clean, and adequate for worship
   c. Social hall adequate for social and educational meetings
   d. Modern parsonage with land for productive home equipped with furnace, deep freeze, and water heater as a minimum
   e. Blackboards, chairs, tables, pictures, filmstrips, recordings for classrooms, and good hymnals
   f. Sanitary rest rooms
   g. Projector for slides, strips, and films to be available and used
   h. Religious library and denominational literature

From time to time the pastor and the people should evaluate fairly the work and program of the church. If they find they are not making progress they should reconsider their methods. If, for instance, they are not reaching the people with revivals, they should attempt to reach them through study clubs, dinner meetings, or visitation. A method is always subject to change; the objective is not.

A final thought can be expressed in the words of Jesus, "No one who puts his hand to the plow and looks back is fit for the kingdom of God" (Luke 9:62). Except for evaluation purposes, all eyes should be focused steadily on the horizon. The church is going forward. To look back may call forth an unworthy feeling of nostalgia, as the Israelites longed for the leeks, onions, and garlic of Egypt. With eyes forward, let the church move forward.

XVII

FINANCING THE PROGRAM

No PROBLEM IS MORE TALKED ABOUT in town-country church circles than church financing. Well it might be, for unless adequate finances can be found, the modern structure of the church organization will collapse. Money must be made available for building expenses, staff salaries, literature and music, community activities, and to continue the denomination's far-flung mission program.

In town-country churches of less than one hundred fifty resident members the pastor's salary claims a large share of the total church budget. Even so, this amount is frequently less than enough to support him and his family on the level of the congregation's standard of living. Much of the rest of the budget is consumed with the housekeeping needs of the church, and perhaps 10 per cent goes into the denomination's missionary enterprises. The tight squeeze in finances prevents the church from entering into a fuller and deeper program for itself and the community.

The rapid change of pastors is due in part to their small salaries. As a pastor's family increases in size the expenses also increase. Under pressure of balancing the family budget he feels that he needs a larger church, even though it may offer only a slightly larger salary. He then begins to look for another church. Before he is in a position to lead one church, he is moving to another. Meanwhile, the churches are without the continuous leadership which is essential if they are to make healthy progress.

In order to meet their pastor's meager salary some churches neglect to make needed repairs and improvements on their buildings. Small repairs if neglected develop into larger ones. When the church does get around to them the cost is several times what it would have been if they had been made earlier. This extra cost encourages neglect at another place, and the general appearance of the church property deteriorates. What might have been a beautiful building on well-kept lawns becomes an eyesore in the community.

Not only is there evidence of decay in the building and grounds, but also in the equipment of the educational department. Hymnals and pictures become worn and torn, and are not replaced. To save more money, cheaper literature is purchased, but this is found to be cheaper in quality, too. Children accustomed to attending public schools where the buildings are clean, the equipment in good repair, and the books of high quality, find themselves thumbing through ragged lesson materials of doubtful value. Inevitably these children weigh the church in the balances, and find it wanting. Good equipment does make a difference, and it takes money to buy and keep it in acceptable condition.

For a church to become a constructive power in its community, it must carefully study its financial program. There is no need to apologize for this, nor think it is not spiritual, for financing is a necessity for the presentation of the gospel. Three essentials in church finance are people, money, and program.

A Base of Supporting Members

It takes people to finance a church. With but rare exceptions, a church of fifty resident members does not have the base for a satisfactory financial program, nor does a church of one hundred members. Of course, churches of these sizes can gather together their tithes and offerings and pay someone to preach on Sundays. They may even provide him a place in which to live. But this is not financing a church program. If preaching only is the church's program, that program is too limited to be of much effect in the community.

It is difficult to determine the minimum number of members a church needs to finance a worthy program in its community. The consecration of the members, their median age, the wealth at their disposal, the condition of their church buildings, the needs of the community, and the program the church aspires to have all must be weighed to determine how many members are needed for financing a church program. Although sufficient studies have not been made, observation indicates that approximately 350 resident members probably make the optimum size for a church in the town-country area if it is to have a satisfactory program, financial and otherwise. Since the town-country community covers an area of from several to many square miles, and some areas are sparsely settled, it will often be impossible to have 350 resident members in one church. This does not mean that the program is to be financed with less members however, for there are acceptable ways of accomplishing a larger base.

In Chap. X, attention was given to the multichurch fields. Christians have experimented with and developed the denominational community church, the denominational larger parish, the interdenominational larger parish, the federated church, and the community church. Many a poorly-financed church could be adequately financed if it would join with sister churches of its town-country community in one of these multichurch organizations. Their combined membership would often approach the mark and, other things being equal, the financial program would be secured. However, before taking this step, a church should carefully consider its present scope of influence. It might be that it is serving a neighborhood when it should be serving a whole community. In a short time, a change of perspective with its corresponding change in outreach might give the needed membership for adequate finances.

Denominational loyalty, community mores, and the hope of growth may be factors in some areas that forbid the use of any of the above plans. If it seems strategic to keep the church of a particular denomination active, that denomination should provide enough funds to assure the minister an adequate salary.

If any denomination is to fulfill its worldwide mission it must have a ministry which functions effectively. This is obtained only by providing for salaries which will attract a fully-trained ministry. The first claim on the money which a denomination receives from the churches should rightfully be used to pay every minister of the denomination a living wage. A denomination negates its preaching of social justice when it mistreats its own employees by underpaying them. In public education, state and even federal aid is promoted. Surely a Christian denomination must use a similar principle to finance its own town-country churches.

The first task in financing a church is to secure a sufficiently large base of supporting members. Moreover, money with which to finance a church cannot be collected from those who have little or no money. Money comes from the proper exercise of an individual's, a church's, or a community's stewardship. If a church teaches good stewardship, and practices what it teaches, there is reason to believe that the members' incomes, from which a tithe may be given, will increase. For its own sake and for the sake of its witness a church must teach its members good stewardship practices.

SIX STEWARDSHIPS

The Foreign Missions Conference, in an excellent book entitled *The Christian Mission Among Rural People,* listed six stewardships that any church may well take into consideration. Christian stewardship must begin with the land, whence comes man's every possession, including his own body. When the land is exhausted or destroyed life comes to an end. The first biblical command concerned the reproduction of the human body and the care of the natural resources. Psalm 8 sets forth man's relationship to land, "Thou hast given him dominion over the works of thy hands. . . ."

Much of the poverty in town-country America exists because the land has been used carelessly or improperly. Erosion by wind and water has taken a heavy toll of national wealth. Land that should support luxuriant grass is now semidesert because it was plowed for the raising of small grains. Land that should be covered with forests is now streaked with gullies because in ignorance and greed, all the trees were removed. Rivers that should be available for recreation and teeming with fish are filled with untreated refuse and silt from upstream cities and farms.

It is the task of the Christian, through wise stewardship teaching, to help all town-country people to recoup the land losses. The hour is late, and this should be done in this generation. All who deal in any way with the land must be taught the Christian view and use of land. When this is accomplished there will be enough money to support the church program.

The second principle of Christian stewardship is the development of the abilities of the individual. Notwithstanding the sentimental wish that all the boys of a farm family might be kept on the farm, the fact is that there is no way in which the farms can absorb all the males that are born there. Today there are less than five million farms and their number is decreasing. Moreover, not every boy born on a farm has the innate capacity to become a farmer. Individuals have whatever they have by the grace of God, and this is for the purpose of serving their fellow men. Such gifts call for the investing of life where the most good will be accomplished. It is reasonable to believe that enough consecrated lives invested in the town-country areas could make for the world a new nation within one generation.

Many town-country communities are destitute of workers in the fields of medicine, nursing, business, banking, education, the ministry, art, music, industry, and many other community services, for the individuals who have such aptitudes have migrated. If the community is to have a satisfactory life these losses must be replaced. Even the churches have suffered as they have failed to help people to develop their abilities, and have even sometimes encouraged them to migrate.

Rather than try to keep the boys on the farm, the realistic approach is to help every child to recognize his God-given abilities, develop them into acceptable skills, and invest them for the enrichment of town-country life. The church need not feel disappointed if a few of these go to the cities, for such a move is their inherent right. The town-country community will be greatly enhanced if the church can encourage the young to remain not on the actual farms but near the farms.

A third stewardship principle is that of guarding the cultural resources that have been inherited from past generations. For Americans, these include a democratic-republican type of government, public schools, family-managed farms, art, music, churches, the Bible, and separation of church and state. Along with these priceless inheritances are also the many customs gathered from three score or more of nations, as people have come from all parts of the world to dwell in America. This American phenomenon is unique on the earth.

Christian stewards should cultivate this rich heritage for the glory of God. In the spirit of Christ, they must man the offices of the community, maintain schools at the highest possible level, and teach the Scriptures to young and old. By their being good stewards of their cultural resources, the community will grow in the knowledge and grace of the Lord. Thus the town-country community becomes a more desirable place in which to live, and its resources will increase.

Christians should see themselves as stewards of their bodies. This is a fourth principle of stewardship. According to the Apostle Paul, the human body is the "temple of the Holy Spirit" (1 Cor. 6:19). It is not to be mistreated or abused with either too much work or too much play. It is to be respected, so that it may be used as the temple for which it was designed. It must be properly nourished and protected against disease and accident. Christian parents will make sure that their children are given the opportunity to establish satisfactory homes and reproduce themselves in children, who, in turn, will be well cared for.

Happily, the stewardship of the human body may cause town-country churches to gain a new concept of medical support. This may necessitate church action to establish young physicians, nurses, and their families in homes in the area served by their churches. For why should the church send medical missionaries to the far places of the earth if it overlooks the health of the citizens at home? Why should it teach the value of Christian homes and do nothing to aid in their establishment? A Christian concept of stewardship of the body will not ignore these facets of life.

Fifth in the list of stewardships is time. It is the most fleeting of all resources. It must be used as it passes, or it is forever lost. Looked at from another angle it is always used, either for good or bad. The Christian must know how, and be willing, to use his time for good purposes. Properly used, along with the other resources, time will renew the physical appearances of town-country communities. Drab, ugly places may come to be places of beauty and charm. Likewise this stewardship will remake the spiritual, social, and mental aspects of life. Time is on the Christian's side because he will thoughtfully and carefully use it.

The difference between a winner and a loser often is that the winner continues for a few seconds longer than the loser. The difference between a successful Christian witness and a failing one frequently lies in the proper use of the minutes as they glide by.

This discussion of stewardship finally comes to that which most commonly is associated with Christian stewardship: money. If the reader has followed the sequence of thought in this chapter, he will readily understand that money is the outcome of the proper use of the preceding five stewardships. Lack of money in the long run comes from an unchristian use of these resources. Men have little money in town-country areas because Christians have been *poor stewards* of natural resources, abilities and skills, cultural assets, body, and time. They will have money at their disposal when they become good stewards of these other things!

Money received by Christians is not to be squandered, but is to be used intelligently. Rightly speaking, every cent a Christian has is God's money and must be handled as such. Christians should carefully invest their funds not only where they will be safe and make a fair return, but where they will yield most for the kingdom of God. All religious institutions need financial support. The foremost of these institutions are the churches and their far-flung missions. How much should a Christian return directly to his church and its mission enterprises? Over the years it has seemed that one-tenth of a family's net, or real, income is the beginning, from which further giving may spring. If all the Christian families in town-country communities were to give a tenth of their incomes there would be no shortage in the coffers of the churches. After giving a tenth, a Christian should proceed to more abundant giving in proportion to the blessings he has received. Legalistically giving a precise tithe is the Old Testament concept of giving; the free giving of a tithe plus more offerings for institutions of religion and charity is the New Testament concept of the stewardship of money.

The church should lead the way in showing men how to care for their finances. The most ethical, business-like methods known should be used in the raising and spending of church money. In past generations churches have obtained money by the use of many devices. Some of these were the church tax levied by government, lotteries, scrutinizing the public tax rolls and taxing each member accordingly, bake and rummage sales, and the systematic estimation of needed revenues and the voluntary pledging of members to meet these needs. It may be assumed that there is no justifiable way to force people to support the church. It seems consistent with the idea of Christian stewardship to lead people to estimate their church's needs and value, and voluntarily give of their resources to pay the bills. In a church or parish which has a workable constitution provision has already been made for some group to carry responsibility for making a suggested annual budget, and for its presentation to the church.

BUDGETS AND PLEDGES

Many town-country churches have expressed their fear of a budget. This may exist because of some former unhappy financial experience, and the budget became the target for blame. Every church member should understand that a suggested budget is only *an attempt* to predict, or estimate, the amount of money needed to carry the church's program for the next twelve months. A suggested budget, in so far as possible, lists every item of expense the church anticipates. There can be no criticism of this. The real budget is determined *after* the church's financial resources are known. Only then does it become the church's authorization to its officers to spend the money accordingly. The following is a suggested town-country church, or parish, budget outline. It should be studied carefully, in light of the question, "What are the needs of our church?" Recommendations by those who plan church programs should be sympathetically considered.

CHURCH (PARISH) BUDGET FOR YEAR 19___

For Our Church Home (s)

Custodian (s) .... $_____
Utilities and Fuel .... $_____
Repairs and Improvements .... $_____
Insurance .... $_____
Service and Supplies .... $_____
Miscellaneous .... $_____

For Our Pastoral Ministry

Salary .... $_____
Travel on church business .... $_____
Honorarium .... $_____
Parsonage Upkeep .... $_____
Retirement .... $_____

For Our World Mission

Our Share of Denomination's Mission Budget .. $_____
Institutional Budget .... $_____
Other Benevolences .... $_____

For Our Worship and Service

Music and Supplies .... $_____

For Our Christian Education Work

Church School .... $_____
Youth Groups .... $_____
Equipment .... $_____
Materials .... $_____
Special Projects .... $_____
                              Total Amount $_____

Once a church has agreed upon the total amount of money
it needs, the next logical procedure is to have each member to
determine his fair share of that need, and pledge that, by the
grace of God, he will seek to pay to the church this sum week
by week or, in some rural areas, season by season. Many plans
to secure these pledges have been tried. No better way has
ever been found than for every member to be visited by a fellow member, confronted with his financial responsibility to
his church, and asked to meet it.

Every member should pledge his fair share and a church has
a right to expect this of every member. Any who will not promise to do his part at the time of their professed conversion
should not be admitted to church membership. Most church

covenants specifically indicate that all members agree to provide their fair share of the needed money for church operation. If every member tithes, and gives a major portion of his tithe to the church, optimum-sized churches will have abundant funds for a well-rounded program, including world missions and community enterprises.

The Every Member Canvass

Excellent material on the Every Member Canvass is now available from most denominational headquarters. Over the years, American Baptists have worked out and thoroughly field-tested an eight-step approach to the adequate solicitation of every member of the church for funds to support the church's program. This program has been adopted by several other denominations.

There is a tendency for pastors of smaller churches to by-pass the Every Member Canvass because of the small size of the church or old antagonisms within the church, by saying "The Every Member Canvass is all right for the big city church, but it won't work with our people." The truth of the matter is that the Canvass, carefully thought out and organized, *will* work in the small church. Some of the most notable gains in giving and renewed interest in the church have been made by the smaller churches in town and country.

If the local congregation is being subsidized, the denomination will probably insist that an annual Every Member Canvass be taken under the direction of a qualified stewardship official. This is all to the good, for in some situations when the Canvass has been completed it has been found that the church can pay an adequate salary without subsidization.

Special Offerings

Even when pledges have been made and enough money is coming into the treasury to pay the bills the subject of the stewardship of money should be kept before the people, so long as it is not overdone. There is an appropriate time in the fall of the year, as the agricultural harvests are taking place, for a harvest festival service. One feature of this service could easily be a thank offering. Here is an opportunity for the people to say to the Heavenly Father "Thank you for your loving care!" Easter is an ideal time to suggest that because Christ sacrificed his life Christians ought to sacrifice themselves to advance his kingdom. A sacrificial offering, perhaps dedicated to some mission project, may be received by the church and thereby the spiritual level of the church will be raised.

THE LORD'S ACRE

In the depression days of the early '30's thousands of rural churches closed. Dumont Clarke, of Asheville, N. C., conceived the idea of each Christian farmer setting aside one acre of land to be dedicated and marked by the church as "The Lord's Acre." This acre was to be carefully planted, cultivated, and harvested. When its produce was sold the entire amount was to be given to the church. The idea gained prompt acceptance and men working in factories and in businesses felt that they should have a similar project. They agreed to give their first hour's earnings of each week. Beef raisers set aside a steer as the Lord's and when it was sold gave the proceeds to their churches. Some churches have rented land and their men have donated labor, tools, seeds, planting, cultivating, and harvesting, and the entire proceeds have then been placed in the church treasury. Many other projects have been worked into the pattern of The Lord's Acre. It is an acceptable means for securing funds for special projects *over and above* the tithes and offerings of a congregation. It is less valuable when it takes the place of tithes and offerings. It should not be used by a church for more than three or four years in succession. Judiciously organized and promoted, it may build a new parsonage or new church school rooms, and at the same time it will teach the stewardship of land, time, and talents.

Finally, when financing a town-country church the members must make sure that the church has a worthy program. People will not long pour their money into an institution that has ceased to render significant service. This consideration is so important that it calls for a whole chapter of treatment.

PROTESTANT CHURCHMANSHIP
for RURAL AMERICA

PART THREE

PASTORAL
ADMINISTRATION

XVIII

A DIVINE SUMMONS

WHEN JESUS CALLED THE TWELVE he said "You did not choose me, but I chose you and appointed you that you should go and bear fruit and that your fruit should abide; so that whatever you ask the Father in my name, he may give it to you" (John 15:16). Having chosen them he broke through their indifference and dullness of mind, winning all except the betrayer to undying loyalty to his cause. Thus he moves today. He has a way of breaking through man's conceit, selfishness, and ambition. This may come in early youth like the unfolding of a flower or it may come in middle age like a violent thunderstorm. However the call may come some accept it joyfully while others turn sorrowfully away.

The life men live on earth is a gift from God. It is a gift with a purpose which fits into the overall program of God. Paul expressed it well when he said "I appeal to you therefore, brethren, by the mercies of God, to present your bodies as a living sacrifice, holy and acceptable to God, which is your spiritual worship" (Rom. 12:1). God lays upon all men everywhere the responsibility of using for his glory what he has already given them. Their lives, each with its unique possibilities, are to be used for the service of mankind in the framework of the present day.

The call of God differs with each person. Some are called to be sentinels in a stormy world. They are to be modern Noahs, confronting their generation with the judgment of God. They are to be Jeremiahs, assured that God has called them to speak

231

to a fickle, undulating people. They are to be Nehemiahs, for-saking high positions of leadership in strange places to rebuild the walls of Jerusalem. Of such men the writer to the Hebrews said "They were stoned, they were sawn in two, they were killed with the sword; they went about in skins of sheep and goats, destitute, afflicted, ill-treated—of whom the world was not worthy—wandering over deserts and mountains, and in dens and caves of the earth" (Heb. 11:37, 38).

To others there comes the call to perform the unglamorous and prosaic acts of which all great movements are made. Such is the work of a pastor. He calls from home to home; he teaches the children and young people; he attends endless meet-ings; he counsels with disgruntled and neurotic people. The preaching which he does two or more times a week has little of romance, the high, thrilling call of the Old Testament prophet, or the missionary in a foreign land. Yet, all of these tasks are significantly part of the work of God which he has been divinely called to perform.

It is the Christian duty of every man to decide, often with the aid of many interested people, what God would have him do. The prayer of Saul on the Damascus road may well be used by every Christian: " 'What shall I do, Lord?' " (Acts 22:10). To determine the will of God is not an easy matter. God does not speak to any two individuals in exactly the same fashion. But there are characteristics which accompany every call of God. When there is a need to be met he calls some individual whom he has already endowed with the suitable talents. He disturbs his mind and heart until, frequently, unable to rest, he says, like Isaiah, "Here I am! Send me" (Isa. 6:8).

There are people who recognize that they possess unique abilities, but who feel no compulsion to help fellow men around them who have great needs. They are satisfied to let the need go unmet or to permit someone else to carry the burden. But others experience uneasiness before the need and the rec-ognition of their abilities. This uneasiness, the work of the Holy Spirit, will not leave them until they throw themselves into the application of their abilities to the needs of the hour. It behooves every man to search his soul to see if he is doing what God would have him do.

MANY CALLINGS

Within the church's far-flung program there are many avenues along which diverse talents may be used. These offices are all honorable and necessary to the development of the kingdom. There is need for men and women to leave their homeland to labor in faraway places. There is equally great need for men and women to work in the sprawling cities, where Christianity has not done well. Large cities are comparatively new in human society and Christians have not learned well how to evangelize them. Moreover, there is need for men and women to give themselves to a ministry among town-country people. This area has been, and continues to be, the seedbed of the world. It is here that Christianity has its brightest hope for sustained success.

Both at home and abroad, there are many kinds of human needs which can be met only through church-related vocations. Aside from the position of pastor, a partial listing of these callings would include the following: evangelists, directors of Christian education, directors of Christian centers, medical missionaries, educational missionaries, agricultural missionaries, military chaplains, institutional chaplains, office secretaries, administrators of institutions and denominational organizations, accountants, journalists and writers, research analysts, audio-visual technicians, religious dramatists, teachers in Christian schools, and university pastors. The field in which an individual serves is a matter between himself and God, and no other man has a right to criticize him for the field he chooses.

In addition to full-time paid vocations there are within a church many places for volunteer services. These are honorable and ought not to be overlooked by one who seeks to do God's will. The church loses a good deacon when he becomes a poor pastor. Before anyone believes that he is called to the pastoral ministry, foreign mission work, or any church-related vocation, he ought to see if he can satisfy the divine compulsion by ministering along one of the volunteer avenues, while he supports himself and his family by other employment. The work of the church cannot be done by a paid ministry which is unaided by volunteer workers! The kingdom needs both.

Those who give their full time to religious work should receive a salary which is sufficient to meet living needs. They and their families should be able to live on or near the level which prevails in their community. It is, however, an accepted fact that in this world mankind's greatest benefactors often are meagerly paid while the frivolous run away with the monetary prizes. Baseball players and prize fighters receive more pay than religious leaders, a sad commentary on our materialistic civilization. Every man then should be sure of his calling, and so be spiritually prepared for the hardships of the battle, be it fought on a town-country, urban, foreign, or home mission field. A prospective minister should be alert to the possibility of the conflict extending throughout his entire life.

Protestant ministers do not generally work alone; most of them are married. There is much to be said in favor of the married ministry. The church and the community benefit by the inspiration of a Christian home established in the parsonage. Contrariwise, if this home fails it may cast a blight over the work of the church and hinder other homes in their development. A married ministry costs more than a celibate one. A Protestant church is expected to support the pastor, his wife, and their children. The pastor will be expected to send his children to college. All of this must be paid for by the church and denomination he serves.

The married pastor needs, more than any other professional man, a fully co-operative wife. She must be a Christian and in full sympathy with the work in which her husband is engaged. It is not necessary that she be schooled in theology, Christian education, or church administration. It is, however, desirable and necessary that she be experienced in the art of homemaking, child care, and getting along with people. In the agricultural area it is imperative that she practice the productive home techniques which will give the home financial stability. More important still, she must be spiritually bound to her husband and his work. She must be willing to sacrifice when necessary, that the kingdom might be advanced.

Unless a man's wife is willing to support his work with all her mind, heart, body, and soul it is doubtful if that man should enter the pastorate. It would be better for him to remain unordained and find some volunteer work to do. As such he might serve as a lay preacher. If a foreign mission board suspects that a candidate's wife is unwilling to co-operate with him he will not be appointed. The same standard should prevail at home.

Denominations, boards, and churches have different ways of determining where a man may work. The foreign mission boards, with more than one hundred years of experience behind them, are most careful in their choices of candidates for mission work. First of all, age limitations and health considerations are to be met. The educational attainments of both man and wife must be reviewed. The candidates are carefully screened by psychological tests. Finally, after a trial period, they must win the approval of their co-workers. Such requirements may be frustrating to the man who feels that he is called of God. However, the boards are not acting foolishly, but in the light of long experience.

Some of our denominations are so organized that supervisory officers or bishops appoint pastors for local churches. If a man is appointed to a field which he likes and in which he feels that he is doing God's will, he may request permission to continue therein. If he is unhappy or ambitious for promotion he may request relocation in a "better" church. Other denominations leave the selection of a pastor to the local congregation. This method seems to have as many dangers and pitfalls as the appointed method. It requires churches without pastors to raid churches that have pastors. This does not create good feeling between churches. Pastors who want to change pastorates frequently have great difficulty in finding a church. They too rely upon the influence of friends in order to obtain a call. Such a system opens the door for the fast, smooth talker, with his strong protestations of spirituality, to prey upon unsuspecting churches. Many a church has called such a character only to find itself in the hands of bad leadership, and perhaps hopelessly divided in a year's time. After this the hireling moves to another field. All, including the man who is interested in becoming a pastor or in moving from one field to another, the denominational officers charged with placing pastors in churches and other responsible positions, and the pulpit committees seeking pastors, would do well to seek carefully the will of God, for God has a design for every congregation and every laborer.

Although prayer is necessary to find God's will for the leader of a church, it is by no means the only instrument. Each church or position to be filled should be carefully studied to determine its needs. Each candidate should likewise be studied to determine, as nearly as is humanly possible, his ability to match the needs of the church. Meanwhile, responsible parties within the denomination should set up reasonable, realistic standards for the ministry, by which the churches should then abide.

It is no little thing to enter the ministry. It is no little thing to become pastor of a church. Therefore, let the decision be made with deliberation and in co-operation with all agencies that are concerned; and when the decision has been made let the minister remain until God takes the initiative in making a change.

XIX

A TOWN-COUNTRY MINISTRY

THERE WAS A TIME when the town and country ministry was limited to a small church in a village, hamlet, or the open country. A severely circumscribed and limited neighborhood was served. Only occasionally could the services of the minister be community-wide. The emerging town-country community, with boundaries pushed out to include the adjacent open country and several neighborhoods creates opportunities for a clergyman to enjoy a most satisfying ministry. The area to be served and the nature of the services needed provide ample opportunity for him to give full time to his calling and exercise his talents to the full.

The greatest single hindrance to the development of a strong town-country ministry is not the low salaries, as so many people have assumed, but the psychological craving of human beings for recognition by their fellowmen. Every person wants to do something in life that is important. Rural life has been disparaged for so long that there is an unconscious stigma attached to it. There is a feeling that one who lives in a rural situation cannot be important. Even good rural Christians have informed young pastors, in one way or another, that if they are good they will not be expected to remain. They imply that those who do stay are of inferior quality. Town people have taken a similar attitude. They feel their pastor should be moving on toward the city, otherwise he must be inferior. This feeling defeats the best efforts of good men time and again. A minister is a human being before he is a minister of Jesus Christ. In spite of his higher unselfishness he often finds himself acting and reacting like the rest of mankind. He desires the same recognition which other people have. He wants his work to count. Because it is easier to go with the current than against it, to follow the thinking of others than to be original, he assumes that the way to obtain importance is by the city. To the city he goes. This flight to the urban centers need not take place. A satisfying contribution to life *can be made* in the town-country areas and a competent town-country minister *can know* that he is important.

There is great satisfaction to be gained from working among town-country people. They are not second-class citizens, but are some of the choicest souls God ever created. To be sure, some may wear poor clothing and use poor English, but these are not the things that count for the most. First, they reproduce themselves, with numbers to spare, whereas most large urban populations do not. This simple fact has been overlooked by many church planners. Second, rural people, as a group, have an inherent vigor and intelligence that mark them wherever they go. Their young people often outstrip in earning power those born and educated in the city. This power properly harnessed in the town-country area, could make a world of difference and permeate the whole of American society. Third, rural people, as custodians of the natural resources, hold in their hands the destiny of the unborn generations of the world. It is the farmers, fishermen, miners, and lumbermen who are making the future of this nation, and not the politicians. Of course, they are being assisted by the scientists who are taking a long and careful look at the natural resources. Finally, it may be noted that rural people are the guardians of democracy. Indeed, it is extremely doubtful if democracy can survive solely in an urban culture. It is at home in town and country.

The town-country minister who painstakingly fills his office will exert an influence for good not only in his parish but far beyond it. His influence, like that of John Frederick Oberlin, may extend on to the far reaches of the world. In the years to come he will be an example, a power, and an inspiration. The importance of a faithful town-country minister should never be underestimated.

SOME ADVANTAGES

As we look at a town-country minister and at the one-to-ten thousand people who are in the area of his concern we may note advantages which he enjoys that may be denied the urban minister. A town-country minister is surrounded by people who, more than he will ever know, want to respect him. They would like to think of him as being the best living example of God to be found in their community. They know they are soiled with the cares of this world. They know they often fall before temptations. They would like to have one man of whom they can say "There is a Christian. That man has been with Jesus." Even where the laymen fail, they expect the minister to walk and behave as a disciple of Jesus of Nazareth. They are shocked by a minister who stoops to tell smutty stories or engage in doubtful deals. His every word is weighed; his every act is watched. Unknown to the minister, these words and acts become topics of conversation in many homes. When a minister measures up to the standard which town-country people set for him, they copy his ways. The words of his public prayers become their private prayers. His way with his family becomes their way with their families. Lives are fashioned by his unspoken words and unconscious examples.

However, it should be clearly noted that people can only comprehend what is spoken to them in a language they understand. Town-country people have their own language. They weigh their ministers in their scale of values, not in his. Except for the business and professional classes, they are inclined to think of work as being only physical labor. If their minister's hands are soft and white, their respect for him will be lowered, unless he proves himself in some other way. They think of recreation in terms of family gatherings, basketball games, and community activities. If the minister knows nothing of such activities, he is not speaking their language; as a consequence, they do not fully understand him.

The town-country minister has the added advantage that, of all the active men of the community, he is almost the only one who has time to study. By the very nature of his work, it is expected that the minister will be a scholar. He has the opportunity to read extensively, and to explore ideas which were barely touched while he was in school. He may now go into the depths of Bible study and theology to make a profound contribution to the living, growing church of Jesus Christ. He has time also to write, thereby sharing with his parishioners and many others the fruits of his study, the convictions of his soul, and the warm hope and faith of his heart. Through writing he enlarges the limits of his parish for his thoughts move around the world by the magic of printing.

THE MINISTER'S STRATEGIC SITUATION

The town-country minister is privileged to move among all groups in his community. He finds an open door when he calls on the wealthy of the avenue and also when he visits the poor who live on the other side of the tracks. In the Protestant tradition, it is expected that he will call, and his arrival is awaited hopefully at almost every door. Unfortunately, many wait in vain for the call that never comes. The professional and business people see in the minister an equal. He is welcome in their offices and places of business. He touches the farmers, the manufacturers, the laborers, and the sharecroppers. He can know at first hand the problems, hopes, joys, and sorrows of all groups, if he will do the necessary calling. Finally, the town-country minister has fellowship with people in all age-groups. The children, the young people, the young adults, the adults, and the aged, too, are his. No other man but the village physician is privileged to be so intimately acquainted with so wide a variety of people in the community in which he lives and works.

This means that as Christ's ambassador the town-country minister is an intermediary between people. If trouble develops between farmers and merchants, he is able to interpret one side to the other. If there is trouble between the elders and the young people, the minister knows both sides and can be the peacemaker. There are great possibilities for serving Christ in such a series of intimate situations. The peace of eighty million people is in the hands of town-country ministers who love them. Because they have these contacts, and are in a position to understand, rural ministers may lead many to a better day.

The town-country minister is important because he touches the lives of many people in the crises of their lives: at birth, conversion, marriage, and death. He is their leader in corporate worship. It is in these hours that people are deeply stirred. Then it is that results are achieved which could not have been brought about through thinking and planning alone. The minister who is in touch with his people in these great moments can help to mold them after the pattern of Christ.

The town-country minister is in the enviable position of being able to remake a church and the community as no other man can. If he has the spirit of the pioneer and the gift of imagination, he may move a dirty, unwholesome place toward his dream of a colony of heaven on earth, and steadily lead his people to its realization. Today, as never before, the tools and resources are at hand for the growing of great Christian communities. The minister is the key man in this potential growth.

It has been a common complaint, too often expressed with bitterness, that the minister in a town-country parish foregoes recognition. This, too, is a false assumption. To be sure, too few town-country ministers serve on the national boards of their respective denominations. But a town-country minister does gain the recognition of his co-laborers and churches. For, no sooner does he demonstrate that he is a good minister than a city church extends him a call. This is thought of as moving up in the ministry, and town-country pastors accept it as their rightful due. Right or wrong, this is recognition. It is this that keeps town-country pastors off many denominational boards, for by the time they have attained enough age and experience for satisfactory board service, they are no longer town-country pastors.

When town-country pastors demonstrate their ability and stay on the job long enough to do acceptable work, state and national organizations are only too glad to elect them to their boards. These men are in great demand for denominational service. Frequently, national magazines feature the work of town-country pastors. Few city ministers receive such recognition. Colleges and seminaries are constantly looking for outstanding pastors they can honor as "Rural Pastor of the Year." After all, what recognition are ministers to seek, the recognition of men, or of God? The seeking of the recognition of men may be the antithesis of doing the will of God. If anyone is disturbed about not receiving recognition, perhaps he ought to examine his own heart as well as his work.

While, as in all work, there are hardships and disappointments in the town-country ministry there are, nevertheless, unique advantages for extending the gospel to hundreds and eventually to tens of thousands of people around the world. To minister for Christ in a town-country area is not to minister in a graveyard, or on a barren desert, as some have supposed, but in the midst of a virile, prolific people whose lives reach out into time and eternity.

Here is work worth doing with all of one's might.

XX

MAKING BOTH ENDS MEET

BENJAMIN FRANKLIN ONCE MADE an observation to the effect that happiness was better assured if one spent a penny less than earned, whereas unhappiness came from spending a penny more than earned. The minister's care of his own finances may be of greater significance to him and his family's well-being than doubling and raising the funds for the church budget. His failure to be financially solvent may cause domestic stresses that can seriously curtail his effectiveness.

A minister of the gospel should be adequately paid for his services and he should be as diligent about his work as the farmers, county agents, teachers, bankers, and housewives of the community are about their work. A minister is receiving adequate remuneration when he receives enough money, supplies, and services to provide for his family as well as the average family of his congregation is provided for. The cost of necessities varies from year to year and from place to place. They may also vary with the size and ages of the pastor's family. In addition to personal and family living costs the church should also provide the necessary funds to enable the pastor to carry on his professional duties. For example, when an automobile is needed for pastoral calling the church should pay the automobile expenses.

Some ministers are so slipshod and careless that they constantly live in the midst of financial dilemma. It is even rumored that occasionally there has been a dishonest minister. To the shame of the ministry they have left debts behind them when they moved. However, in too many cases the dishonesty was not the minister's but the congregation's in withholding a rightfully earned salary. No church can be excused from being fair-minded and Christian in fixing an adequate salary. Well-dressed church members, who live in good homes and drive expensive cars, often pay only a dole to the church, thus compelling their pastor to live as a second-rate citizen. Such people need a new understanding of what is involved in Christian stewardship and a change of heart.

The pastor himself can exert upon the church much influence which will affect his financial welfare. It is his duty to bring the church to the place where it can pay a salary commensurate with the accomplishments of a well-trained minister. He is not wise when he encourages or forces a church to adopt a program which it cannot carry honorably. Too often a town-country church is reputed to have a full-time pastor, whereas the pastor tries to subsist on half-time pay. Frequently such a church should join in a larger parish, by which a broader membership base could support the financial load.

There are occasions when a minister must put modesty aside and recall the passage, " 'Ask, and it will be given you; seek and you will find; knock, and it will be opened to you' " (Matt. 7:7). Often when a minister asks, seeks, and knocks on the congregation's door he helps not only himself but the pastor who follows after him. If the minister does not mention the salary at the proper time and place the members may assume that he is happy and well provided for. Then, simply for lack of courage to speak, the pastor may either resign or try to continue to live on a substandard level which leads to his going hopelessly into debt. Meanwhile, the church drifts along with inadequate leadership for the lack of a few hundred dollars more for the pastor's salary. Churches, by their treatment of the pastor, need to command the respect of the community.

THE PRODUCTIVE HOME

A pastor's productive home is one of the most promising ways for maintaining solvency and for helping him on his field. Aside from the consideration of an adequate cash salary it has values other than monetary. The productive home may be defined as a home in which all the members of the household co-operate to produce and process as large a share of the necessities of life as possible, not depending upon the cash income of one or more members to purchase these necessities. The family then produces much of what it consumes. Production is as wide as the talents and resources of the several members of the family. Thus it is not necessary for one member to earn all the money, which is then spent by all members on consumer articles.

The productive home has several distinct advantages to its credit. The family can enjoy fine, wholesome foods at low monetary cost. The high cost of food today is not in the food itself but in the processing, transportation, advertising, merchandising, profit, and taxes. The farmer receives only about thirty-eight cents of the food dollar. If a home can produce a goodly portion of its food supply, it saves these costs and makes that money available for other uses. Canning methods and the modern deep-freeze make preservation of ripe, home-grown foods simple, efficient, and quite inexpensive.

It is possible, through the proper use of a productive home to lift and maintain a high level of health in the family. Health is conditioned on more than good food. It flows from a sense of contentment. As the members of a family willingly share chores and work, there develops among them a spirit of appreciation and a sense of security. Contentment brings emotional stability and mental health, which maintain or improve the physical fitness of the family members. Thus a constructive spiral is formed, and the welfare of the whole family is raised.

In the fast tempo of twentieth-century living, time must be given to recreational pursuits. Often recreation is thought to be something outside the home and family circle, such as attending a movie, a ball game, "teen town," or games in the church hall. These have their values and are not to be overlooked, but they are not the whole of healthy recreation. The productive home which tries to be self-sustaining will seek to develop its own recreational outlets through hobbies, such as music, art, writing, and by using the home as a frequent gathering place for friends.

The minister who is conscientious in his study, in his preparation of sermons, and in his calling and administrative work, will discover that an hour a day in the garden or in caring for livestock has great recreational value. In this work his taut nerves have a chance to relax and his world comes again into proper perspective. It is better for the minister to express his ire with a hoe on garden weeds than with his tongue on the board of deacons or the Sunday congregations.

The productive home develops the children's talents. When a child is born, no one knows what talents he may possess. He is sent to school where he is expected to stay on an educational assembly line for eight, twelve, or sixteen years, during which his talents may or may not be discovered. In some shy boy or girl there may be a new Abraham Lincoln or another Florence Nightingale. In a productive home, with parents and children working, playing, and praying together, there is a chance for free expression by all members. Reasonably sensitive parents will note the special aptitudes of their children and encourage them. As a boy tries to keep the household machinery and his car in repair, he may discover that he has mechanical abilities. Or he may display abilities in public speaking, debating, and dramatics. This new-found talent may be the beginning of his start toward the ministry or a career in government. A girl may show unusual aptitude for drawing, writing, dramatics, or homemaking. The home should be, and rightfully is, the determinative factor in most people's lives. The Christian productive home offers unique opportunities for the development of abilities into highly useful skills.

This development of talents need not be confined to the children and youths of the homes. The productive home is ideal for the discovery and development of talent in adults too. Late in life many people have become adept at newly-discovered avocations, not the least of which was Grandma Moses with her rustic art.

Recently there has been a trend in which commercial interests have tried to usurp the place of the home in every possible manner. The home is then reduced to a service station where its members come only to change clothes, to eat, and sometimes to sleep. But in the productive home that makes use of modern technology, there is more than a mere possibility that a change to a better mode of life is at hand and a new culture about to be established. The pastor who demonstrates in his own home this new way of living may well be at the fountainhead of one of the most significant changes of the twentieth century.

It is always the duty of a pastor to help his people rise to a higher standard of living. Whether he desires it or not, he and his family are strong examples for the people of the parish. If the productive home gives the pastor and his family a higher standard of living, then, by being copied, it places his people also on a higher level. Many low-income people could enjoy a much higher standard of living if someone would teach them how to use their resources better, including their skills. A pastor and his family, by using a minimum of words and a maximum of living, are ideally situated to show people a better way of life.

Finally, the pastor who works with his muscles as well as with his brain has a contact with laboring men which professionals alone seldom have. There is an unbridged chasm between the pulpit and the villagers who seldom go to church. The Apostle Paul, a highly educated man, bridged it in his day by going into the market place and arguing with the people. He spoke so they could understand him. And is it not significant that Paul was a tent maker? If the pastor can talk intelligently about his livestock, his garden, or his shop, he achieves rapport with the people all around the church. From this point he can, if he will, move to more serious conversation which will lead to changed minds and habits.

Besides property, the minister needs certain qualities if he is to have a productive home. These may be called four "willingnesses," of which the first is a willingness to break with the established pattern of urban life, which is based on a money economy, and strike out on a new way of living. He needs the willingness to be called queer, for many who see a pastor's productive home will slyly ridicule him. They will say that a pastor is worthy of a "better" field of labor where such physical work is unnecessary. It is easy to yield to this flattery and to self pity when the thermometer stands high on a July day and the garden must be weeded. He needs also a willingness to be a pioneer, for the productive home suggests a frontier to be conquered. Pioneer forefathers knew the productive home as a matter of necessity and filled with drudgery. It is the modern man's privilege to reopen this frontier aided by a dozen modern labor-saving devices. Finally the pastor should possess a willingness to organize time and resources and use them to the best advantage. This calls for discipline, regularity, and promptness that some ministers lack.

Suggestive Home Requirements

In addition to these four spiritual values, there are material requisites for operating a productive home. The first of these is land and a house. There is a difference of opinion as to who should own the property: pastor or church. For many years it was thought that the church should provide a parsonage. But at some time along life's way a man ought to gain an equity in productive property, and for that reason not a few pastors advocate that the town-country minister should own his own land and house. They also argue that other values may come to him and the community from his land and home ownership that would not be evident if he lived, rent free, in a parsonage. Others believe that the church should provide the house and land. In many instances this has proven to be wise and workable.

The difficulty in owning property is the financing of a home on the limited salary of the town-country minister. After his education the pastor has little or nothing with which to buy a house. His income remains low for many years, allowing little chance to accumulate cash reserves. Meanwhile the cost of living increases with the coming of children. Obviously a church that does not provide a parsonage should increase its salary enough that the pastor can afford to secure suitable quarters.

Regardless of who furnishes the property, there should be a substantial house and a piece of land of from one to five acres. The house should be among the best one-third of those in the community. It should be equipped with certain permanent items, provided by the church. The following are suggested: furnace or other heating equipment, electric or gas range for cooking, water heater, deep-freeze box, and/or root cellar for storage of vegetables and fruit. The minister should furnish certain items of personal equipment for inside use. The list includes the following necessary items: durable furniture for all the rooms, cooking equipment, adequate refrigeration, canning equipment, flour mill, laundry equipment, sewing machine and barber tools.

After the town's population passes 2,500 it is difficult to locate the parsonage on land of greater area than a town lot. If so, the pastor may purchase a few acres at the edge of town for a garden, orchard, and livestock. In time this property will increase in value.

Outside the house it is proper for the church to furnish a small barn and a garage for the pastor's car. Edward and Carolyn Robinson advocate a 16′ x 30′ building and claim that this, when properly arranged, will take care of the animals and fowls that the productive home needs for its use. [1] In productive home parlance, *"we do not produce to sell but to use."*

The pastor will, of course, own his livestock. According to his needs this will include a milch cow with calf or a goat with kids, thirty hens for eggs, fifty broilers, a few turkeys for the holidays and for gifts, rabbits (two or three does and a buck will suffice), three or four colonies of bees, and perhaps squabs. If the location permits, two pigs a year may be included.

A few hand tools are desirable and necessary for the care of the garden. A modern rotary type garden tractor may be added to the equipment, for it is possible to do in an hour, with power equipment, what might take a full day to accomplish with a hoe. At the same time the soil will be kept in better condition.

Woodworking tools and shop equipment, as well as musical instruments, art equipment, and weaving looms, may be added to suit the talents of the members of the family. These help to provide recreation and develop skills in growing boys and girls. Parsonage life has been the beginning of many careers in the arts, because the necessary equipment or musical instruments "happened" to be available in the home.

[1] Robinson, Edward and Carolyn, *The Have-More Plan*, Box 501, Noroton, Conn.: E. N. Robinson, 1946. Reprinted by The Macmillan Co., New York.

TIME AND EFFICIENCY

An unfounded criticism encountered when there is talk of operating a productive home is that it will take too much time, and there is already too much work to be done. It will take a full day, six days a week, for the housewife to carry out her part of the productive home. This is not unreasonable, for this is her work and she will be more helpful if she carefully carries out the tasks of the productive home than she would be if she tried to do a portion of her husband's work, such as typing, mimeographing, and calling on the parishioners. Also the productive home can be made more profitable than a job outside the home would be. This is not a life of drudgery. There is excitement in it and there will be time for social and church affairs.

It is assumed that the pastor already puts in at least eight hours of honest work each day for the church. How much more time, then, should the husband spend as his part in his productive home? Experts seem agreed that, except for the busy gardening season, or when the berries are ripe and need picking, the productive home will require about two hours a day of his time, depending upon the type and size of productive home he operates. He may charge this time to recreation. One missionary with a cow, chickens, turkeys, and a garden commented, "It's good for me to get up at five-thirty in the morning and milk the cow. I feel better all day for doing it."

Since the productive home operates on the philosophy that the whole family works, how much time should the children spend as their share of its projects? There is no definite figure, of course. But every child should have responsibilities each day. These chores should be of a productive nature with a minimum of monotonous labor. Where there is more than one child, the work should be rotated so that one child will not have all the difficult jobs. As the family grows, there will be need for additional projects. The children add them to their tasks, one by one. A twelve-year-old will be helped physically, mentally, and spiritually by an hour of work to perform daily.

The techniques for operating the various phases of the productive home are described in so many books, magazines, and

that we need not go into details. One of the best books is
newspapers that we need not go into details. One of the best
books is *The Have-More Plan* referred to above. It has come
from the experiences of two people who had the four willingnesses previously mentioned. Thoroughly tired of the type of
living forced upon them by a large city, they could see the
value of many things which town-country people often overlook. Although any attempt to carry out all of the suggested
projects would take the joy from the work, the minister and
his wife will enjoy searching the book page by page, item by
item, to discover those things which they might do with greatest profit. The United States Government seems to have one
bulletin on every conceivable subject of interest to the agricultural and do-it-yourself family. Most of these are free and may
be secured by writing your congressman. Farm magazines are
also a rich source of help. It was in the *Farm Journal* that an
article appeared on using geese to keep the weeds out of a
strawberry bed without hoeing. Geese will not readily eat
strawberries, but they do love the weeds. Thus the patch is
weeded with the minimum of labor. Some readers were so
interested that they tried it, then found a profitable sideline
in the raising of geese! Such is the way of progress.

No pastor should try to live in the town-country area without becoming acquainted with the county agricultural agent
and the county home demonstration agent. These persons are
paid to help people solve problems in agriculture and home
management. They feel complimented when they are con-
sulted, and are eager to give any help they can. They usually
keep abreast of the latest ideas in gardening, farming, and
homemaking.

PERSONAL FINANCIAL MANAGEMENT

The minister should be beyond reproach in his personal
finances. No matter how eloquently he preaches, or how faithful he is in calling on the sick, if it is rumored that he is heavily
in debt he automatically closes the door of opportunity for
reaching some people and his influence for good is curtailed.

We live, however, in a capitalistic society where money is
used to improve one's standard of living. The purchase of a

car entails such a heavy outlay of cash that it is usually considered necessary, if not profitable, to pay for it over a period of from eighteen to twenty-four months. The purchase of some furniture or equipment and occasional family emergencies may be in the same category. When such capital expenditures and emergencies occur it is usually better to finance the project from the church's credit union or from the local banks than to do so through finance plans of small loan agencies, which usually charge very high rates of interest.

Charge accounts in local and nearby city stores are seldom economical because of the tendency to buy more than is really necessary. The credit union idea has been tested over a long period of time, and a minister would do well to see that one is organized and maintained in his church.

For the protection of his family, the education of his children, and for his retirement, the minister should have a carefully planned life insurance program. There are three main types of life insurance, each valuable in its place. *Ordinary Life* or *Straight Life* is the most common type of all insurance. It provides for the payment of a sum of money on the death of the person insured. It provides for final illness and burial expenses, and the remainder may be used by the survivors. Because of its cash surrender value it is often recommended above any other type of life insurance. *Term* insurance insures for a specified period only and is payable only if death occurs within that period. A rather heavy policy carried while there are minor children provides for their security in case of the death of the wage earner. *Endowments* emphasize the savings features. Premiums are paid at the conclusion of these payments or at death, whichever occurs first. In the year each of his children is born, if the minister takes out a fifteen-year endowment policy on himself he can work toward financing, in part at least, that child's college education. Because the minister will probably live in rent-free houses during his active ministry he can take out an endowment policy which will help him to secure a home of his own when he retires. A $10,000 endowment policy begun at the age of thirty and carried until age sixty-five will cost approximately $200 a year.

Some counselors recommend that a minister carry life insurance equal to two-and-a-half times his annual salary. In times of need he can then borrow adequate amounts on it, repaying when circumstances are more favorable.

Ministers are seldom paid wages that enable them to save enough money to live comfortably when they become too old for service or if they are suddenly incapacitated. In order to offset this, the major denominations have set up retirement or pension plans for their ministers. In some denominations it is obligatory that a minister belong, while in others it is optional. Surely no minister who has a concern for his own and his family's future would want to be outside his denomination's retirement plan. Usually the church, the denomination, and the minister each contribute a fraction of the minister's salary to the pension fund. The total averages 11 per cent in most plans. Then at the age of sixty-five or seventy, when the minister retires, he receives an income for as long as he lives, based on his average salary during the years that he has been a member of the pension plan. In some denomination's pension plans, there are insurance features which give protection to the widow and the children under eighteen years of age in case of the minister's death.

All denominations have been aware that the retirement funds paid to ministers are not adequate unless they are supplemented by other income. In 1955 this condition was greatly improved when the law made it possible for clergymen, as self-employed persons, to be eligible to become insured under the government's Social Security Program. A clergyman who elects to be covered by this old-age and survivors insurance will pay a Social Security tax, but becomes eligible for substantial disability and retirement benefits, including certain monthly payments for widows and orphans. This amount, with the denomination's pension payments, plus the insurance program to purchase a home, should make it possible for a minister to retire gracefully and render service to his fellowmen as long as he lives. Under existing laws, the retired clergyman may earn a certain amount each year in addition to his Social Security payments without any penalty and more than this amount with only a partial penalty. He may serve as a pastor, as an interim pastor, or he may do other kinds of work.

Detailed and extensive as these insurance and pension plans are, they omit the health hazard. The minister should join the Blue Cross Hospitalization Plan and Blue Shield Medical Plan or some comparable, reliable group that he may be assured of adequate hospital care for himself and his family. At least one denomination co-operates with the Ministers Life and Casualty Union of Minneapolis, in a Family Health plan, which provides hospital and surgical protection, loss of time insurance, and substantial payment in case of accidental death of the minister. The minister pays a premium in keeping with his salary and his denomination pays the balance.

In summary, a minister cannot be too careful about his handling of money. The mishandling of money will detract from his ministry. The careful handling of money will strengthen his ministry and provide for him and his family a self-respecting way of life and a reasonable degree of security for the sunset years. The time to begin planning for the future is now.

XXI

THE MINISTER'S TENURE OF OFFICE

A MINISTER NEEDS TO BECOME ROOTED in his community and in his church over a long period of time if he is to grow in the confidence of his people. When John Frederick Oberlin was questioned about leaving Walbach he replied: "I shall not be leaving Walbach. It has taken me ten years to know the people and what to do. I must have another ten years to correct my mistakes, and then time to fulfill my plans." As he continued to be the pastor at Walbach for over sixty years the churches prospered under his devoted care, as he grew in skill, grace, and wisdom.

There seems to be a relationship between a pastor's length of service in a church and the number of members of the church. The trend of modern society is to associate value with bulk. Therefore there seems to be an unattractive limitation of prestige in serving as a pastor of a small church. The human thing for a pastor in this situation to do, as he seeks greater prestige, is to seek a larger church.

As noted in an earlier chapter, rural churches tend to have limited memberships, the average resident membership being less than 150. Town churches, situated in a larger concentration of population, tend to be larger. As towns approach the maximum size of ten thousand population the churches move toward the optimum membership of 350.

Town-country churches have consistently had short-term pastorates. Where a long-term pastorate prevails, the size and vitality of the church is above the average of churches of sim-

255

ilar background. Sparse population alone cannot be blamed for the smallness of churches, although it doubtless has a bearing on their condition. Where churches in sparsely settled areas have had long sustained pastoral care the churches have grown. Surveys of sparsely populated areas have repeatedly shown that there are many people in these communities untouched by the churches of the area. Evidently the pastor who stays for only a short time does not stay long enough to win them. The pastor who stays wins such people, and his church grows.

LONG PASTORATES

Some pastors remain with their churches for many years. This is generally considered to be wholesome for both the pastor and the church. It is the sense of dedication that inspires most pastors to remain for a long period of years. Such pastors serve effectively, through hard and good times, because they believe it to be God's will that they stay in their particular places. As a rule, they were not hasty in accepting the call of the church, but sought earnestly to learn if this might be God's chosen place of service for them. When they accepted the responsibility they concentrated on the task at hand and found therein a challenging work to do. They devoted all their time, strength, and wisdom to it, for it was the Father's will for them. As the work developed they took pride in it, and moved steadily from one project to another. Such ministers are the men who give Christians hope in the advance of the church against the powers of darkness, for they are moved by the Spirit of God to give to the world a good witness of the faith.

There are some conditions under which long pastorates are undesirable, for long tenure in itself is neither good nor bad. What happens during a pastorate is of the greatest significance. A pastor of a large well-paying church may remain because he can find no other church that offers a higher salary or more prestige. Accordingly he makes every possible effort to keep his congregation happy so that he can remain with them.

Some pastors remain with one church over a long period of years because they are without ambition for either the church or themselves. They have settled themselves into a comfortable rut and do not want to be disturbed. The church, under such a pastor, may show signs on every hand of deterioration, such as lagging attendance, dwindling finances, run-down property, and flagging spirit. All too frequently these signs are overlooked, or the blame is placed on some situation or person beyond control, while the pastor remains with the dying church. Sometimes there are members of such a church who will take steps to force the resignation of the pastor. If they are not successful they become branded as trouble-makers, and, after a few unpleasant experiences, they withdraw from the church or resign themselves to tolerating the *status quo*. Meanwhile, the church continues to decline.

There are many reasons why pastors terminate their services in churches. Some, as they grow older, feel that the burdens and wider responsibilities are too heavy for them, and they resign to accept smaller, less demanding situations. Such a withdrawal is more likely to occur when a man has served in a long pastorate than when he has had only a short tenure.

Short Pastorates

There are reasons why many pastorates are of short duration. Not all of these reasons can be discussed in this book. Perhaps the one thing which most often causes men to terminate their services with a church is a sense of futility that comes with the failure to develop a sensible program. In seminary days these pastors were taught to "preach the gospel." They imagined themselves as preachers who would command the attention of a large, imposing congregation every Sunday. When they became pastors they found that few were the people who came to hear them preach. Then, half-heartedly, they tried a few gimmicks of one kind or another to whip up enthusiasm. Failing to fill the church even then, they began to look for another field of labor where, unfortunately, they would preach the same sermons and repeat the same mistakes! Had these men been able to conceive a substantial long-term program of preaching, teaching, counseling, and serving they would have escaped this sense of futility and perhaps remained for years as good pastors.

Other men leave a church because they did not come to stay; they came to fill a gap in their climb up the ecclesiastical ladder. They accepted a small rural church as a starting place, a town church as the next rung on the ladder, and hoped soon to be called to an urban church of great prestige. When they secured a call to a larger church, it was with a sense of promotion to a better job and a renewed desire to push on at all cost.

The eagerness for promotion may also stem from a different attitude. Some ministers may be ashamed to serve Christ in a rural area, for, in their mistaken code of values, they believe that rural people are inferior to urban people. Since they wish to stay with rural people no longer than necessary lest they, too, be marked as inferior, they resign the pastorate of the rural church as soon as possible.

Many a pastor has left his field of service with a heavy heart because of financial necessity. It is understandable that a minister must receive for his labors enough money to support his family. From the time the first child is born in the parsonage until the last has completed college the minister's expenses steadily increase year by year. This indicates that the minister's salary must increase year by year, or he will be compelled to neglect his family obligations. Too many churches are willing to ignore such a need. They do not offer the pastor well-deserved increases in salary.

A few ministers move frequently because it is easier to do so than to prepare new sermons. In a new field they will be well received for a year, they will coast along for a second year, and then they will seek a new place in the third year. These men are mentally and spiritually bankrupt!

Other men move from a field because they are confronted with insolvable problems. These problems may be inherent within the field, or they may be of the pastor's own creation, such as a problem arising from his preaching or his conduct toward his people. A solution may not be impossible, but it may be beyond the powers of the pastor in question.

Still other men leave a church because it is God's will that they do so. Life is a school in which both ministers and laymen are enrolled. From successes and mistakes a good minister learns valuable lessons. The time may come when the lessons learned on one field can be used with much profit on another field, or even in a different line of endeavor. Thus, in order that a man's experiences may be used to the best advantage, it may be God's will that after even a short period of work in one church he should move to another church or into some other kind of Christian work.

This, then, is the question which a minister must answer: "Am I in the ministry to try to live in ease and refinement, or to turn the world upside down for Christ?" There are certain facts which any man ought to consider and weigh carefully before he enters the gospel ministry. If he is convinced in his mind and heart that God has a place for him, he must be content to serve only in that place, and in no other.

To Serve or to Escape?

It was the service motive that sent Jesus on his mission. "The Son of man came not to be served but to serve" (Matt. 20:28). He poured out his life for people who neither appreciated him nor understood what he was trying to do. In but a brief time, he went to the cross with all of its physical and mental sufferings. But even as the suffering of the flesh took hold of him he prayed "Father, forgive them; for they know not what they do" (Luke 23:34). His life motive was to serve the people as God had planned: "My food is to do the will of him who sent me" (John 4:34).

The Apostle Paul, highly educated and acquainted with the "best people," left all to become an itinerant preacher of the gospel of Jesus Christ. Many were the days on which he might have turned back with bitter words about people who did not appreciate him. But Paul did not turn back! Like his Master, he felt that he had a mission to perform and he did not cry because the price was high!

Jesus told his disciples not to put their hearts and minds on the accumulation of material things and worldly honors, but to seek first the kingdom of heaven. His words might well cause some ministers to have a feeling of uneasiness: "For the Gentiles seek all these things" (Matt. 6:32). There is a spirit abroad, even within the ministry, that does not speak well for the future of the church. It is the spirit of the Gentiles. It

is seeking the chief seats, being known among men, and pos-
sessing worldly goods. In modern phraseology this is material-
ism, the predominant sin of the day, fostered by high-powered
advertising. Ministers have come to be appraised by the size
of the churches they serve, by the salaries they receive, and by
the cultural tone of their congregations. Some executives speak
of promotion in the gospel ministry! How can such a thing be?
Do they not recall the conversation Jesus had with his disciples
at Capernaum? Jesus asked them: "What were you discussing
on the way?" They were ashamed and looked at one another in
embarrassment, "for on the way they had discussed with one
another who was the greatest." And Jesus said: "If any one
would be first, he must be last of all and servant of all" (Mark
9:33, 34, 35).

If any minister could find a field with no problems there
would be no need for a minister in that place. In the ministry
men are where they are because there are problems to be faced.

When ministers come face to face with a problem, they can
do one of two things: They can face it realistically and, by the
grace of God, solve it; or they can run away from it. To face
problems seems to be the logical, Christian thing to do. For
that cause ministers were born! The problem may be some
little thing that a brief, frank conversation will cure. On the
other hand, it may be a tremendous obstacle to progress, with
roots which extend far back into the past and branches which
will shade the future for years to come.

If there is anything to prayer and the gospel of love, problems can be solved. Most of the great achievements of the material world originally were problems to be solved. We enjoy
today's blessings because yesterday's people solved problems.
It is recorded that after Edison had made some six hundred
tests and experiments seeking a filament for the incandescent
bulb an assistant said: "Let's quit. We have made over six
hundred tests and we know no more than when we started."
Edison is said to have replied: "We know there are over six
hundred things that will not work. Let's go on." They went on
and found the long sought after filament! When ministers
seek the answers to problems with prayer and love they have
a good chance of resolving them.

The other way to handle problems is to run away from them. Under this method the church, the minister and the community all lose. When a man faces the fact that he ran away from a problem instead of solving it, something evil happens to his soul. He thinks a little less of himself. He may take refuge in boasting about what a fine church he now has, but inwardly he knows that he ran away from a problem!

Ministers grow by overcoming obstacles. This is the way athletes are trained. It is the way the body builds up immunity against disease.

Some time ago there appeared in a professional magazine a story of a minister who, when he was about fifty years of age, wanted desperately to leave his church for greener fields. But at fifty this is a difficult thing to do, for churches foolishly want only young men as their leaders. When this minister found he could not get another church he decided to build a new one— out of the old one. For the first time in his life he studied himself to find if he had any faults which might hinder the progress of the church. By the grace of God he found some, and made the necessary corrections! Next he looked the problems of the church full in the face, and wholeheartedly set to work at their solutions. Before he reached his retirement age he had the kind of a church he once had sought for in vain! He was a bigger man because of this experience. And the kingdom was enriched with a better church. If the fault is in the church, a minister does not correct that fault by moving. If the fault is in the minister, then in leaving he carries the fault to the new field and repeats there the same general pattern. The pattern of problems generally follows a minister from field to field. Progress comes only when problems are solved, not dodged.

THE ADEQUATE DURATION

The question as to how long a minister should remain on a field now presents itself. It sounds quite orthodox to reply that he should remain until the Lord calls him to another field. But such sham orthodoxy offers an unsatisfactory answer because that which is called the voice of God may be only a convenient excuse. At some time, most pastors have had people say to them, "It was God's will!" Maybe so, but often it did not look that way to the pastors who knew the conflicting desires and interests of those people. In the same fashion, a minister will sometimes say that it is the Lord's will that at this time he leave this unprofitable field for a better position where the people are kinder and have more money. Maybe so, but this outwardly pious remark calls for close scrutiny.

Another answer to the old question is that a man should remain on a field as long as he is green; i.e., growing. If a pastor keeps growing spiritually and mentally, he may keep right on, year after year leading his church forward. Both pastor and people will be happy. A minister once complained bitterly to fellow pastors that his church was not responsive to his preaching and leadership. In his tirade (for it was that) he said: "I can't understand their hardness. I am giving them the same sermons I used effectively thirty years ago, and I can't touch them!" He did not know it, poor impoverished soul that he was, but thirty years ago he stopped growing. The people of his generation and the new generation had moved on and left him behind. His leadership had gone by default! It was already past time for him to leave the field. Moreover, it was past time for him to leave the ministry unless he was willing to pay the price of growing again!

There are a few ministers who seldom read a new book, write a new sermon, or switch their minds to a new thought. They can only fall back on the art of rearranging old prejudices. And this art is not confined to men who are over sixty years of age. Too many younger men have lost the power to remain green; they are already brown with old age! As long as a man remains green, and applies himself to the program of the church, there is progress. A minister who keeps his growing edge alive may profitably remain as pastor of a church for many years. But, on the other hand, because he keeps green God may have other work for him.

It is proper for a minister to ask himself when he should move. The soundest answer to this is that a minister should move when God takes the initiative and indicates in no uncertain terms, that he has a work for him to do at another place. As a man grows in his work there are specialized places of service which he might well fill. When the job seeks him he may rightly feel that God is pointing him out for that position. The recognition of God's voice must, of necessity, be left to each individual. No man has a right to judge another at this point.

Let God and the church members take the initiative in a pastor's moving. Carefully and with all their spiritual powers, the minister and the people should listen for God's voice. If a pastor is thinking of leaving a field, he might with much profit discuss his contemplated action with some of his people. They might concur. They might disagree. Perhaps all would see things in a different light after such a discussion. After a free, friendly exchange of ideas the pastor's feeling that he should sever the pastoral relationships may be confirmed. If so, satisfactory arrangements can be made for the severance. On the other hand, the frank facing of problems by pastor and people might be the very means of their solution. From the conversations there might easily come a renewed feeling of fellowship and closeness that would enhance the pastor's work.

The church is defeated in the true evangelizing of America until gospel ministers, after the spirit of John Frederick Oberlin, say that they want a work to do that no one else wants, a work that will not be done unless they do it; then earnestly seek God's will for their lives and remain with the work until God indicates clearly that he wants them elsewhere. The ideal seems to be that a minister should seek his field of service carefully, with much prayer and meditation, and plan to stay with it for the rest of his life. Then great churches will dot the land, great ministers will speak from their pulpits, and great Christian communities will be developed.

XXII

THE LIBRARY AND STUDY HABITS

THE FARMER, IN ORDER TO HAVE profitable crops, understands that he must discipline himself to till the fields in proper season with tested and proven methods. The merchant knows that if he would earn a fair return on his investment he must attend to his store when business is available. The day laborer realizes that if he is to receive a pay check he must be on the job and at the disposal of his foreman every working day. Likewise, the minister must understand that to lead his people aright, he must discipline himself to spend adequate time in the development of his intellectual and spiritual life. No running hither and yon will ever compensate for deficiency in study and prayer.

In one sense parishioners feed upon the mind and spirit of the minister. People of all kinds and descriptions attend the services of public worship. They attend of their own free will, because they are spiritually hungry. They come hungry, and they will receive little nourishment from the minister who has neglected his study all week, then, on Saturday night, has hurriedly thrown together a few thoughts for the morning sermon.

THE PASTOR'S STUDY

A town-country minister, to be at his best, must have a place which is set aside for study and meditation. Rather than an office it should preferably be known as a study or library, for these terms suggest study and meditation. In the rural setting, it is usually located at home rather than in the church.

264

The study should be on the first floor of the dwelling and, if possible, in one of the front rooms. At the same time it should be separated from the rest of the house. It should have both an outside and an inside entrance in order that the minister may be readily accessible to his people. Parishioners should not find it necessary to climb a flight of stairs and then be shown to some back room in order to see their minister. And when they do find him, there should be a combination of both privacy for conversation and protection for the minister.

A study in the home calls for co-operation of all members of the minister's household. The sooner the minister secures this co-operation the better. His wife and children must learn to respect his hours of study. This may call for some energetic teaching by husband, father, and minister.

The minister's wife should learn that when people call on the minister they are not also calling on her. She is not the spiritual consultant. Her husband is a professional man who must often deal with delicate and confidential matters. By keeping to herself she will help him in his difficult work. A minister cannot afford to have a jealous wife. If the call from a parishioner develops into a social call, the minister may need the help of his wife. After the conversation has continued for a little while, she may invite the social caller into another part of the house and continue the visit while the minister returns to the discipline of his study.

The minister's study should be neat, clean, and as comfortable as possible for efficient work. Because it is a public relations project it should be, in so far as possible, presentable at all times. A deranged study does not suggest creative activity, but random and almost irresponsible methods of work. As to the furnishings, the minister will need a desk with proper lighting, and a desk chair. He will need his books so arranged on shelves and desk as to be easily accessible. He will need a comfortable reading chair and a chair or two for visitors. With his typewriter, filing cabinets, and perhaps mimeograph machine and addressograph he has all the equipment he really needs in his study. He now has the place and the physical tools for creative work. As for decor, a few good pictures may be placed on the walls, as the minister's fancy and pocketbook dictate.

A rug or two on the floor will add a touch of comfort, and of course there will be displayed in a prominent place the parish map to which the minister will frequently refer.

STUDY PRACTICES

The next logical question is how much time a minister should spend in his study. This question cannot be answered by a definite, arbitrary statement, for some men grasp and develop an idea quicker than others. Some men read and write faster than others. One man may require five or six hours to do what another can do in four. The time spent in study varies with each individual.

The hours from six to eight each morning are for personal use, with thirty minutes to an hour devoted to morning chores related to the productive home. When these chores are completed, including his own grooming, the minister is ready for his day's work.

It seems to be the consensus of opinion among ministers that the hours from eight until noon, five mornings a week, are ideal for work in the study. In some far-flung parishes and in certain types of mission work such a time schedule is not possible, and other schedules must be worked out. During the four morning hours the minister may engage in such activities as Bible study and the reading of serious books and professional magazines. He will also, in these hours, plan and write his sermons and addresses. The planning of church work may also be done during these study hours. Correspondence and the mimeographing of bulletins should be done at some other time.

This time schedule represents twenty hours of study each week. If any minister will seriously conform to this schedule he will spend a thousand hours a year in study. He can thus become the equivalent of a new man in the pulpit in the second year. In these study hours it is determined whether a minister will remain green, or dry up and turn brown; whether he will be a leader of his church, or a mere hanger-on.

The study is not the proper place to read newspapers and popular magazines, valuable as they may be. If the minister has popular magazines scattered about the house he can in a leisure quarter of an hour pick them up for quick reading. He may be surprised at how much can be read and absorbed in this manner. Some brief articles may even be read during television and radio commericals. There is always the possibility of evening reading, which is ideal for the reading of magazines and fiction. It is not how long a minister stays in his study that counts, but what he does while he is there.

Although a rigid schedule of study in the morning hours is imperative it must be recognized that the study or library is not the only place where the minister can or should study. Nor are books the only things to be used in the study. One writer has put it well in these words:

> It would never satisfy me to get my knowledge of my people and their problems from books of psychology, sociology, and economics. Next to the Bible and my own Christian experience, the most used and valuable adjunct in my study would be my parish map and a file with a set of cards for every family, every person, for whom I should be responsible as an ambassador of Christ. To aid my memory I would enter on the cards all the important personal, biological, psychological, sociological and economic facts obtained by me in personal acquaintance with each person and each family. My sermons would grow on the farms, in the barns, in the houses, and on the highways of my parish.[1]

This sound advice does not apply to the two- or three-year pastorate. No man with the urge to move is going to study his people as Galpin has suggested. On the other hand, the man who does so will be keenly aware of the life of his people, and will unconsciously minister to their needs when he calls and when he conducts worship.

Commendable also are the special offerings of the land grant colleges and seminaries. For years these institutions have given special courses for rural ministers. They keep him in touch with contemporary rural movements. Some seminaries offer summer study for ministers. For the man who has been out of school for a few years, or for the man who wants to pick up a few hours toward an advanced degree, the seminary courses are an opportunity he ought not to neglect.

The town-country minister, if he is to be a good pastor and preacher, must not satisfy himself with the study of only books

[1] Galpin, Charles J., "If I Were a Rural Minister" (New York: American Baptist Home Mission Society, Town-Country Work, Bulletin No. 3, 1940).

and people. By close observation he must study the earth and as much of what it contains as he can observe. The rural minister, of all people, must have his eyes open to observe and meditate upon God's workings through nature. From this study he may draw many illustrations for spiritual lessons. His preaching will then have a ring of authority which it could not have from the mere reading of books. It is to be noted that Jesus observed nature and from it drew His parables. The rural minister should strive for such mastery.

BOOKS AND OTHER HELPS

What books should the minister own? A good beginning collection would be the English Bible in several translations, a Bible dictionary, a concordance, a few books on theology, a good commentary, and books of good sermons. Books on various phases of church work and the Christian life may be added. Some ministers will want to add volumes of poetry, while others will prefer history, science, or biography. As men vary in their likes and dislikes, so will their libraries vary. The American Baptist Rural Church Center, Green Lake, Wis., has issued a folder, *Twenty-Four Books for Town and Country Pastors.*[2] These books might well be included in a town-country minister's library.

The United States Department of Agriculture issues from time to time a *Rural Reading List.* This is a listing of helpful books and pamphlets on such subjects as agricultural economics, rural sociology, political science and history, creative living, education, religion and philosophy, home economics, and science and technology. Books on such subjects are the kinds a town-country minister should buy and study, in addition to books of a more religious type.

It is important that the minister should learn very early in his career how to classify his books and how to file in a systematic manner magazine articles, news stories, pamphlets, and sermons. A great amount of valuable educational, inspirational, and illustrative material is available in the many popular and professional magazines that are offered to American readers at low prices. The pastor will read much of this material and feel

[2] This list may be secured by writing the Rural Church Center.

profited by it, and will promptly forget it unless, wisely, he files it so that it will be easily found again when needed. If he selects sagaciously and widely, in a few years he will have at his command an increasingly valuable collection of material covering all phases of church and community life. This file may easily constitute for him the most valuable part of his library, for this material is his own in a sense that other materials are not.

The securing of books is a problem for most town-country ministers. In order to obtain religious books it is helpful to belong to a religious book club. This permits one to examine monthly offerings and occasionally buy a needed book. Annually four or five good books may be secured in this manner. Varying with different book clubs, a bonus book will be received for each four or five purchased. This may be as many books as a minister can afford during one year. Some denominational presses offer a 10 per cent discount to ministers who enroll in their book clubs and buy as many as four books a year. Used book stores are a good low-cost source for the purchase of old but good books.

Paper-bound reprints of excellent books are available at the newsstands as low as twenty-five cents a copy. A minister would do well to invest several dollars in these books while they are available.

An excellent opportunity for obtaining books is the state library. In most of the fifty states any citizen may read almost any book by asking the local librarian to request it from the state library. If there is no local library, a citizen may himself write to the state library for a book or books. Not only will the state librarians send the books, but in some cases, on request, they will outline reading courses. Many schools and theological seminaries have circulating libraries through which a minister may obtain books for the asking by paying the postage.

It is usually possible for an energetic minister to organize among his ministerial friends a book club. Ten or twelve ministers may form an efficient reading club, though a smaller number may band together in one. After soliciting and securing the consent of the men to join in the club, the next step is to draw up a list of good books. Each minister then buys one book and during the month reads it. Let us say this is done in September. On the predetermined date, September 30, he mails the book to a previously determined club member. A day or two later, on October 1 or 2, he receives a book from another member of the group. He reads this book and mails it to his man at the end of the month, October 30. This system continues month by month, until in the twelfth month, August, he receives back the book he purchased and with which he started. If the club has twelve members, he has read his own book plus eleven others during the year. Thus, for the price of one book, plus postage, he reads twelve books. If the reader makes adequate outlines, copies pertinent passages, and intelligently files these notes he has valuable material at his fingertips when he needs it. The book club may be even better than owning the book, for too often the owned book is not carefully read.

Magazines and papers play a large part in the cultural life of America. The town-country minister should read a daily newspaper, and his denominational papers, both state and national. He should read also one good religious technical magazine, one religious news magazine, one cultural magazine each month, and a scholarly journal each quarter. It is necessary for the town-country minister to read these magazines while he reads the Bible, for through the reading of periodicals he keeps abreast of current events and thinking. Through Bible reading he is then able to interpret and to evaluate present-day happenings for his people. The one last word to add to this phase of the town-country minister's studying is that he should read as widely as possible. A minister must be careful that his reading is not confined to one side of any question. Generally speaking, he should read anything that is fit to read, for this is good for mind and soul.

WRITING

Another significant phase of the town-country minister's study program is writing. There is creative value in writing, and there is value in creative writing. Few workdays should go by without the minister trying to express himself clearly through the medium of writing. This can be done, in part, through letter writing. Common courtesy requires a professional man to keep his correspondence up to date. The answer to a business letter should be in the mails not later than the second day following its reception. One man set himself to the task of writing at least three hundred words every day.

Is it any wonder that he became a good writer with the promise of a brilliant career? Good writing calls for keen discipline. For most people it is not easy to write, but it is an art that every town-country minister must resolutely try to master, for he is often called upon to write for the papers and magazines of his community. If he feels that he has no talent for writing he nevertheless should learn to write as he would learn any other task he must perform.

The writing of sermonettes provides another means of gaining writing ability. These often can be used in the local newspapers. The minister may also develop original illustrations, taking his subject from nature and the community life about him. And, of course, he will gain real experience if he writes in full his sermons as they are to be delivered. Moreover, he should write his prayers, seeking to express himself clearly and forcefully. Even though he does not read these prayers verbatim he will achieve a style that makes them meaningful to the congregation.

By setting apart hours of study the minister deepens his intellectual and spiritual life in order to feed his people. Therefore, the matter of study should be taken seriously.

Routine Duties

In its place and work the church office overlaps the study. The office maintains the membership records and it is the center from which the church reaches out to homes on the farthest edges of the parish. Although a large or medium-sized urban church may have its office in the church building, the study will perform double duty as an office in the majority of town-country churches, for the minister himself has the dual responsibilities of being pastor and administrator.

Some churches are able to employ a competent secretary for routine office work, including the mimeographing of bulletins and news sheets, but usually the town-country church is unable to bear that much extra expense. However, there may be a woman in the congregation who is, or was, a secretary, who would volunteer to give a day a week, or perhaps three afternoons a week, to this kind of work as her service to the church. This plan would relieve the pastor of certain time-consuming details and free him for more constructive use of his time. In a larger parish of more than two churches a secretary is the first logical addition to make to the parish staff.

The pastor should plan the secretary's work carefully, so that she has time to finish it when it is needed. It is poor policy, and most damaging to morale, to assign work to a secretary only a few minutes before it is needed and then expect it to be done well. He must be firm about the quality of work he permits to go from his office. All letters must be brief and to the point, correctly punctuated, with all words properly spelled, with not more than one erasure per letter, and that neatly done. Mimeograph work must be legible and neat, free of blots and smears.

Church records should be securely kept, regardless of the size of the church. The clerk of the church has charge of the church constitution with amendments up to date, the church roll, and minutes of church meetings. The denominational publishing houses have excellent record books for all purposes, and they should be used. The financial secretary and the treasurer keep the financial records of the church in their homes. Each officer turns all materials over to his successor.

It is wise to provide a suitable place for the safe keeping of old records. It would be well, in many cases, for the church to rent a safe-deposit box in the local bank for the storage of valuable records. Another plan is the installation of a small fireproof safe in the church office. Also, historical libraries operated by states, counties, local communities, and religious denominations, are glad to provide safe-keeping for very old records. These records, the history of the church, are valuable, and never should be lost.

The minister's study and office may be likened to a hydroelectric generating plant which serves a vital area. It is in the plant that the waters are impounded, directed through turbines, and transformed into electrical power. The power is then sent out over the wires to schools, factories, business houses, and a million homes. It is used to turn the wheels of industry. Even so the study and office may represent the spiritual generating plant of the community. If knowledge and spiritual insights are not impounded, transferred into power, and distributed to the community, nothing will happen and the community may become spiritually bankrupt.

XXIII

THE MINISTER GOES CALLING

THE TIME THAT A PASTOR gives to calling on the people is next in importance to the time he spends in his study. The most effective churches are those in which the pastor purposefully calls on the people, learns at first hand their hopes and frustrations, then ministers accordingly. Some pastors have neglected this time-honored practice and as a result their work has lost much of its effectiveness.

There are two basic reasons for making a pastoral call. A minister calls in the homes because of what he can do to and for people. He is charged by Christ to take care of the Christians, to bind up their wounds and inspire them to purposeful living. He is also charged to win the unconverted. These things he can do best, as the New Testament leaders did, by calling on the people where they are, in the market places or in their homes. There is a great gap between laboring people and the church. The only way this gap can be bridged is for the clergy to go into their homes and their places of work. This is going out to the highways and hedges, and compelling people to come in (cf. Luke 14:23).

The second reason for making the pastoral call lies in what the call contributes to the pastor himself. To be a successful pastor the minister must keep "green." He cannot do this by the reading of books alone. He cannot do it by remaining in the study, important as the study is. He can do it only by calling on people in their homes, in their places of business, and during both their work and their play, learning from them how they react to life situations. Every call is an educational experience for the visiting minister. For example, he may read many books and theorize until doomsday about the poor, miserable sharecroppers, migrant laborers, or Navajo Indians, but he begins to know them only when he visits their shacks and receives their timid invitations to sit at their tables to meals of fat pork, corn bread, and sorghum molasses. As he sits in the midst of their poverty, and sometimes filth, he becomes aware of how they live and how dispirited they are. He may see glimmering a faint glow of hope which, in spite of the poverty and dirt, has not been extinguished. Perhaps he can remember that it was said of Christ "he will not break a bruised reed or quench a smoldering wick" (Matt. 12:20). After such an experience, the sermon of a true minister of Jesus Christ will take on a new poignancy and depth. Henceforth any program which he advocates will be different, for it will be tempered with understanding and compassion.

At the other end of the social scale are the rich people. They look happy, sleek, and contented as they pass on the streets and are seen in church. They are often envied by the poor. It may be that they are happy. But in their homes the minister learns that the rich and proud may be very lonely too. He discovers frustrations therein which are not to be found even in sharecroppers' homes. Sometimes he finds blasted hopes, with contemplated suicide only a few months or weeks away. These poor people, so rich in worldly goods, also need the ministry of the man of God. He learns from both the hungry poor and the heartsick rich that he must make of himself a herald of the good news of Jesus Christ.

TYPES OF PASTORAL CALLS

There are different types of pastoral calls, and one cannot handle any two in quite the same way. The first type of pastoral call may be named the introductory call. A church has a reception for its new pastor and his family, and he tries to remember as many names as possible. Soon afterward, it is necessary for him to call on all the members for the primary purpose of becoming acquainted with them and their families. He should visit not only the members but all of the church's known constituency; i.e., all those families that are enrolled in any auxiliary of the church. It is an excellent procedure for the senior deacon or some other member to accompany the pastor on these calls to introduce him to the people. After a census has been taken, and a full list of the church's constituency compiled, those not called on previously should receive visits from the pastor and perhaps also from lay members.

As new people move into the parish the pastor should be one of the first to call on them and welcome them to the church's activities. If the deacons and others will keep him informed of changes in their neighborhoods it will enable him to be the first representative of any agency in the community to call on a new family. Because the introductory call is for the purpose of establishing a link between the new pastor and the people of church and community, the minister's wife may, if convenient, accompany her husband on the call. Usually the minister is wise in not taking his children.

The introductory call does not necessitate Bible reading and prayer. However, if the conversation develops during the first call so that these seem natural and logical, one or both may be used. It is always prudent to be prepared beforehand for such Bible reading, but also to avoid anything that might cause a strained atmosphere. The minister is calling to become acquainted and to prepare the way for many future calls as he leads this family in the Christian way. To do this he should make every word pleasant, meaningful, and free from controversy.

A second type of call is made for the purpose of keeping in touch with all the people. Here, for example, stands a church at the center of the community. Although some people attend the church services almost every Sunday, others almost never attend. To be sure, meager contacts may be made by letters, bulletins and the newspapers, but these are seldom adequate. In order to keep in touch with all of the people a pastor must go into their homes often, and through his personality and his interest in them make them aware of the church's concern. To do this, he must be of some service to them when he calls. The least he can do is to read the Scriptures and pray for them according to their needs.

On these calls the pastor must seek diligently for ways and means of bringing the people into the fullest possible relationship with God and the church. Though he must not hurry them, his ultimate aim is the complete surrender of every member of the household to Jesus Christ. He is seeking to lead his people to a better practice of the Christian faith. He will use any honorable means that will draw their interest to Christ and the church. If it seems timely he will introduce some biblical thought into the conversation and close the visit with a sincere prayer for the family. If his acquaintance has been of such length that he can do it freely, he will in his prayer mention each member of the household by name, especially those who are in military service, at college, sick, or away from home for any other reason. On some of these calls the minister's wife, by her personality and interest in feminine things, can be of great help to the church. There are a few situations where, for her husband's protection, she most assuredly should call. However, there are some cases in which she should not accompany him. A sensitive pastor will recognize these.

There comes a time in the ministry of every pastor, as in the work of a farmer, when he is privileged to harvest his crop. He has been preaching to people. Young people have shared their experiences with him in youth meetings. Children have been instructed in the Sunday school sessions. He has married young couples. Death has come into some of the homes and he has officiated at the funerals. Through these experiences he has been privileged to converse intimately with his people. He has been sowing seeds and praying that there might be a good harvest. How heedless it would be if he did not attempt a harvest! This is accomplished as the faithful minister calls on individuals and patiently seeks to lead them to a commitment to Jesus Christ as their Lord. Because this method is personal, better and more lasting results are obtained by it than by holding a series of revival services where the entire congregation is addressed at once. If a pastor is keenly aware of what is happening around him and is faithful in his task of calling, decisions will be made for Christ throughout the whole year, although a heavier harvest may be expected at such seasons as Christmas, Easter, and Pentecost. Here again the technique of the call will be planned according to the needs of each individual. From previous calls the pastor has a picture of the spiritual condition of the person he is seeking to win, and he deals with this person in the light of these facts. It is seldom advisable for the minister's wife to accompany him on evangelistic calls, for privacy is needed at such times.

Occasionally a minister needs to call upon his people for business reasons. Let us assume there is some problem or project in the church that needs the attention of the brethren. Sometimes it can be introduced into a business meeting without previous preparation, and often this is the best procedure. But frequently it is sensible for the pastor to inform the brethren individually of a problem and help them to search carefully for its solution. Perhaps there are a number of things they would like to say to him which they might not want to say in an open meeting. The pastor may even consider it to be appropriate to plant a few seeds in their minds. For example, let us suppose that the pastor wishes to promote interest in a good work. He will think out, before calling, how he can best go about this. Why should they be interested? What can they get from its successful accomplishment? What part should each one play in the project? In the light of this reasoning, and as tactfully and winsomely as possible, he makes his approach to the people. This kind of work can usually be done most efficiently if the minister is not accompanied by his wife.

Whenever there is sickness or death in a home, the pastor is expected to call and offer his spiritual help, hope, and consolation. Although it is impossible to offer a full discussion of pastoral counseling in this book, it should be pointed out that the more the pastor knows about the relationship between physical illness and spiritual maladjustment, the better. He should try to keep abreast of the latest ideas and findings in the fascinating fields of mental illness and psychosomatic medicine.

Before calling upon a sick person the minister should explore his own mind as well as his written records, that he may be familiar with every aspect of the patient's life and attitudes toward God and his fellow men. During the call there may be a brief conversation in which the patient does most of the talking, the pastor asking a few pointed questions. Gradually a pattern of the patient's real need develops in the pastor's mind, and he analyzes the situation as quickly as he can. Perhaps the sick one is harboring some guilt, enmity, or anger. Perhaps a prayer of confession asking for forgiveness is in order. God will not forgive a patient's sin until the patient has forgiven those who have sinned against him. The minister therefore offers a Bible reading, a cogent statement, and a prayer that will help restore the person's faith in God and in his fellow men. Often when some spiritual maladjustment is erased the accompanying physical illness may be cleared up or alleviated. The minister can thus work hand-in-hand with the medical doctor.

As the medical profession moves more and more of its patients into hospitals, the minister will find that he must make many hospital calls. Here, as in the home, he will attempt to minister to the spiritual needs of the patient, using the Bible and prayer as the spirit leads. Knowing beforehand whom he will see, he will prepare his mind and heart before calling.

Soon after settling in a field, the minister should become acquainted with the supervisor and head nurses of the nearest hospital or hospitals. Only in extreme emergencies will he ask them to exempt him from the rules which they have established. If the minister's techniques are right and he is helpful in the recovery of patients, the hospital staff will heartily welcome him to the hospital. If on the contrary he makes a nuisance of himself and hinders the recovery of the patients he may find the doors gently but firmly closed in his face. Moreover, if he establishes right relations with the hospital officers they will repay him for his thoughtfulness by notifying him of patients that need his care. Sometimes these will be his own parishioners who reached the hospital without his knowledge and sometimes they will be strangers without a well-defined religious background. A friendly head nurse who informs him of their presence is rendering a helpful service both to the patients and the minister. He will always express his appreciation for this courtesy.

Some cautions are to be observed by the minister as he deals with the sick. He must remember that he is the minister and that his area is that of the spiritual adviser. He must remember that there is a real place for the medical doctor and the psychiatrist, and that he is neither of these. Never is it his privilege to recommend a different physician from the one chosen by the family, and never may he prescribe or suggest the use of any favorite medicines or drugs. The pastor should attend to his own area of responsibility, then promptly leave. Usually he can accomplish his task more efficiently and completely if his wife does not accompany him.

The minister should immediately call in any home in his area where death has entered and the home is not served by some other minister. He can do little except express his sympathy, sincerely and briefly, to the bereaved. If he is to conduct the funeral services, he should talk over the arrangements with the proper persons. Then he should close his visit with a prayer that God's blessings may rest upon the family, if this can be done gracefully. It is often true that silence is better than much speaking.

Although it is seldom proper for the pastor's wife to accompany her husband on sick calls, it seems to be very much in order for her to accompany him to a bereaved home if the family is well-known to both the minister and wife. She may be able to offer some words of comfort or communicate an attitude of sympathy more effectively than her husband can. Her presence will also be helpful in preventing a bereaved woman from showing unseemly attachment to the minister who has consoled her in time of sorrow.

As more and more small business establishments and industries come into town-country areas, an increasing number of town-country people earn their livelihood in the industries rather than on the farms. Already the minister has learned to call at the farms; why should he not, by the same reasoning, call at the places where the men work? He may go into all the legitimate business houses and industries of the community at least twice a year. He should become acquainted with the managers and with the men and women who work under them. He will learn their names, and greet them by name on subsequent calls and whenever he sees them on the streets. Nothing sounds so good to a person as his own name.

When calling in small plants, the minister will be careful to make his presence first known to the man in charge and determine whether or not he is welcome to enter the factory. Naturally, it is helpful to be on the best of terms with him. Then the minister walks through the shop with him and speaks here and there to the workers. A few questions at a machine as to what it is and how it works are in order. A word of greeting and cheer to each workman will not be amiss. But the minister must remember that these workers are being paid by the hour and that it costs money to operate modern machines and tools. Therefore he should not take up the time in any unnecessary conversation. The important thing is to let the laboring men and their supervisors know that he is interested in them. This kind of call may open the way for bringing whole families under the influence of the church.

When the industrial call is nearing its end, the minister may stop briefly in the office of the manager who may be a Christian, even a member of the minister's church. If the minister has noticed something in the factory that appeals to him as thoughtful and helpful to the men, it would be excellent strategy to compliment the manager on it. Being human, he will appreciate it.

The men who manage industries are harassed by pressure from two directions. Labor pushes for rights and privileges on the one hand; stockholders push for profits and larger output on the other. It is not an enviable spot in which to work. Many managers are striving to conduct their shops along Christian lines. In the office of the manager, the minister may well close the interview with a few words of prayer to the end that God's blessing may be upon such a man as he strives to do Christ's will in his shop. After the second or third call, the manager may want to discuss some of his problems with the minister who cares enough to call at his shop. In many cases industry has expressed a need for chaplains, and some businesses have their own chaplains. In town-country situations, alert and understanding pastors will supply this need without being hired by industry.

In the town-country area, the public schools provide a means of reaching people. The small, one-room school is still in existence in many parts of our country. It will continue in some places for many years. A minister misses an opportunity to be of service to his community if he fails to call regularly in these schools. The teacher may be a young girl in her first teaching position, frightened as she faces a roomful of children, five days a week for eight or nine months. She may be lonesome and very homesick. If the local pastor calls for a few minutes just before school closes in the afternoon and remains for ten or fifteen minutes to chat with her, he may give just the attention she needs to bolster her courage and help her through the year. Moreover, such a call may be the means of aligning the school and teacher with the church. It is humbling to a minister to remember that this teacher will be before her pupils as much in one week as the minister himself will be in a whole year. To win her confidence and respect is good strategy. To win her to Christ and church, is a victory for the kingdom.

After a call in a school, the minister may be invited to speak at a P.T.A. meeting. He should accept the invitation, for it may give him the opportunity to touch the lives of ten times as many people as he would reach at a prayer meeting.

Let the minister also go calling in the consolidated grade schools and in the high schools, and become acquainted with the principal and all the teachers. If they ask for any co-operation he should go the second mile to give it. If the minister is chary of criticism and prodigal of compliments it may surprise him how the attitude of the school community will change in his favor.

FURTHER TECHNIQUES

Notwithstanding the fact that several types of calls have been named and their techniques touched upon briefly, there are some additional suggestions which will be found to be practical. A pastor may go into a home, business, or school for a specific reason. He may find the people saying they are glad to see him, and then have them talk endlessly and rapidly about nothing. They may do this quite innocently. On the other hand, they may be exerting a quickly-planned strategy to prevent the minister from coming to the point of his call. Then the minister must tactfully guide the conversation in the way he wants it to go, striving to accomplish his purpose or purposes. How is he going to do this? He will need to be much in prayer even as he talks. He will need to know, completely and intimately, the people. He may need to use artful techniques to keep the reins of conversation in his own hands.

In evangelistic and stewardship campaigns, the illustrated turn-over chart has proven to be a valuable adjunct to the caller. This device may be used for more things than evangelism and money raising, and the resourceful minister will not miss the opportunity to adapt and use it in many types of calling.

One of the quickest ways for a minister to ruin his effectiveness in the community is by talebearing. If he gossips he will not be welcome in the homes of the parish. There are some people who will unceasingly question and cross-examine the pastor about the affairs of their neighbors. The minister must not yield to the pressure of their curiosity. Whatever he learns in any home is to be regarded as a strictly private possession which is not to be shared. If the minister finds it necessary to speak of any one he must be sure that what he says is both good and true, something he would be glad for them to know he said.

It is a strange quirk of human nature that some church members, and others too, are glad when the church is not doing well. The earnest minister will not add to their joy by telling them how badly the brethren treat him and how poorly his best efforts are being rewarded. Expressions of self pity or criticism of the church will do no good and may do much harm. Surely there is something good in the church program that a minister can talk about. He may speak of his hopes and dreams for the future. He may sell them on the positive, constructive features of the church's faith and program.

How strange it would seem if the plumber called to stem the cause of a flooded basement did not use his tools, or the doctor in a sickroom did not open his bag. It would be equally strange for the minister to call in the place of spiritual need and not use the Bible and prayer. The Bible is a greater book than its most ardent readers know it to be. It deals with all of the basic problems which confront mankind today. The minister, therefore, should carefully plan his use of the Scriptures as he prepares his calls. By so doing, when he comes to the closing moments of his call he will be in a position either to read, or better still, to quote some gem of Scripture that will bring light to a darkened mind and soul. The Bible should be used not only to end a call. If correction and enlightenment are needed it should be introduced early into the conversation as a basis for the discussion. During the evangelistic call it may be the basis for the major portion of the conversation.

Although there are a few situations in which it is wise for the pastor to take his wife with him when he calls, it is usually a disadvantage for him to be accompanied either by her or by his children. There are those who would try to extract from her some bit of gossip which they could not learn from the minister himself. Moreover, if she is carrying her part of the responsibility for the productive home she will be busy enough. Much as the minister may love his children, they, too, can be a source of disruption during a pastoral call. The minister is a professional man and people are reticent about conferring with him on intimate, personal, and spiritual matters in the presence of his family.

There will come a time when some members of the church will invite the pastor to bring his family and spend a day with them. The minister accepts such an invitation, of course, unless there are previous engagements of greater importance. He rearranges his work so as to get it all done on time, and takes the day or half day for this pleasant social call. It may be a deeply enriching experience. Although not many days can be spent this way, a few may be so used to good advantage.

It is easy for the minister to call in the homes, talk pleasantly with the lady of the house and then be on his way with another call marked to his credit. But for the sake of propriety it is better and more profitable for the minister to stop first where he knows the men are to be found. As he visits with them in their barns and fields, he may even pick up a tool and work with them. This approach will go far toward discouraging the idea that the church is run by women. Perhaps a neglect of the men is the reason for many churches being run and attended mostly by the women. The men will not be won by the minister calling on their wives.

The Protestant minister has a good reputation. This may be regarded as a double compliment when it is known how many possibilities for straying from the straight and narrow way are placed before him. Hardly another man in the community has the freedom and access to the homes of the people that he enjoys. Therefore, he should guard that honor and abstain from the very appearance of evil. Some ministers tell risqué stories, especially when they are in the company of men. Mistakenly, they imagine that this will cause them to be looked upon as "good fellows." Actually, when the minister tells an off-color story he is lowered in the hearer's estimation and he has lost a strategic advantage which he previously held. No matter what the nature or place of the call may be, the minister must strive to uphold the dignity of the cloth by his every word and act.

XXIV

PREACHING THE GOSPEL

PREACHING IS VITALLY SIGNIFICANT. Through the 1900 years of the Christian era, preaching has been and still is considered to be a highly important religious act. Much good has come from it, and it must not be minimized. In the Old Testament there are numerous references to preaching. The writer of Psalms 40:9 says "I have told the glad news of deliverance in the great congregation." Because the word "preach" means to discourse or speak on a religious subject, it would be impossible to think that Noah and his sons could build the ark and be surrounded by curious people without discoursing on religion. The prophets preached with a very deep sense of urgency. They saw that unless there was genuine repentance the nation would fall and the wrath of God would descend upon the people of Israel.

In the New Testament, preaching gave evidence of a new power and glory. Jesus went about teaching and preaching. The dusty road, the side of the well, the mountain side, and the fisherman's boat were pulpits for his sermons. On the day of Pentecost, when Peter and the other apostles preached, three thousand souls professed faith in Christ. Although not all the credit should be given to this one sermonic effort, it did serve to bring in a rich harvest after three years of the Master's work. There were yet other harvests to come by preaching. All the apostles preached from time to time. So did the deacons. Indeed, Christians who were scattered because of persecution in that first century went about preaching the word.

PREACHING IS EFFECTIVE

Why is preaching important? Why has God ordained that it have such an important part in the extension of his kingdom? It is because the human voice, reinforced by Christian personality, is mighty to change lives. Those who, out of curiosity, have listened to speakers have sometimes changed their whole way of thinking and acting. Napoleon could win hardened soldiers with but a few words. They died for him by the thousands. When Hitler addressed the multitudes they were as putty in his hands. Former President Franklin Delano Roosevelt had similar qualities. Amid the sharpest national emergencies he gave his fireside chats, and the whole nation was calmed. In such cases the listener's change in attitude came not because of logic or new thoughts, for often the logic was false and the arguments timeworn. But there were qualities in the voices and personalities of these men that swayed millions for better or worse.

Preaching is important as a means of guiding religious thinking. How else can the people be guided? To be sure, the influence of a good example is significant. But an example alone, without words which explain it, is not enough. Preaching explains and reinforces the good example of Christian living. Too few people read the Bible as they should, and even if they did they would still need a preacher to set forth the meanings and to enlarge upon and explain many passages.

Moreover, preaching is a way of generating faith within others. Faith is contagious. When the preacher witnesses to his faith, through preaching, many who hear him believe. Thus the faith professed is passed from one generation to the next through preaching.

Better preaching in town-country pulpits will do much toward bringing about the changes that are needed for more wholesome living. The needed preaching is not to be confused with some of the nice homilies delivered in American churches today. Neither is it to consist of pointless storytelling, moral lessons, and long appeals to accept Christ. The stronger preaching will include fundamental doctrines and much biblical material. Preaching alone may not bring about the needed changes, but it will help.

PREACHING REQUIRES PREPARATION

A second major emphasis is that good preaching calls for intense preparation. Voluble speakers do not, *ipso facto,* make good preachers. Not shallow babbling brooks, but deep-flowing rivers carry the traffic of the nations. The lack of preparation accounts for much poor preaching. Preaching worthy of its place in the Christian ministry calls for intense preparation of at least three kinds.

The first kind of preparation for preaching is the care of the body. The minister who is overly tired, anemic, overweight, physically frustrated, or otherwise sick does not preach convincingly, however well and thoroughly he has studied. It takes physical strength as well as mental and spiritual strength to preach well. This problem would be simplified if the only work required of the minister were to stand in the pulpit and preach. However, the preparation of sermons, the pastoral care of the people, and the holding of many organizational meetings take their toll of strength. The body, like any other instrument, must be in good condition. Although this book does not pretend to be a treatise on health, a few basic rules can be given.

Do not pamper the body. It is fearfully, wonderfully, and efficiently made. It can adjust itself to many things, and as it adjusts it grows stronger. It need not be shielded from every wind that blows.

Be temperate. Some ministers who would be horrified at the thought of taking liquor into their bodies commit the same basic sin by eating, playing, or working intemperately. Recent health reports indicate that as many as 40 per cent of American adults are more than 10 per cent overweight. This fact is probably one reason for the high incidence of heart diseases. The preacher should be temperate even in his eating habits before he preaches temperance to others.

Eat wholesome food. By wholesome is meant a balanced diet with meat, cereals, vegetables, and fruits; food grown in soil that has the elements needed for the making of nutritious foods; and food with little refinement and cooking.

Work and play. Be sure to do both if you would remain healthy. Sometimes preachers boast that they must work seven days a week. No man is indispensable. Such a boaster is either a poor organizer, or feeble minded, or he harbors an overweening sense of his own importance. If any man would do effective work, and keep his body strong, he must balance his work with play.

Get enough sleep. The preacher, like other men, needs about eight hours of sleep out of every twenty-four. If this cannot be secured in one unbroken stretch one or two brief naps during the day should be utilized to make up the deficiency. Even with eight hours of sleep a night, a quarter of an hour's relaxation at noon, or before the evening's activities, will renew the strength and sharpen the wits.

Walk whenever possible. If the home where you should call is a mile or more into the country, go on foot. When a person walks his head should be kept up and his chin tucked into an imaginary high collar. This holds the abdomen in and causes a man to walk uprightly and with dignity, as his Creator intended him to walk.

Thinking should accompany walking. Every bird, flower, tree, and sound should be identified. Meanwhile, such problems as sermon texts, illustrations, and how to deal with the subject of your call can be solved. The ideas which thus come will prove far superior to the third-hand thoughts and illustrations which might be gathered from books. To walk to a pastoral call is a means for improving health, for developing serenity of spirit, and for solving problems, all of which help to make for better preaching.

Learn to forget. If the preceding rules are conscientiously followed the minister may dismiss all thoughts of the state of his body from further consideration until such time as something calls itself to his attention. God has made the human body so that it can carry on and do the work it should do with a minimum of trouble. When given a chance it will hold in reserve, and then expend at the proper time, all the energy necessary for good pulpit work.

A second kind of preparation for preaching is to give attention to the development of the mind. That which goes into the mind will eventually come out in preaching and in conversation. If the minister lives on mental rubbish, it will eventually appear in trashy preaching. He must force his mind to work through study, observation, and the reading of good literature. The best preaching comes from wide reading and close observation of conditions in the parish. He must never preach what he himself does not believe, for such preaching has a hollow sound.

Eventually every preacher must find his own best way of preparing sermons. When he has discovered that way, he should stay with it and develop it to the point where it serves him well. Many good preachers have found nothing to be more effective than writing the sermon in full previous to preaching it. When this method is employed the sermon themes must be selected well in advance of the preaching dates. Six months ahead is not too long a time for their selection. The themes should be reviewed daily so that they are kept freshly in mind. As the preacher then goes about his daily reading, he will have relevant thoughts which he should jot down on cards or slips of paper. Illustrations will appear from the most unexpected places. Some of them may be quite original. These, too, should be jotted down before they are forgotten, and properly filed for the time of actual writing of the sermon.

On the Monday preceding the Sunday when a particular sermon is to be delivered, the preacher intensifies his reading in the field of his sermon subject. On Wednesday, or Thursday at the latest, with all the necessary reading done, the sermon is carefully outlined. On Friday the actual writing of the sermon from introduction through the conclusion is completed. On Friday night the sermon is laid aside, not to be seen again until Sunday morning. At that time it is read aloud. Notes are made on 3 x 5 cards, poetry that has not been memorized is copied, and the preacher is ready to preach. This order of sermon preparation calls for discipline, but it produces sermons that far excel any that might hurriedly be thrown together on Friday or Saturday.

The mind must not be under pressure all of the time. It often works best when it seems not to work at all. There must be periods of rest, of apparent mental idleness, during which the mind, unhampered by imposed duties, has a chance to wander and dream. This, too, is thinking. Here is an additional reason for seriously encouraging recreational pursuits as well as pastoral calling in sermon preparation. Moreover, it is a further argument for the productive home, for this daily gives the mind a period for rest, and perhaps for thought.

The third kind of preparation for preaching is in the realm of the spirit. Sermons with the ring of divine authority do not come from men who neglect prayer and meditation. Neither do they come from men who do not practice, with patience, the teachings of Jesus as found in the Sermon on the Mount. Men can effectively preach love only when they themselves love. Men can effectively preach forgiveness only when they themselves forgive. An unloving and unforgiving pastor has little to offer his people. Unless he loves the people he is a noisy gong or a clanging cymbal, regardless of how much preparation he has made in body and mind. Intensive spiritual preparation for preaching is made when the preacher walks by faith each day. Does he walk by faith in regard to his physical care? In solving his problems? In launching his work?

THE CONTENT OF PREACHING

Valid preaching presupposes the leadership of the Holy Spirit. The Holy Spirit is active in ways men do not always understand. He may inspire the discovery of atomic energy, the unifying of Europe, and the nationalist movements of Asia, the Near East, and Africa. He may well be in the desegregation movement in the United States. Many phases of the revival our grandparents prayed for are now being realized in the earth. In answer to their prayers the Holy Spirit is moving with power in this generation.

Jesus promised: "But the Counselor, the Holy Spirit, whom the Father will send in my name, will teach you all things, and bring to your remembrance all that I have said to you. And I will pray the Father, and he will give you another Counselor, to be with you for ever, even the Spirit of truth" (John 14:26, 16-17). Did Jesus mean that this Spirit should be "the Spirit of truth" in one area only, or in all the perplexities of life? Surely in all the perplexities. Here then are two definite promises: The Comforter will be given to Christ's followers; and he shall teach them, for he is "the Spirit of truth." These two promises should mean much to the town-country preacher who is supposedly cut off from the main stream of culture.

Not everything that suddenly comes to mind is necessarily the teaching of the Holy Spirit. Ministers are on solid ground when they raise questions about the activities of the Holy Spirit, for it is written: "Beloved, do not believe every spirit, but test the spirits to see whether they are of God; for many false prophets have gone out into the world" (1 John 4:1). Authenticity of the leadership of the Holy Spirit may be ascertained by a careful study of the Scriptures. It is well to ask: "Does the message I am about to preach reflect the teaching of the Scriptures?" If a secure and unforced base for an action or thought cannot be found in the Scriptures, it should not be uttered until there is a more direct leading.

On the spur of the moment or in an emergency the Spirit does not fail Christ's servant. Neither does he fail to lead in planning long ahead. In fact, he is honored when ministers plan their work far enough ahead to permit their limited bodies and minds to catch up with his leading.

Before leaving this subject we may be reminded of the words "Do not quench the Spirit" (1 Thess. 5:19). After the minister has earnestly sought the leadership of the Holy Spirit, has tested and proven "the spirits," and has before him that which he has written and which he believes to be the Word of the Lord for this occasion, he comes to the hour of the delivery of the sermon. He looks over the assembly and is dismayed to see some parishioners whose presence he had not anticipated. Or perhaps there are denominational or political dignitaries in the congregation. He suddenly feels that he cannot preach so simple or direct a message to so distinguished and discerning an audience.

Is it not possible that, while the Holy Spirit was active in his life, he was also active in these other lives and now he has brought all the parties concerned together? His best plan is to preach that sermon in all kindness and love, and leave the results to the Holy Spirit.

Town-country preaching calls for speaking to the mind and heart of the congregation. A minister should never underestimate the mentality of town-country people. They are accustomed to thinking in concrete, practical patterns. They have problems and they solve them. They do not panic. They take reverses in stride as something to be expected. The man who attempts to preach condescendingly to these people will probably soon be looking for another place to preach. They are worthy of a minister's best thinking. He need not fear thinking too deeply for them. His real problem is to put the message in language they understand. Greek is best left in the study, along with any semiscientific jargon that happens to be popular at the moment.

The use of illustrations from nature, from community life, (as long as they are not personal, and do not cast reflections upon any), and from the daily chores will open town-country minds to the minister's thoughts. Town-country folks are quite responsive to stories from nature. Jesus illustrated eternal principles with simple nature stories. The minister has much to learn from his nature parables.

Preaching to the mind is only a part of the minister's task. He must also preach to the heart. There are times when the preacher needs to stir deeply the emotions of his congregation. It is like plowing deep and stirring up the subsoil of the soul. There is a place in preaching for tears, for laughter, and for righteous indignation.

Town-country people have problems. The minister need not conjure up theoretical problems out of nothing. If he deals with the every-day problems of the people he will have enough material for his sermons.

Problems should be dealt with in the idealistic terms of the New Testament rather than in the rationalizations of the world. For example, Christians have rationalized their conduct in every war. Yet, the Master said ". . . all who take the sword will perish by the sword" (Matt. 26:52); and "Love your enemies" (Matt. 5:44).

Men often rationalize their conduct in order to excuse what they want to do. In a certain church most of the members, the town's leading citizens, worked for a distillery. At no time did the preacher speak out against the liquor interests. It is the Master's ideas that should be preached in love, for in the final analysis it is not what the minister thinks about this or that problem, but what the Word of the Lord says that really matters.

There probably is no social problem of our day that is not directly or indirectly dealt with in the Scriptures. Newspapers, magazines, radio, and television commentators are continually giving to the public their views on social problems. Their suggestions are shaded by their prejudices, their sponsors, and the nature of the products they are trying to sell. They are not idealistic in a Christian sense. But people today need to hear what the Bible says. Therefore the preacher must exalt the Christian idealism of the Bible as he deals with the problems of life. After all, the Bible in its most radically idealistic statements is more genuinely realistic than the hardheaded businessman or the cynical militarist.

People seldom make sweeping changes in their thinking and conduct after only one presentation of the facts. Even though a sermon may be logical and beautifully delivered, those who hear the truth for the first time are not likely to make radical alterations in their manner of living because of it. Much repetition of the same truth is essential. This is the method used by modern advertisers to induce people to buy things which they do not need nor want, and for which they do not have the money. Hidden persuaders hammer away on the consciousness of the public through every conceivable means, again and again, and sales mount. Dr. Harry Emerson Fosdick practiced this in his preaching. He would take one thought and present it three times in three different ways. Such an effective pattern in preaching was used by Phillips Brooks, Alexander Whyte, C. H. Spurgeon, H. S. Coffin, and George Truett. Town-country people do not shift easily from one position to another. It takes constant repetition to induce them to change their modes of thinking or ways of doing.

There is need for giants in town-country pulpits. The emerging town-country community with its unparalleled opportunities for building a Christian civilization demands constructive leadership from the pulpits of the land. Preaching is one of the great arts. The minister may profitably devote much time and effort to practicing it. He will be richly repaid for all the time he gives to perfecting his sermonic skill.

XXV

ETIQUETTE, FUNERALS, AND WEDDINGS

A CHURCH IS KNOWN by its minister's behavior. In his own mind he may minimize the importance of his conduct, but those who see and hear him do not minimize it. It seems fair to observe that the most apparent way in which the world can appraise Christ's work is by the conduct of his ministers.

The first place for the display of good manners is in the home. For an institution to prosper, or even to survive, there must be some authority guiding it. The biblical concept of the Christian household is that the husband, the father, shall be the human authority.[1] This does not call for dictatorial decrees, changed with every veering breeze, to coerce the family members. It does allow for careful thought and discussion by man, wife, and children, followed by a proper ruling which will be enforced. It is not wise for children to be permitted to do as they please. This is the father-minister's responsibility, aided, of course, by his wife.

On the whole, minister's families seem to be well-behaved. Occasionally some minister fails to discipline (teach) his household. When a few fail, the entire profession is blamed. Children of the parsonage should be an illustration of healthy boys and girls growing normally into useful adulthood. They are not, and should not pretend to be, paragons of virtue. No more should be expected of them than is expected of children of other Christian households. But occasionally a father feels that because he is the minister his children should be a model for

[1] Ephesians 5:22-24.

other children of the community. They are, therefore, denied participation in innocent and borderline school and community activities. In the long run this restriction may do more harm to the spiritual and moral development of the minister's children than any wholesomeness it may engender as an example to the community. The children must not be exploited to advance the professional standing of the father. They should be reared in a normal, wholesome atmosphere where courtesy, truthfulness, and cheerful self-discipline are accepted standards of conduct. The parental aim should be for the children to grow as Jesus grew, "in wisdom and in stature, and in favor with God and man" (Luke 2:52).

The first social responsibility of the minister is the feeding, clothing, and housing of his family. These he will be expected to do on a restricted budget. He need not be discouraged at this, for most people live and work on restricted budgets. By careful management and the wholehearted co-operation of all concerned in productive home activities his family may be dressed in good taste, his home substantially furnished, and wholesome food made available for every meal. What more does he need?

In another chapter recreation will be discussed at considerable length. It is only referred to here to say that in some areas of the nation the prevailing culture forbids certain practices that are in good taste elsewhere. Usually it is best for the minister's family to abide by the local mores until the family is well enough established to venture to change them. Conforming in this way is not hypocritical, but is only being thoughtful of the feelings of others.

GOOD MANNERS IN CHURCH

The second place for the display of good manners is in the church. The minister's relationship toward the members must receive his careful consideration. These are the people who have hired him to discipline, instruct, and lead them in their spiritual growth. If he does not please them he may be dismissed. But sometimes if he pleases them he may displease God. What should be his attitude toward the church members when caught in such a dilemma?

Good manners require that the minister be courteous to every member of the church. Life is not so short but that there is always time for courtesy. The members of the congregation are God's children. Every one of them, however imperfect, belongs to God. Indeed, they may be no more imperfect than the man who assumes to discipline them. This the minister must always remember, that he may remain humble. Members of most churches are accustomed to handling their own business affairs, making decisions, and getting along with people. For the minister to assume that he must make all the decisions in the church, and tell the members how to conduct every step of their business and civic life is to be discourteous to them.

There is something about a high-powered automobile that seems to bring out the worst side of people's characters. An automobile driver has a ton and a half of steel, powered by a 300-horsepower motor, in his power. If for one moment this juggernaut runs out of control it may take the lives of innocent people and destroy much property. Insurance can replace the property, but it will not replace lost lives or relieve the suffering of mangled bodies. The minister can show rare courtesy by the way he drives his automobile.

To be a good pastor, a minister must be in position to receive the confessions of the people. Since in Protestantism there is no priestly confessional, the people must seek out a confessor in whom they can confide and from whom they may seek guidance. If they believe the minister will keep in confidence that which they tell him, they will seek him out and bare their souls to him. Such trust must never be violated.

It is almost impossible for a minister to have a uniform relationship with all members of his church. Even Jesus had an inner circle among the disciples. This raises the problem as to whether or not a minister should make close friends of some members. If he stays on a field for a considerable period of time it is almost impossible for him and his family not to have close friendships with some church members. Some have tried to solve the problem by making close friends only outside the membership of the church. This casts a reflection upon the members as if to imply that they would be unworthy as friends. Others have said that, while the minister is the friend of all,

he himself has no close friends. For a few this may be the answer to pastoral friendship inside and outside the church.
Friendships within the church need not be detrimental to the
pastor's ministry, provided he does not neglect any member
of the congregation in his work. Although he regards some as
friends, he must not show partiality. Indeed there is danger
that he may even overlook his ministerial duty to his friends
and fail to counsel them wisely when they need him most.

A minister has contact with many people, some of whom are
Christians with shades of belief different from his own people's,
and some who are not Christians. His conduct toward them
will go a long way in lifting or lowering the church he serves
in the estimation of the community.

To reaffirm and enlarge upon the previous thoughts on courtesy it should be noted that no man or woman is so insignificant
or degraded that he is unworthy of courtesy from the minister.
All are potential children of God for whom Christ died. Be
courteous. Be kind. Such conduct may be the means by which
the Holy Spirit will convict sinners of their sins. There are
other people who are intellectual snobs, or financial bores.
Again, courtesy may be the Holy Spirit's warm method of melt-
ing hearts of stone or misunderstanding.

For most ministers whether to join lodges and service clubs
is a personal choice, although some denominations deny their
ministers this privilege. There is something to be gained in
social contacts if a minister belongs to a good service club or
fraternal order, provided he does not neglect other features
of his work. But there is much to be lost if he forgets his position and stoops to conduct beneath the dignity of the cloth.
Occasionally a club will sponsor some community activity
which is contrary to the ethics of the church and which may
reflect adversely upon the minister. At such a time the minister may, with courtesy, but firmly, voice his objections to the
project, stating clearly why he objects. As he grows in the estimation of his fellow club members, he may find that they will
refrain from planning objectionable pursuits. Certainly, every
minister should belong to the local ministerial association and
do what he can to promote co-operatively the kingdom work.
He cannot, however, commit his church without its permission.

COURTESY TO OTHERS

It is never seemly for a clergyman to criticize other servants of the Lord within or outside his denomination. As long as there are diverse backgrounds in the Christian framework there will be ministers whose personal habits differ from one another. Some may smoke freely; some will partake of alcoholic drinks; others will shun not only tobacco, but will look askance at coffee, tea, or some soft drinks. Many such differences are more cultural than theological in origin. However different another church or minister may be, it does the cause no good to run down any of them. For a minister to speak in a derogatory manner about other ministers is unthinkable!

In general the Golden Rule applies in the minister's conduct and attitude toward other clergymen. If this rule is followed when he leaves a field, he will not return to officiate at weddings and funerals and he will not correspond with members advising them what to do and what not to do. He will treat a retired pastor in his church as though he were his father.

When a visiting minister is to fill the pulpit the pastor will arrange carefully for his entertainment and honorarium. The visitor comes as his guest, as well as the guest of the church, and every possible courtesy must be extended to him. For an honorarium the visitor is entitled to his travel expenses to and from the church, entertainment, and a sum to reimburse him adequately for the day's labors. This last-mentioned part of the honorarium should be about one-half the pastor's pay for the week if two services are held, and about 20 per cent less if only one service is held and there are no other responsibilities.

Denominational representatives, too, often visit churches in the discharge of their duties. Naturally, and because of their positions, the minister shows these men and women every possible courtesy. They should be met at the train or bus, and, when their work is finished, returned to the place of transportation. They should be comfortably housed. Usually a hotel or motel gives more privacy and rest than a home. However, in many parishes there are quiet homes with guest bedrooms where a traveler can gain his needed rest.

One more matter reaches over all the areas previously discussed. It is the telling of stories or anecdotes. Stories enliven a conversation. But they may also reveal some things the storyteller does not want known. Although it has been said that a pun is the lowest form of wit, there is a form of so-called wit that is much lower than the pun. It is the supposedly humorous story that reflects on any person because of some handicap. Daily those who are afflicted suffer as the unafflicted will never know. Often a cheery smile hides a breaking heart, deep resentment, or frustrations. To hold one's weakness up to ridicule is cruel treatment indeed and is wholly unworthy of a minister of the gospel.

Business Ethics

Since "the love of money is the root of all evils" (1 Tim. 6:10), it is not to be expected that a discussion of ethics would omit the money topic. Like everyone else, the minister has money problems. For some the problems originate in too small an income, for others in improper handling of money, and for still others in covetousness.

On accepting a call, the minister should have a clear understanding with the church regarding salary, fees, vacations, secular work, and retirement. When terms have been agreed upon all parties are obligated to abide by both the spirit and the letter of the agreement. The minister is employed by the local congregation. Unless he is instructed by the church to do otherwise, he is bound to give six days of honest work each week. For example, to hold revival meetings for another church and accept pay for such service is unethical, because the minister is already being paid for his time by his own church. An exception to this might be made if his own church recognizes that it does not pay him an adequate salary and places a clause in his contract permitting him to seek such additional income. Even so, if he were to spend the same time on his own field he might develop it sooner to the point where it could pay him adequately.

For its own good, a church should give a minister an annual vacation of from two to four weeks. Notwithstanding, it is questionable ethics when a minister stretches a vacation of specified length by adding the six days before and after it. Likewise it is unethical for a minister to preach for another church while his own church is giving him a vacation. Vacations are given so that the laborer might be refreshed as he rests from his labors. Otherwise, his church might as well keep him on the job.

There are town-country parishes in which the salary is so small that the minister must engage in other work to make ends meet. Without such an arrangement some churches would not have pastoral leadership. The minister teaches school, clerks in a store, drives a school bus, or does other work for which he is paid.

Before a minister enters into such relationship there should be a clear understanding with the church and with the secular employer as to how much time each job will require and how much pay he will receive from each. It goes without saying that no man can adequately care for two full-time jobs. A minister who gives full time to schoolteaching must give to the church the time that should be used for recreation and personal needs. A church that permits this, or a minister who desires it, may be engaging in a penny-wise and pound-foolish economy which threatens both his effectiveness and his health.

In money dealings with townspeople ministers are doubly vulnerable, for many people gauge every value by money. For this reason it is highly advisable for the minister to pay all bills promptly. Except when purchasing durable equipment such as a refrigerator, a stove, or a car, it is wise to pay all merchandise and services promptly and in full. If indebtedness becomes necessary it is more in keeping with a Christian order for the pastor to borrow from his church's credit union than to expect non-Christians, or businessmen who belong to other denominations, to finance him.

In many areas it is customary for businessmen to give ministers a 10 per cent discount on purchases. It may be acceptable for the Christian merchant to favor his pastor in this way, although there is some doubt that this is the best way to support the ministry. But for the minister to *expect* others to do this is certainly uncalled for, because it is not their responsibility to support him.

FUNERALS

It is when the minister is conducting a funeral or a wedding that he is seen by more people than when he is conducting most other services. Therefore these are the times when he is most open to appraisal.

A minister is expected to conduct burial services for people of the community other than his own church members. Those who die as Christians, even though they were not active in a church, present no particular problem. In such cases the pastor may use the funeral service as a means of emphasizing the Christian hope of eternal life. But there is some question as to whether or not the minister should conduct a Christian service for people who made no profession of Christianity. American Protestant custom dictates that human bodies are always buried with at least a prayer, although prayer is of no benefit to the dead. Because of this, the Protestant minister hardly dares to refuse to officiate at any funeral. Nevertheless in doing so, he must not offer non-Christian mourners the comfort of the Christian faith nor in any way infer that the deceased was a follower of Christ. Furthermore, it is not proper to hold such a service in the church unless no other building is available and the home is not easily adaptable.

A deceased Christian should not be unduly eulogized. A few words will serve to show proper respect. However, in such funerals the full comfort of the Christian faith may be extended to the family and friends. They may be reminded of the words "I am the resurrection and the life; he who believes in me, though he die, yet shall he live" (John 11:25).

Funeral procedures and customs vary greatly, depending upon the funeral director, the minister, and the section of the country. Insofar as possible, the wishes of the family of the deceased should be followed. Although the use of the funeral home is increasing, the family may desire to have the funeral service held in the church, and if the deceased was a Christian this is appropriate. In any case, procedures should be as simple and unostentatious as possible. If the service is to be held in the church building of the neighborhood where the deceased resided, the following procedures will be found to meet the requirements of Christian faith and courtesy.

At about noon the mortician brings the deceased's body to the church and places it in the front of the sanctuary. The casket is opened and the floral remembrances appropriately arranged. From that time until the hour of the funeral service friends come to the church to take their parting view of the body. At the announced hour of the service, the organist begins to play. The funeral director closes the casket and places upon it the family's floral spray. The family of the deceased is ushered to the section of the church reserved for them. This is usually in the front pews nearest the pulpit so that the minister may the more easily speak to them. The soloist or quartet are seated at the same time. The officiating minister and any who are to assist him take their places in the chancel, whereupon the minister opens the Bible and reads from it his

Opening Sentence, such as "I am the resurrection and the life; he who believes in me, though he die, yet shall he live" (John 11:25). He then offers the brief

Invocation, beseeching the Holy Spirit's comfort and help in this hour.

A Hymn by the singers may precede the

Scripture reading, which may take from three to five minutes. It is then proper to offer the

Prayer, giving special attention to the needs of the mourners. This is followed by a brief

Message, which may begin with a few eulogizing remarks concerning the deceased, then go on to speak of the Christian's assurance. The service of twenty or twenty-five minutes is brought to a close with the

Closing Prayer, and

Hymn

After the hymn the mortician moves the casket down the aisle to the church exit. It is proper for the pastor and his assistants, followed by the pallbearers, to walk immediately in front of the casket. At the door the pastor pauses to allow time for the family, mourners, and others to prepare to follow. When they are ready, at a word from the mortician, the pallbearers lift the casket from the catafalque and bear it to the funeral car, or if the cemetery is near by, to the grave site. The minister leads, and remains on the right side of the procession.

At the grave the minister stands behind or at the head of the casket, and reads from his service book some appropriate lines of Scripture. He closes with a brief prayer and a benediction.

This concludes the service, and the minister may now speak personally to the immediate members of the family and withdraw. The mortician will disperse the assembly, and his helpers will finish their work.

For the non-Christian the mortician's chapel or the home of the deceased is the appropriate place for the service of separation. If the service is in the mortician's chapel, then the place for the casket is determined by his custom and the design of the room. The pastor may suggest that the casket be closed before he starts his portion of the service, but here he is subject to the direction of the mortician more than he is when he is in his own church. The same general order of service may be followed as in the burial of a Christian, using great care not to suggest that the deceased has obtained a rest unsanctioned by the Scriptures.

This is not the time for an evangelistic appeal. Everything that is said and done should be in such a spirit that the minister will be welcome in the home of the deceased a few days later. In the quiet of their home he may talk with them of eternal things. They may have many questions to which they have sought in vain for answers. Thus the funeral of a nonbeliever may become the means by which the Holy Spirit brings a wandering soul to salvation.

In his conduct of the service the Christian minister must maintain the posture of dignity. This is a time of deep sorrow, even a time of tragedy for the family, according to circumstances, but Christians have a hope that washes out the sorrow.

WEDDINGS

Unlike funerals, weddings are usually a pleasant chore for a pastor. This is more than true if one or both of the parties are members of the officiating clergyman's parish. If he has known the young people over a period of years, and has been instrumental in their development in the Christian graces, he may take great satisfaction in uniting them in marriage and helping start another Christian home.

Young people should need little spiritual counseling when coming from a church that has a proper educational program. If they are from Christian homes they have been conditioned for marriage over a period of years. There may be, however, opportunity for the pastor to meet with them once or twice for an hour or so to discuss the responsibilities and privileges of Christian marriage.

Those who come to the pastor with license in hand, wanting to be married at once, are a problem. This is not an infrequent happening at the county seat. Hasty marriages are seldom advisable. The laws of most states guard against haste by demanding a health certificate which takes a few days to secure, and a lapse of time between applying for the license and its issuance. Even so, the pastor may know nothing about the couple until they appear at his door asking that he marry them. When this happens he can do one of two things. He may refuse to marry anyone who comes in this fashion; or he may question them, and if he finds nothing irregular, counsel them on the seriousness of this step and perform the wedding. By his counseling it is barely possible that some little good may come, but he ought not to expect much. The minister should remember that to refuse to marry a couple because of his own beliefs, when the state has sanctioned their marriage, is to set himself up as a judge of their right to be married. There could be some embarrassing consequences for the minister in some cases; in West Virginia for instance, where he is the state's legal officer for this function. The minister may well have a form of ceremony for professing Christians, with all the beauty and significance of the Christian faith, and another for nonprofessing persons, designed to satisfy the state, but without the religious emphasis.

The ideal place to perform a Christian marriage is in the church where the young people worship. The second best place is in the bride's home. Every effort should be made on the part of the pastor to make this a memorable event in the life of Christian young people. To assure against an embarrassing *faux pas* at least one rehearsal should be held. Just before the rehearsal, the pastor would do well to meet the couple and go over, line by line, the marriage ceremony which he intends to use. In this manner the couple will know not only what they are to do in the ceremony, but, more important, what they are promising one another for life. Such preliminary coaching will give the event a deeper meaning than if they heard the words for the first time when taking their vows.

As to which ritual to use, most ministers' service books carry two or three suggested orders, any one of which may be appropriate. It is usually better to use one of these carefully prepared forms with its time-honored language than to try to make a new one. The old forms have the sanction of usage and of beauty.

It has been customary to hand the pastor some monetary token of appreciation when he has conducted a funeral or performed a wedding ceremony. Although only a few ministers gain from this source a considerable sum in a year's time, it puts all ministers in an unfavorable light. It would be better if the minister could say, especially to those of his congregation, that there is no charge and a gift cannot be accepted, for this is a part of the church's service. That would be to say in essence, the services of the church are not for sale at your convenience.

In either funerals or weddings the pastor stands, in a circumscribed sense, between the people and God. When he performs these sacred offices he can strengthen the bond between man and God. He can do no more, and let him be sure he does no less.

XXVI

THE MINISTER AT PLAY

IT BECOMES INCREASINGLY EVIDENT that men who carry heavy loads by which the destinies of millions are determined or greatly altered find it necessary to rest systematically from their work. It may be axiomatic that the heavier the load, the more need for periods of relaxation.

In past generations, rural people frowned upon play. The nature of farm work and narrow Calvinistic teachings caused many to believe that play was sinful. Nevertheless, there are sufficient suggestions in the Bible to justify the planning of times and places for rest and play. The third commandment (Ex. 20:9-11) shows this to be true. Moreover, Jesus says to his disciples " 'Come away by yourselves to a lonely place, and rest a while.' For many were coming and going, and they had no leisure even to eat" (Mark 6:31). These were days when Jesus had many important things to do. The people were pressing hard upon him for healing. The disciples were in need of instruction and needed to be supervised as they ministered to people. His time on earth was soon to run out. Some men would have found this to be a wonderful opportunity to vaunt their busyness. But in that hour Jesus said "Come away . . . and rest a while." His modern disciples, hectic and frustrated, would do well to listen to his counsel. It is doubtful if any of them, with all their activities, are as hard-pressed as Jesus was in the days of his flesh.

At first glance it might seem extraordinary for a church to give its pastor a paid vacation of fifty days each year. This

307

means a month and a half in which to relax, play, and plan. Impossible as this may seem, every church offers, and expects its pastor to take, a minimum of fifty-two days of rest each year. The command that instructs laymen to rest one day out of each seven does not exclude ministers. The minister who does not observe this one-out-of-seven days of rest violates God's instructions. Unless he observes a day of rest each week he cannot counsel his people to observe the Sabbath.

Ministers frequently speak of "blue Monday" when they gather for the ministerial association's meeting. And why should it not be blue, when they worked steadily from Tuesday through Saturday, then went into the most strenuous day of the week tired and hard pressed? By exerting themselves to the limit on Sunday they are exhausted on Monday. But is it necessary that they be "blue"? If Saturday were used as a day of rest Sunday would be a joyful day.

If the minister has a family, Saturday is the ideal day for rest. The children are free from school responsibilities and the family may enjoy the day doing those things a family can do well together. The proper use of Saturdays calls for both planning and discipline, for the minister must make sure that all preparation for the Lord's Day has been completed by Friday night. There will be no such things as late Saturday-night sermon preparation and bulletin mimeographing. The minister's wife will need to discipline herself, too, to make sure that all the heavy cooking is well out of the way by Friday.

The proper use of any day calls for planning. If Saturday comes upon the minister's family without their knowing what they are going to do, they will merely loaf and come to the end of the day with a sense of frustration. There are many places not far from home that a family could and should see. In a dinner conference these might be listed by the family and specific Saturdays set aside to visit them. Likewise those things the members of the family would like to do as a family and as individuals should be listed.

THE ANNUAL VACATION

The minister who is considering a call to a church should have an understanding with the people about his annual vacation period. For town-country ministers this may vary from ten days to a month, and may be with or without pay. The trend now seems to be toward granting the pastor one month of paid vacation each year. This month is intended to provide an enriching experience for him which in turn will enrich the church. The church should continue to pay the pastor during his vacation, in order that he might be a better workman for them. This consideration almost automatically rules out his preaching elsewhere, or going to school during this period, for such things are in the line of his regular work and violate the purpose of a vacation. Instead of preaching, he can worship in a church where he is not known. This can be done profitably in churches of denominations other than his own. A Baptist minister might enjoy the experience of worshiping in an Episcopal service, and an Episcopalian might equally profit by attending a Baptist service.

A thirty-day vacation calls for careful planning beforehand if the time is to be utilized to the fullest extent. The fact that money is not available for a trip to the seashore, the mountains, or across the continent need not forbid a thrilling vacation. There are scores of places of interest within a hundred miles of every home. It may be that a whole month's vacation at one time is not practical for either the church or the pastor. Summer may not be the best time for a vacation. Sometimes two shorter vacations may be taken, one just before school starts in the fall, and the other immediately following the Christmas activities in the church. Whether the vacation lasts for thirty days, one day, or one hour, it is not for the purpose of loafing, but that the vacationer may take on additional growth.

One of the most common types of vacation is travel. Travel is not as expensive for a family as it may sound, for by renting a motel with kitchenette each night the family can prepare all its own meals at no greater cost than at home. Some families carry camping equipment and stay at state parks and similar places. If the vacationers are observant and talk freely to the natives, the family will return with a deepened appreciation of the size, variety, and beauty of the country. They will have a better understanding of the customs of people in different areas.

If circumstances should forbid all travel there are still cultural values and any one of a hundred hobbies that will add immeasurably to one's stature. The time can be used at home doing those things one had always intended to do if only there had been time, such as refinishing furniture, or fishing in a local stream. A hobby like astronomy, botany, geology, bird study, anthropology of North American Indians or Negroes, music, painting, or sculpturing might offer a special appeal. These may be pursued for an hour at a time, for a whole month, or over the years, as time permits. Picnics, visits to historical places, and visits to the city with its museums, rare plants, parks, and theaters may be considered as wholesome recreation for the town-country minister and his family. They add to the enjoyment of life. They enrich the minister's sermons.

Recreation can have practical monetary rewards. The man who takes a wholesome vacation and returns to his church tasks with renewed vigor and faith will be a better pastor and will stand a better chance of receiving an increase in salary than if he had not taken a vacation. Also, daily and weekly recreation may be centered around the productive home, the projects of which may offer monetary reward. The minister may take over some of the cooking and baking in his own household as a hobby. This also could have monetary rewards as his wife is set free for a short time to rest or to do other work, such as family sewing. Some ministers have discovered that they can combine recreation and the furnishing of a home by securing good furniture from second-hand stores and giving it only minor repairs and refinishing. Careful workmen have thus furnished their homes with substantial and tasteful pieces. One minister specialized in antiques which he carefully refinished and later sold at a neat profit. Photography is one of the crafts in the productive home. There is fun and relaxation to be gained from seeing a picture evolve all the way from nature to its printed form in a magazine.

A minister will be copied by his congregation. People will imitate him as he demonstrates in his living that certain types of recreation are wholesome and contribute to his and the church's growth. When a minister takes a rest for an hour, day, or month, he thereby shows his people how to rest. This, in itself, is good work, for the people need wholesome rest as well as the minister.

There is need for wholesome recreation in every town-country community. In spite of much talk about recreation it is still a neglected art. With the coming of the forty hour work week, and prospects for thirty-five hours or less in the next decade, the need for wholesome recreation is vastly increased. Mark A. McCloskey, speaking in 1944 from the Office of Community War Service, was emphatic in his statement that war-born accelerated programs of all kinds have confirmed recreation as a legitimate public responsibility, on a par with such other services as education, health, and welfare. The passing of the years has given additional weight to this observation.

XXVII

ARCHITECT OF THE TOWN-COUNTRY COMMUNITY

IF A TOWN-COUNTRY MINISTER is willing to pay the price of leadership he can be the architect of his community, for no other man has so strategic an opportunity to guide its development. If he falters before this opportunity community life will assuredly go on; but it will be mediocre because it will then lack the spiritual qualities that would make of it a great community.

At the turn of the twentieth century all-weather roads were few. The farmer and his family knew the overwhelming dullness that comes from hours of drudgery and months of loneliness. Many farm children could attend school for only a few months each year. There were sincere hardworking doctors, but medicine was poorly developed, and the graveyards had too many headstones for babies under two years of age. It might be reported that they died of some such malady as "summer sickness"; the nature of cholera infantum and cholera morbus seems to have been unfamiliar then. Women also died young. It was not unusual for a farmer who became widowed early in life to remarry two or more times. Caricatures depicted the farmer as a backwoods yokel to be ridiculed. The drudgery and poverty of the farm drove many young people to the villages and towns where life was thought to be better. But these places could care for only a small fraction of them, so many moved on and became lost in the large cities. Many of these made good in business, industry, and the professions, but while they were doing so they failed to rear families which would perpetuate the family name.

In a half century the picture has changed in most of rural America. Good communications have been established with the rest of the world. Hard surfaced, all-weather roads have put farmers on wheels the year around. The telephone, radio, television, and daily paper permit even the most remote farms to know what is happening in the rest of the world soon after it happens.

Electricity, now in most farm homes, has taken a heavy load from the farm family's back. It pumps and carries the water, cooks, washes, irons, and lifts heavy loads at the barn. This old-time drudgery sent mothers prematurely to their graves. Although schools are not yet all they should be, the consolidated rural school is a far cry from the one-room district school of 1900. With few exceptions, the children are in school at least eight or nine months a year.

No longer is the farmer the dull, beaten-down "Man with the Hoe." Today's successful farmer is an active participant in the agricultural revolution, one of the greatest revolutions of all time. To be a successful farmer he must be a mechanic, agronomist, veterinarian, scientist, businessman, and politician, all molded into one man.

A shift has come in the population balances, too. If the term "rural" means farms and towns with a population of less than twenty-five hundred, the percentage of rural population in the United States moved from 95 in 1790 to 36.6 at present. Moreover, a change has also come within the rural population. Those living in hamlets and villages number thirty-one millions while those living on farms number twenty-three millions, a ratio of about 3 to 2. The growth of the villages and towns can be accounted for by the desire of people for a better place to live, and by the increase of their small industry. But unfortunately it is doubtful if the villages have improved as places in which to live at the same rate as the farms have improved. As desirable places to live, farms have increased rapidly, while villages of less than 1,000 population have too frequently become less desirable as places in which to rear a family.

In 1908 America's rural life was oriented around the neighborhood. These neighborhoods were determined by the distance a team could haul a load in a day. They were of necessity small and limited in their opportunities for rich and varied living. Those who lived in places of denser population looked down upon these neighborhoods. But these years have brought a change that could hardly have been foretold in 1908. The old-time neighborhoods are passing rapidly. With their passing, there emerges the town-country community that embraces from three to a dozen or more neighborhoods of the former type. People in these new areas are finding that they now have much in common, including adequate trading facilities, employment, recreation, schools, and worship opportunities. This emerging town-country community gives promise of providing all the values of the former neighborhoods, plus the stimulation of wider, more varied contacts.

The end of material progress in town-country areas is nowhere in sight. Much improvement is still desirable in the way of schools, hospitals and clinics, housing, industry, transportation, and a more equitable distribution of wealth. These will come. Then what? Nineteen hundred years ago, Jesus put his finger on the crux of the meaning of life when he said "A man's life does not consist in the abundance of his possessions" (Luke 12:15). American culture has not yet caught up with the Master's thinking.

Into the town-country community comes the Protestant pastor. What is his task? He may increase the attendance at public church services and by various means increase his church roll. He may put on a building program and enhance the property of his church. He may join the service clubs, attend all public meetings, speak frequently, and always champion the winning cause. Thereby he may become known as the most popular preacher in the county. For his reward he may be called to a larger church in a larger place where he will be expected to repeat, on a grander scale, his past performances. But what of the town-country people and Christ's observation about a man's life? If the people's vision is characterized by more and more material grandeur they are like the fool of Christ's parable.

A pastor comes into the town-country community with the weight of considerable advantage on his side. He is thought to be a man of high religious ideals. Although the people may not fully understand religious ideals, they nonetheless respect his high office. Furthermore, he is backed by a religious organization whose oft-reaffirmed motive is to be God's witness and instrument for the redemption of the world. The church members are, in theory if not in fact, committed to this redemption. The church may have in its membership the most influential citizens: men and women whose words are carefully weighed, and whose advice is followed.

The pastor is paid to take time to study community needs carefully and devise methods for accomplishing proper changes in community living. As a man of prayer and meditation he may be expected to speak with wisdom and judgment on community problems. Better still, he knows how to keep silent when silence is necessary. On his arrival in the town-country community, he will, in all probability, find no plan in effect for the development of the community except perhaps for increasing its wealth for the benefit of a few. He may find that the community contains deep-seated cancers of strife, jealousy, ill will, and hatred. He may find covetousness among the older citizens, and immorality and drunkenness among the young adults. He will find that some citizens live in luxury while others exist in squalor because their skin pigmentation is different or they speak with a foreign accent. He will find that some send their children to college and their sick ones have the advantages of the latest in medicine, but that others must take their children from school when they are sixteen years of age and endure sickness with folklore remedies until death sets them free.

Into such a programless community the town-country pastor comes. With the abundant resources at hand, he can work out a scheme that will give the community a taste of the kingdom of God on earth. He can help the people to bring into realization, in large measure, the kingdom for which Jesus prayed and for which he taught his disciples to pray.

The practical one will ask what kind of picture is presented by this future town-country community with its world-wide influence. That is, what will the community of the future look like? Who can see clearly enough to answer this?

The essence of the great community of the future can be understood if one puts together all the pleadings of the Hebrew prophets for a nation of righteousness, the insights of Paul in 1 Cor. 13, and encloses them in Christ's Sermon on the Mount. From this material the architect must strive to design for his place and day *the community*. It will never suffice that he simply pray "Thy kingdom come, Thy will be done, On earth as it is in heaven." He must plan, and plan, and plan. Then he must work without ceasing that God's will may be done in his little but far-reaching part of the world.

APPENDIX

PROGRAM SUGGESTIONS
FOR TOWN-COUNTRY CHURCHES

WINTER-NIGHT COLLEGE

The Winter-Night College, originally developed and used at Honey Creek, Wis., is an effort at Christian education for adults, beyond the usual concern of the Sunday church school. The college may take any of a number of forms. The Honey Creek college was sponsored by churches of the area, and financed by a modest enrollment fee, subsidized by the Wisconsin University Extension Service, and Midland Wholesale Co-operative. The format used six Monday nights of the fall, before Thanksgiving Day, with the following schedule:

7:00-7:50—Six classes meeting simultaneously.
1. Church music (A chorus was organized, which later sang at a number of churches).
2. Advanced Bible study—"What the Bible Means To Me."
3. Family—man, woman and child.
4. The co-operatives.
5. Soil conservation.
6. The small vegetable garden.

8:00-8:15—Chapel period, all classes assembling in Community Hall auditorium for announcements, hymn, Psalm, and prayer.

8:15-9:00—Forum.

Address by an outstanding authority on subjects of interest to the community. In this case speakers were secured from Wisconsin University, The Midland Wholesale Co-operative, Garrett Biblical Institute, and the Public School Administration.
1. Co-operation a way of life
2. The future of town-country communities
3. The rural school
4. The family farm

317

5. Wisconsin rural communities - Which way?
6. Christianity the dynamic

9:00-9:30—Questions from the audience directed to forum speaker.

A logical follow-up is to organize small discussion-action groups, continuing the study in the areas where greatest interest has been shown.

HOME DEMONSTRATION AND COUNTY AGRICULTURAL AGENT

Almost every county of the nation has a County Agricultural Agent and a Home Demonstration Agent, provided co-operatively by the federal, state, and county governments. In some, a third person is in charge of 4-H Club work. For the most part these people are dedicated to the task of lifting the cultural and economic level of town-country life and are well trained for their work. Although they must be impartial in their approach to religious groups, nevertheless any time a church requests their services they will do all humanly possible to comply with the request.

The Home Demonstration Agent is an expert at helping solve family problems and organizing study-action clubs. The County Agricultural Agent is equally adept at helping the farmer or gardener with his problem. A minister would be well advised to cultivate an acquaintance with these people and work with them in building a more Christian community.

VOCATIONAL GUIDANCE

It is important that a pastor know what vocational guidance, if any, the local high school offers its students. If no guidance is being given, or if some phases such as Church vocations are omitted, then a friendly talk with school authorities may help to initiate it. If this fails, pastors of the community may organize their own "vocations week" and in co-operation with a nearby college arrange for aptitude tests to be given high school juniors and seniors. Various corporations provide vocational pamphlets free of charge. One of these, the New York Life Insurance Company, has prepared an excellent series. Such materials may be given to the students, in addition to suggestions for further vocational reading, which the Public

Library will doubtless be glad to assist in preparing. Further emphasis may be given by pastor and/or laymen from pulpit.

If the high school does offer vocational guidance (and the better ones will), the church may co-operate at a suitable time by presenting, in worship programs and in church bulletins, Christ's claim on human life and talents. It is important that when the school provides vocational counseling, church-related vocations should be fairly presented. If this practice is not possible, on an interdenominational basis in the school, the church should offer supplementary guidance.

CREDIT UNION

The modern Credit Union Movement was started by the Lutheran layman, Frederick W. Raeffeisen in 1849, as Brotherhood Credit. As a means of encouraging savings and supplying credit at low interest to the small borrower, modern credit unions are so effective that industry has encouraged their employees to organize them. The Roman Catholic Church, seeing their value, has also encouraged many parishes to organize. Some Protestant churches have done likewise. In some cases the ministers of a state have organized credit unions to supply themselves credit in the purchase of cars and in meeting emergencies.

The credit union effectively encourages regular savings. Only *one dollar per week* deposited in the credit union equals fifty-two dollars a year plus interest. Such a saving, if carried from age 30 to 65, with the accumulated interest, at 4½%, which is not unusual in credit unions, would equal approximately $6,000, a tidy sum to supplement one's retirement fund. And at the same time, this money is doing extra duty by financing the purchases of other members.

Credit unions are regulated and protected by both state and federal legislation. For additional information and help write the National headquarters, CUNA - Credit Union National Association, Madison, Wis.

FATHER-SON PARTNERSHIP

Sooner or later the ownership of any privately owned farm or business must pass into hands other than those now holding the reins. Often these periods of transition come at times which are far from ideal. Either they come so abruptly through sudden inheritance that the son is not prepared for his new responsibilities, or the father's active ownership and direction extends so far into old age that the son's initiative is stifled. These changes are not only hard on the family; in a small community, they are hard on the church of which the family is part.

There is much to be said favorably for passing the ownership of farms from father to son at a time when the son can invest the best earning years of his life in the enterprise. A most effective solution is in the forming of father-son partnerships, permitting control of the farm to move in orderly fashion from one generation to the next. Land-grant colleges have done research on this problem and issued their findings in pamphlets that may be had free for the asking.

Small business may likewise be passed along within the family structure.

VILLAGE INDUSTRY

The advent of electricity and good roads to our villages means, among other things, that industry no longer needs to be located in already overcrowded cities. In fact, small communities with labor surplus, good transportation, adequate power and water supply, are prized today for plant relocation, especially if they are also located near attractive recreational areas. Churchmen, looking to employment of their young people in the home areas, have formed committees of interested citizens to lead in exploiting the opportunities of their area. The State Industrial Commission (name varies in different states) is a rich source of help and should be contacted by pastor and committee. Where possible, the churches of an area should cooperate in developing and securing industry for the village, rather than one church going it alone.

Not all industrial potential lies in encouraging moves from the outside, however. Some authorities feel many communities overlook their best opportunities for a broader economic base in not encouraging, in various ways, local youths to start their own enterprises.

HOME STUDY CLASSES

Problems of the home are so numerous and complex that Sunday school lessons cannot cover them adequately when they devote only one or two sessions a year to the study of family relations. *The Christian Home in a Rural Setting*, C. R. McBride, (Judson Press, 1949) was prepared expressly for use by parents who wanted to give time, other than in the Sunday school hours, to a discussion of home problems. Other materials are available from denominational and interdenominational sources. Colleges, universities, and social agencies have on their staffs people qualified to speak on the theme of family relations, from infancy to old age. The concerned pastor should have no great difficulty in organizing study clubs utilizing the excellent resources now available.

HOME DEDICATION

When a young couple are married, and move into their first home, Christian friends may gather and hold a service in which the new home is dedicated to the high purposes of Christ's kingdom. As a part of the dedication service they may give an appropriate picture for the wall of the home or an attractively bound Bible.

A similar service may be held when a couple moves into the first house they have purchased, or one they have built. A further and significant adaptation of the program is the case of a non-Christian home becoming Christian and rising to the occasion publicly in the Christian dedication of this home.

HOME OBSERVANCE OF SPECIAL DAYS

The Christian Home in a Rural Setting contains suggestions for significant observances which may be held in the Christian home for each Lord's Day, Christmas, Lent, Easter, Rural Life Sunday, Harvest Festival, and the birthdays of each member of the family. This is one means of carrying the faith into this Christian citadel, the home.

THOROUGH STUDY OF COMMUNITY

Not much can be done for the improvement of community life until there is an awakened and informed citizenry. These two ends can be accomplished, in part at least, by responsible persons making a careful study of their community. The sociology departments of the land-grant colleges, as well as denominational home mission agencies, in all probability will be pleased to help in such a study or at least to suggest reference books. *Small Town Renaissance*, by Richard Waverly Poston, is an inspiring factual account of what a community can accomplish.

In addition to studying what the church's community *is*, some people may be interested in discussing what it *ought to be*, in relation to the teaching of the church. This would be an excellent experience for some who have seldom thought of the community as being of God's creation.

COMMUNITY COUNCIL AND CALENDAR

The Community Council consists of the heads of the various community organizations, meeting regularly, usually once a month, to appraise the welfare of the community and suggest activities that might be undertaken by various groups within the community that would contribute to the welfare of all. Pastors have helped to organize these. Such a council helps to co-ordinate the efforts of all the different religious, civic, and school groups.

In addition to this they serve as a community co-ordinating council, preparing and publicizing a community calendar, in which the more important activities of the area are listed, such as those of schools, churches and civic clubs. Such a calendar answers the frequent complaint of pastors that "The school takes all the children's time," or "This town is clubbed to death." Both complaints indicate a conflict in scheduling community activities. Having agreed to a scheduling of activities, each group then should abide by its decision and not plan activities that conflict with other groups. If an unforeseen activity becomes necessary, it is scheduled in consultation with other groups to assure a free date.

MINISTRY TO ALL GROUPS

Even with the best of intentions to serve all people of a community some groups are frequently overlooked, such as inmates of the county jail, residents of county homes and private rest homes, people living in trailer camps, migrant agricultural laborers, non-agricultural work crews, and those folk on "the other side of the tracks." These people ought not to be overlooked, but pastor and/or the laity should carry the hope of the gospel message to them.

GLOSSARY

Words are valuable only when speaker and listener, writer and reader, agree on their meanings. The following terms and words, commonly used in town-country circles, are used as defined in this glossary, unless otherwise indicated at the time of use.

CITY. (See *urban*.) An aggregate of 10,000 or more people.

COMMUNITY. An aggregate of people with similar living conditions who are reasonably self-sufficient in such basic needs as trade, employment, recreation, education, and worship, and have the "we" spirit, a sense of concern for one another.

COMMUNITY CHURCH. A church belonging to no denomination and assuming to minister to the religious needs of a community or neighborhood. In some areas it is called a union church.

COMMUNITY DENOMINATIONAL CHURCH. A church of any denomination that assumes to minister to the religious needs of members of several denominations within the community, but which holds intact its relationship to its own denomination.

CO-OPERATIVES. Voluntary organizations by which people attempt to (a) market their produce at an advantageous price to themselves (producers' co-operatives); (b) purchase their needs for less than the market price of commodities (consumers' co-operatives); (c) provide for themselves credit and saving facilities (credit unions). There are also hospital and medical co-operatives, housing co-operatives, burial co-operatives, and the Rural Electrification Administration (REA) through which co-operatives are organized for supplying electricity to rural areas.

CORPORATION FARMS. Farms owned by corporations and operated by managers.

COUNTY (*agricultural*) AGENT. A person employed by the United States Department of Agriculture to bring information from agricultural experimental stations to those in the county who claim his services. He is expected to lead and organize agricultural interests so as to achieve better farming, better business, and better living.

DENOMINATIONAL CHURCH. Any church that claims to be part of a religious denomination and is accepted by the same.

DEPARTMENT OF THE TOWN AND COUNTRY CHURCH. A department of the Division of Home Missions of the National Council of the Churches of Christ in the United States of America. It is charged with developing the rural program.

EROSION. The rapid process of soil removal brought about by interferences with nature's normal balance between soil building and soil removal.

FAMILY FARM. In brief, a farm owned and operated by the members of a family. For more detailed explanation see *Rural Christians and Natural Resources,* by C. R. McBride. (Philadelphia: The Judson Press, 1949), p. 69.

FARM. The Census of 1960 defined a farm as ten or more acres with gross sales of fifty dollars or more in agricultural products; or if the unit is less than ten acres, gross sales of $250 or more.

FARM BUREAU. An association of farm families co-operating with the extension services of the state agricultural colleges and the United States Department of Agriculture in the employment and support of county agents in agriculture, homemaking, boys' and girls' club work, and in carrying on an educational program under their leadership. The membership is open.

FARMERS HOME ADMINISTRATION. A government agency made possible by the Bankhead-Jones Tenant Purchase legislation (1937) to aid farmers in purchasing equipment and farms when credit elsewhere is unavailable.

FARMERS' UNION. Organized in Texas in 1902 as a family organization of farm people. Its chief emphasis is on co-operative enterprises, strengthening the family farm, and a legislative program for betterment of farm life.

FEDERATED CHURCH. Should be called federation of churches. A plan by which churches of two or more denominations agree to work and worship as one unit under the leadership of one pastor, with each unit maintaining its relationship to its respective denomination; usually found in areas of diminishing population.

FOUR-H CLUB. Boys' and girls' club with specific vocational projects in the fields of agriculture, animal husbandry, home economics, manual arts, and sometimes fine arts. The four H's stand for head, hand, health, and heart; promoted by county agent or his assistant.

FUTURE FARMERS OF AMERICA. An organization of rural youth of which the high school teacher of vocational agriculture acts as local adviser; has a comprehensive program of school fairs and exhibits, tours, father-and-son banquets, and social and athletic events to develop morale among high school students interested in farming. The annual national convention is held in November, in Kansas City, Kan.

GRANGE. (The *Patrons of Husbandry*.) Formed in 1867 as a fraternal organization. In the 1870's it rushed into political activities and has continued in them with great interest and power; a mouthpiece for farmers' movement since 1870; oldest and largest farmers' organization in the United States.

HAMLET. A population aggregate of less than 250; usually 18 to 250; at least four residence units, two of which are non-farm houses.

HOME DEMONSTRATION AGENT. A teacher of home economics to women and girls especially in rural homes, paid jointly by federal, state, and county funds.

HOMESTEAD. A home on a small holding of land where a family may preserve the natural bonds of integration and unity.

LAND. All natural resources except man.

LAND GRANT COLLEGES. Through the Morrill Act of 1862 Congress gave to the states public land, with the stipulation that one or more colleges be maintained devoted primarily to instruction in agriculture and mechanical arts.

LAND TENURE. The occupation and operation of a piece of land owned by others.

LARGER PARISH. A group of churches in a community working together through a larger parish council and staff (one or more ministers) to serve the people of the area with a comprehensive gospel ministry.

MIGRANT LABORERS. People who cross state and/or national boundaries once or more a year for work in agriculture. They frequently follow the harvesting of crops across the nation.

NEIGHBORHOOD. Similar to a community, except that the people are less numerous and not to any reasonable degree self-sufficient, as in a community. Here the "we" spirit is usually strong. (See *community*.)

PARISH. The area served by a local church, except in Louisiana where it is a civil division equivalent to a county.

PARISHIONER. One who lives in the area served by a church and is the responsibility of that church.

PRODUCERS' CO-OPERATIVE. (See *co-operatives*.) A voluntary organization of producers for the advantageous marketing of their crops.

PRODUCTIVE HOME. A home that attempts by the labor of its members to produce a high proportion of all it consumes, rather than to earn money and buy such necessities.

RURAL. According to the U. S. Census, people who remain after the urbanites are counted; namely, those people living on farms and in hamlets and villages smaller than 2,500 population. (See *urban*.)

RURAL CHURCH. A church in the open country or in a town of less than 2,500 population.

RURAL FARM. Refers to people who live on farms.

RURAL NONFARM. Refers to people who live in a rural area but not on a farm; except those persons who live in a second house on a farm and who pay cash rent for it.

RURBAN. A term which attempts to describe rural settlements that are being highly urbanized through industrialization and proximity to large cities.

SHARECROPPER. A farmer who pays a share of his crops as rent for his land.

TENANT. A farmer who lives upon and cultivates land owned by another with whom he shares both the proceeds of his toil and usually the responsibility of management.

TOWN. A community of closely clustered dwellings and other buildings in which people live and work; while generally considered a center of population from 500 to 10,000, it is used loosely by rural people for any size community. Sociologists arbitrarily place towns at 2,500 to 10,000 population.[1]

TOWN-COUNTRY OR TOWN AND COUNTRY. Usually synonymous with rural. However, with some religious groups the population runs as high as 10,000 insomuch as sociologists consider towns as population aggregates of 2,500 to 10,000.

TOWN AND COUNTRY COMMITTEE. (See *Department of the Town and Country Church*.)

TOWNSHIP. A geographic division of land which follows meridians, being six miles on each side, and which may be the base of a political township.

UNITED STATES DEPARTMENT OF AGRICULTURE. A department of the federal government charged with improvement of all phases of agriculture and agricultural life in the United States; commonly referred to as USDA.

URBAN. As established by the 1960 Census the urban population comprises all persons living in (a) places of 2,500 inhabitants or more incorporated as cities, boroughs, towns, [1] and villages; (b) the densely settled urban fringe, including both incorporated and unincorporated areas, around cities of 50,000 or more; (c) unincorporated places of 2,500 inhabitants or more outside any urban fringe; and (d) unincorporated areas with a population density of more than 1,500 per square mile. The remaining population is classified as rural.

VILLAGE. As generally accepted, a population aggregate of 250 to 2,500.

YOKED FIELD. Two or more churches, not necessarily of the same denomination nor in the same community, served by the same pastor. The pastor is their only connecting link.

[1] Except in New England, New York, and Wisconsin, where "towns" are minor civil divisions of counties and not necessarily densely settled centers, as are towns in other states.

A SELECTED BIBLIOGRAPHY

PART ONE

Beard, August Field, *The Story of John Friederich Oberlin*. New York: Christian Rural Fellowship, 1946.

Beard, Charles A. and Mary R., *The Rise of American Civilization*. New York: The Macmillan Co., 1959.

Becker, Edwin L., *Disciples of Christ in Town and Country*. Indianapolis: United Christian Missionary Society, 1950.

Brunner, E. deS., *American Society: Rural and Urban Patterns*. New York: Harper and Brothers, 1955.

Burchfield, Laverne, *Our Rural Communities*. Chicago: Public Administration Service, University of Chicago, 1947.

Butt, E. Dargan, *Preach There Also*. Evanston, Ill.: Seabury-Western Theological Seminary, 1954.

Butterfield, Kenyon L., *The Country Church and the Rural Problem*. Chicago: University of Chicago Press, 1911.

Christian Rural Fellowship Bulletin. New York: Christian Rural Fellowship, 1934 ff.

Evans, E. F., *Our South — Its Resources and Their Use*. Austin, Texas: Steck Co., 1949.

Fenner, G. R., *The Episcopal Church in Town and Country*. New York: National Council, Protestant Episcopal Church, 1935.

Galpin, Charles J., *Empty Churches*. New York: Century Company, 1925.

———————— *My Drift into Rural Sociology*. Baton Rouge, La.: Louisiana State University Press, 1938.

Gillespie, J. T., *The Rural Church — Long Range Program of Southern Baptists*. Atlanta, Ga.: Home Mission Board, Southern Baptist Convention, 1956.

Howard, R. L., *Lazyman Rest Not — The Burman Letters of Brayton C. Case*. Philadelphia: The Judson Press, 1946.

Kolb, J. H. and Brunner, E. deS., *A Study of Rural Society*. Boston: Houghton Mifflin Co., 1952.

Lindstrom, David Edgar, *Rural Social Change*. Urbana, Ill.: University of Illinois, 1960.

Medearis, Dale W., *1953 Year Study Book — Disciples of Christ*. Indianapolis: Department Church Development and Evangelism, United Christian Missionary Society, 1954.

Mickey, K. B., *Man and the Soil*. Chicago: International Harvester Co., 1948.

Moomaw, I. W., *Rural Life Objectives*. Elgin, Ill.: General Mission Board, Church of the Brethren, n.d.

Mueller, E. W., *A Profile of the Lutheran Church in the United States*. Chicago: Division of American Missions, National Lutheran Council, 1954.

Osborn, Fairfield, *Our Plundered Planet*. Boston: Little, Brown and Co., 1948.

Parker, Florence E., *The First 125 Years*. Chicago: Cooperative League of the U. S. A., 1956.

Randolph, Henry S., *A Statement to Committee on Management*. Unpublished. National Council of Churches, Town and Country Department, 1956.

————— and Maloney, Alice, *A Manual for Town and Country Churches*. New York: Board of National Missions, Presbyterian Church in the U. S. A., 1950.

Reck, F. M., *The 4-H Story*. Ames, Iowa: Iowa State University Press, 1951.

Report of Commission on Country Life. Chapel Hill: University of North Carolina Press, 1944.

Rich, Mark, *The Rural Church Movement*. Columbia, Mo.: Juniper Knoll Press, 1958.

Rölvogg, O. E., *Giants in the Earth*, (1927); *Peder Victorious* (1929). New York: Harper and Brothers. Novels on early days in the Great Plains.

Rural Education — A Forward Look. Washington, D. C.: 1955 Year Book, Department Rural Education, National Education Association of U. S., 1956.

Sandford, Glen F., *A Statement to the Committee on Management.* Unpublished. National Council of Churches, Town and Country Department.

Smith, Rockwell Carter, *People, Land, and Churches.* New York: Friendship Press, 1959.

Taylor, Carl C. and Others, *Rural Life in the United States.* New York: A. A. Knopf, 1949.

Town and Country Church. New York: Monthly publication Town and Country Department, National Council of Churches, 1943 ff.

Tripp, Thomas A., "Rural Congregationalism in America." New York: *Congregational Quarterly,* April, 1951.

————— *Successful Rural Church Methods.* New York: Town and Country Department, Board of Home Missions, Congregational-Christian Church, 1953.

Williams, Vinnie, *The Fruit Tramp.* New York: Harper and Brothers, 1957. A novel of life with migrant agricultural laborers.

Wilson, Warren H., *The Church of the Open Country.* New York: Missionary Education United States and Canada, 1911.

————— *Rural Religion and the Country Church.* New York: Fleming H. Revell, 1927.

Zimmerman, C. C. and Du Wors, R. E., *Graphic Regional Sociology.* Cambridge, Mass.: Phillips Book Store, 1952.

PART TWO

(See also the special bibliography on Christian education at the end of Chapter XIV.)

"A Balanced Program for Town and Country Churches," "Church Planning Through Discussion Groups," "Check Up on Your Church," and "The Farmers' Winter Night College." A series of pamphlets issued by Town and Country Work Department, American Baptist Home Mission Society, New York.

Adams, Rachel Swann, *The Small Church and Christian Education*. Philadelphia: The Westminster Press, 1961.

Atkinson, C. Harry, *Building and Equipping for Christian Education*. New York: National Council of Churches, 1959.

Bliss, Kathleen, *The Service and Status of Women in the Churches*. London: S.C.M. Press, Ltd., 1952.

Bonner, Hubert, *Group Dynamics: Principles and Application*. New York: The Ronald Press Co., 1959.

Brownell, Baker, *The Human Community*. New York: Harper and Brothers, 1952.

Carr, James McLeod, *Working Together in the Larger Parish*. Atlanta: Church and Community Press, 1960.

Christian Mission Among Rural People, The. New York: Foreign Missions Conference of North America, 1945.

Churches and Church Membership in the United States. New York: National Council of Churches, staff project, 1957.

Conover, E. M., ed., *Building for Worship*. New York: The Interdenominational Bureau of Architecture, 1946.

————— *The Parsonage, Planning and Building It*. 1952.

————— *Rebuilding Town-Country Churches*. 1945. New York: Bureau of Church Buildings and Architecture, National Council of Churches.

Day, LeRoy Judson, *Dynamic Christian Fellowship*. Philadelphia: The Judson Press, 1960.

Douty, Mary Alice, *How to Work with Church Groups*. Nashville: Abingdon Press, 1957.

Felton, Ralph, *The Home of the Rural Pastor*. Drew Forest, Madison, N. J.: Ralph Almon Felton, 1948.

————— *Men Working*. Drew Forest, Madison, N. J.: Ralph Almon Felton, 1949.

————— *New Gospel of the Soil*. Drew Forest, Madison, N. J.: Ralph Almon Felton, 1951.

Foster, Virgil E., *How a Small Church Can Have Good Christian Education*. New York: Harper and Brothers, 1956.

General Director's Report to Executive Committee, The. New York: National Council of Churches, 1957.

Hedley, George, *Christian Worship*. New York: The Macmillan Co., 1953.

Hollingshead, August de Belmont, *Elmtown's Youth*. New York: John Wiley and Sons, 1949.

Holm-Jensen, P. H., *The People's College*. Blair, Nebr., Danish Lutheran Publishing House, 1939.

Hymns of the Rural Spirit. New York: Commission on Worship, Federal Council of Churches, 1947.

Johnstone, Margaret Blair, *When God Says No*. New York: Simon and Shuster, 1954.

Jones, Idris W., *For Christ and the Church*. Philadelphia: The Judson Press, 1952.

Judy, Marvin T., *The Larger Parish and Group Ministry*. New York: Abingdon Press, 1959.

Kuhn, Margaret E., *You Can't Be Human Alone*. Philadelphia: The Judson Press, 1956.

Leach, William Herman, *Handbook of Church Management*. Englewood Cliffs, N. J.: Prentice-Hall, 1958.

Manual for an Effective Every Member Canvass. New York: Council on Missionary Co-operation of the American Baptist Convention, 1957.

Morgan, A. E., *The Community of the Future*. Yellow Springs, Ohio: Community Service, Inc., 1957.

——————— *The Small Community*. New York: Harper and Brothers, 1942.

Rich, Mark, *The Larger Parish*. Columbia, Mo., Mark Rich, 1956.

Ryrie, Charles Caldwell, *The Place of Women in the Church*. New York: The Macmillan Co., 1958.

——————— *Rural Life Prayers*. New York: Commission on worship, Federal Council of Churches, 1941.

Schnucker, Calvin C., *How to Plan the Rural Church Program*. Philadelphia: The Westminster Press, 1954.

Smith, Rockwell Carter, *Rural Church Administration*. Nashville: Abingdon-Cokesbury Press, 1953.

Strum, Roy A., *Research and Survey in the Town and Country Churches of Methodism*. New York: Department of Town and Country, Division of Home Missions and Extension, Methodist Church, n.d.

Tripp, Thomas A., *Successful Rural Church Methods*. New York: Board of Home Missions, Congregational-Christian Churches, 1953.

Williamson, Ralph, *Federated Churches, a Study of Success and Failure*. Ithaca, N. Y.: Cornell University, Rural Church Institute, 1951.

PART THREE

Blackwood, Andrew W., *Planning a Year's Pulpit Work*. Nashville: Abingdon Press, 1942.

Harmon, Nolan B., *Ministerial Ethics and Etiquette*. Nashville: Abingdon Press; Revised, 1950.

Herbert, George, *County Parson: His Character and Rule of Holy Life*. Boston: James B. Dow, 1842. Written in 1632. Still an excellent treatise on the behavior of a pastor.

Leach, William Herman, *The Cokesbury Marriage Manual*. New York: Abingdon Press, 1959.

Maves, Paul B., *The Church and Mental Health*. New York: Charles Scribner's Sons, 1953.

Morrison, James Dalton, *The Minister's Service Book*. New York: Harper and Brothers, 1937.

Poston, Richard Waverly, *Small Town Renaissance*. New York: Harper and Brothers, 1950.

Robinson, Edward and Carolyn, *The Have-More Plan*. Box 501, Noroton, Conn.: E. N. Robinson, 1946. Reprinted by The Macmillan Co., New York.

Schoff, Leonard Hastings, *A New Outlook and a New Culture for Rural America*. New York: Bureau of Publications, Teachers College, Columbia University, 1957.

Smart, James D., *The Rebirth of Ministry*. Philadelphia: The Westminster Press, 1960.

Walker, Daniel D., *The Human Problems of the Minister*. New York: Harper and Brothers, 1960.